VERDICT IN PEKING

OTHER BOOKS BY DAVID BONAVIA

Fat Sasha and the Urban Guerrilla: Protest and Conformism in the Soviet Union
Peking (TIME-LIFE GREAT CITIES OF THE WORLD SERIES)
The Chinese: A Portrait
Tibet
Hong Kong 1997
Hong Kong—Living With the Future

VERDICT IN PEKING

THE TRIAL OF THE GANG OF FOUR

DAVID BONAVIA

G. P. PUTNAM'S SONS
New York

Designed by Richard Oriolo

Library of Congress Cataloging in Publication Data

Bonavia, David, date.
Verdict in Peking.

Includes index.
1. Gang of Four Trial, Peking, China, 1980–1981.
2. Chiang, Ch'ing, 1910–   . 3. Trials (Political
crimes and offenses)—China—Peking. 4. Chung-kuo kung
ch'an tang—Purges. I. Title.
LAW   345.51'0231   83–13931
ISBN 0–399–12803–4   345.105231

Printed in the United States of America

CONTENTS

Imagine that China is a large ship advancing at high speed along a course of socialism but the navigator makes an error and the ship enters hazardous waters, where there are treacherous shoals. At this moment, some of the people in charge of the vessel clandestinely get together, form cliques, commit murder, resort to various foul means to seize the ship and turn the several hundred million on board into their slaves. Under the circumstances, the navigator must answer for his error, but his error is different in nature from those who try to exploit the navigator's error for their own despicable ends.
—Fei Xiaotong, Director of the Chinese Institute of Sociology

If it's going to rain, or a woman has made up her mind to get married, there's not much anyone can do about it.
—Mao Zedong

PREFACE

This book's purpose is to supply an intimate view of how the modern Chinese political system works, especially at times of strain and conflict. What do people say to each other while changing a set of government policies, or plotting to assassinate a dictator? How discreet are they in their telephone calls? Where do they meet? How do they assure themselves of the trustworthiness of their associates? What means do they use to ensure popular support? These are the questions that it is proposed to answer here, through a series of portrayals of Chinese politicians in action.

The raw material consists mainly of transcripts of the trial of Mao Zedong's widow and her associates in the "Gang of Four," and of six other conspirators, who tried to fashion the course of Chinese history according to their own ambitions and ideals—and failed.

The transcripts are taken from the Chinese television broadcasts of excerpts from the trial while it was in progress from November 1980 until January 1981. It must be emphasized that these are only excerpts. Much of the trial proceedings was never broadcast or printed in the press. But relays of court spectators—up to 800 strong, and changing every day—heard testimony and saw the behavior of defendants, witnesses, prosecutors, judges and counsel, and have doubtless described those proceedings to their friends and relatives all over China.

Eventually, perhaps, the proceedings will be published in full. The fullest version existing at present is the official book *A Great Trial in Chinese History* (New World Press, 24 Baiwanzhuang Road, Peking, 1981), which contains much material not broadcast on television, and which has been used to flesh out many areas of background and detail. But *A Great Trial* is so muddled in its presentation, so partisan, and so studded with Chinese names, which the Western reader finds difficult to recall or store in the memory, that it needs the spice of the live human behavior in court, which only the transcripts can provide.

Additional passages aim at elucidating the personalities and former public roles of the defendants, and their policies while in power. These were thoroughly discussed in the Chinese media for more than six months following the overthrow of the Gang of Four in October 1976.

Like all live conversation, the trial transcripts are full of repetitions, confused speech, ambiguities, interruptions, and irrelevancies. Where these do not contribute to our understanding of what is happening, they have been deleted in translation, their existence recorded by ellipsis points. Doubtless some of the translations, which are the author's own, can be challenged.

It is the very raciness of the dialogue that leads me to believe the trial was only to some extent stage-managed. These were not the wooden puppets of the Soviet and Czechoslovak show trials, where every word was scripted in advance. Some of the defendants and witnesses clearly sought to ingratiate themselves, or be relieved of further interrogation, by admitting everything the indictment said of their crimes or complicity. One of the main defendants, Zhang Chun-qiao, refused to open his mouth for the entire course of the trial. Nobody could have scripted Jiang Qing's meanderings and outbursts of rage. Yao Wenyuan speaks as muddleheadedly as a tongue-tied schoolboy. Some defendants tried to talk their way out of charges against them, or seek understanding of their previous state of mind. The very inadequacy of much of the testimony is an indication that the Special Procurators, who prepared the prosecution, were often baffled by the death or disappearance of potential witnesses, the sheer volume of second-rate evidence, and the fading, prison-shocked memories of the accused.

This is not to suggest that the trial was even remotely a fair one. That subject is dealt with in the closing chapter. But the nature of the testimony heard suggests strongly that it is rooted in fact—even if the fact is often luridly embroidered to make a more damning case.

Much of modern China's history is myth—myth that keeps changing in its subject matter and shifting in its purposes. The more recent history is in China, the less clear it is. The passage of years, the death of participants in the historical tableau, and the transformation of the ruling ideology bring a different official picture of recent events every few years. Individual people's contributions to history, or their activity aimed at furthering their own interests or visions, are constantly under reassessment—not least those of Mao Zedong himself.

The trial—a central event in modern Chinese history—represents the view of recent history taken by the ruling Chinese leadership in 1980 and in early 1981. It has supplied many more facts about the political process in contemporary China than have previously been available. The only material that approaches it in detail and intimacy is the series of political documents released during the Cultural Revolution, but while that material is highly informative, it lacks the dramatic immediacy of the testimony and pleas at the trial.

To see someone reliving traumatic events of the past is almost as good as being present when they took place. Tears, cries of rage and hatred, fear, regret, spiritual surrender, and utter defiance are emotions found in the courtroom as often as on the stage. So we shall pull the curtain aside a little way—just enough to see what went on upon certain parts of the Chinese stage in the years 1966–76—the so-called Decade of the Cultural Revolution.

I have taken one major liberty with the transcript. Questions to the accused were posed by different judges and prosecutors, and their names are of little importance to the Western reader. For practical purposes, all the judges and prosecutors pursued one goal—the extraction of admissions of guilt from the defendants. To save a confusing plethora of names, therefore, I have put all the questions into the mouth of a multipurpose judge. The reader who really needs the names of the interrogators can find them in the official Chinese account of the trial.

As in all modern works on China, spelling is a problem. The standardized *pinyin* spelling in official use for the rendering of Chinese words in the Latin alphabet is ungainly and ugly, not infrequently misleading. Nonetheless, it is futile to fight the tide of this style of romanization, and I have compromised to the extent of spelling Chou En-lai as Zhou Enlai and Mao Tse-tung as Mao Zedong, while all other names are in *pinyin* except Chiang Kai-shek and Sun Yat-sen. But it still rankles to see the exotic name Peking rendered as Beijing— so Peking it will continue to be. In general, *pinyin* can be accepted in English if the following rules are observed: *pinyin q* is pronounced like English *ch; zh* is English *j; z* is *dz; c* is *ts;* and *x* (most important) is English *s,* used before front vowels (*i* or *ü*). Before back vowels (*a, e* [like French "neutral" *e*], *o, u*), *pinyin s* is equivalent to English *s*.

PART ONE

1
JIANG QING—
THE EMPRESS IN BLACK

On a freezing November day in 1980, two smartly uniformed young female guards, pistols strapped to their waists, escorted an elderly woman into an auditorium at the central police headquarters on Zhengyi Lu (Justice Road) in the heart of China's capital, Peking.

Walking steadily, her head held high, apparently unconcerned by the curious stares of some 600 spectators already in their seats, she took her place in a special dock facing the broad rostrum, which sloped upward to the back of the hall. The rostrum was crowded to capacity with judges, lay assessors, prosecutors, defense counsel, testimony readers, and other court officials.

The sixty-six-year-old woman, with her jet-black hair that hinted of dye, was the widow of Chairman Mao Zedong. For two decades, until his death in 1976, Mao had treated China as his private property. Drawing on his immense prestige as a revolutionary and military commander of genius, he overthrew or disgraced most of his former top comrades-in-arms in an astounding purge carried out with the aid of millions of students and schoolchildren.

In pursuit of his dream of a totally pure socialist system, with himself at its hub, Mao put the Chinese nation through an amazing series of upheavals in which no one—peasant or field marshal, artist, teacher, philosopher, engineer, or poet—could feel entirely safe. He turned Chinese culture and society upside down and in their place offered his own personality cult. He visualized China as the sunflower perpetually facing him, the sun, in adoration.

Close at Mao's side through those heady days in the late 1960s stood his third wife, Jiang Qing (pronounced "Ching"). A former

Shanghai movie starlet, in 1937 she had joined Mao's band of supporters at the northwest city of Yan'an. Within two or three years
(the exact date is uncertain), she had caught his eye and they had
been married—with the strict enjoinder of his colleagues in the Communist party that she never be allowed to take a political role. Presumably Mao's associates sensed the fierce and vengeful personality
that her unhappy childhood had bestowed upon her, and disliked her
frivolous delight in the values of the picture palace.

How Jiang Qing scorned that prohibition nearly three decades later
is part of the story of China's stormy passage through the twentieth
century. Drawing on her experience as an actress, Mao's young wife
was able to involve herself with cultural work such as organizing stage
shows for the Communist-led troops and party cadres,[1] and she remained active in this field until the early 1950s, when the victorious
Reds were consolidating their rule over the country. Little is known
of her doings from then until 1963, when she launched herself into
the controversial business of modernizing old Peking operas and giving them contemporary political themes. Out of the leftist "reforms"
in the sphere of culture, Mao plotted the emergence of his Great
Proletarian Cultural Revolution, the most extraordinary mass movement in China's long history.

In the early stages of the Cultural Revolution, nobody could have
dreamed then that just ten years after it began in 1966, Jiang Qing
would be on trial for her life before many of the veteran revolutionaries
whom she and Mao, together with other top leftists, had abused and
reviled, imprisoned, driven to suicide or premature death from maltreatment, or exiled to remote corners of central Asia or the fringes
of Siberia, to eke out a wretched existence amid the peasantry.

Nine other people—all men—went on trial with Jiang Qing. We
will see more of them later. Having led Jiang Qing to the dock, let
us watch her courtroom demeanor.

The judge, beginning his interrogation of Mao's widow, asked her
whether in July of 1968 she had obtained a list of the several hundred
top party members who had attended the 1959 plenary session (plenum)[2]
of the party's Central Committee. The Central Committee is supposed
to be the top policy-formulating organ, but actually is the rubber
stamp of the smaller, cabinetlike Politburo, where all big issues are
thrashed out. Plenary sessions are the occasions when the Communist
party assembles all members of the Central Committee to endorse
new policy lines handed down from the Politburo. Though theoret-

ically the plenary sessions are democratic, in practice the sessions nearly always produce 100-percent support for the decisions of the Politburo. On the other hand, the appointments (called "elections") of new members give useful indications of the drift of policy and the real power situation at the apex of the system. The list Jiang Qing was supposed to have obtained was drawn up by Kang Sheng, a Politburo member and head of the internal organs of security. Kang Sheng, a dour and sinister figure, was often called "the evil genius of the Cultural Revolution." (He died in 1975, and in 1980 was in his turn viciously denounced.)

Jiang Qing's evident motive for demanding an advance list of the participants in the session was to enable her to cross off names of people she disliked, and perhaps to pencil in some nominees of her own for membership in the prestigious body.

The judge asked whether she had indeed obtained such a list from Kang Sheng. In a faint voice she replied, "I don't know."

JUDGE: I'm asking you whether it's true or not!
JIANG: It's true, but you've put it wrongly. I must point out that it was normal and legal as a preparation for the Twelfth Plenum [to be held in October 1968]. I mean the important thing is to understand the circumstances.

This was the first of several occasions when Jiang Qing hinted or explicitly stated that the acts for which she was standing trial were performed at Mao's behest or in accordance with his policies and with his tacit or explicit approval. The court consistently refused to accept this argument, though nearly everyone in the audience would have assumed it, quite naturally, to be true.

JUDGE: At that time you were not even a member of the Central Committee—
JIANG: [raising her voice] At that time—
JUDGE: What do you mean by "normal and legal"?
JIANG: [angrily] We— At that time the Central Cultural Revolution Group was having a meeting—that was equivalent to the Party Center.

The Central Cultural Revolution Group was a small knot of hardcore leftists, including Jiang Qing, which plotted action against the hundreds of top officials and intellectuals marked down to be overthrown and abused. By 1968, though, most of them had already met their fates, and it is more likely that the group was meeting to prepare an agenda and lists of names for the forthcoming plenary session.

One man who had already fallen to the storm was Lu Dingyi, a party ideologue and propaganda strategist disgraced in 1967. (He has since been rehabilitated and now holds nominal office as a member of the Central Committee and leading scholar of contemporary Chinese history.)

JUDGE: On September 18, 1968, when you were receiving representatives of the China Peking Opera Troupe, did you say that Lu Dingyi was "a military secret agent"? Did you say that?

JIANG: I think there's been some mistake about this!

JUDGE: Play the recording of the accused Jiang Qing's speech. [Recording is played.]

JIANG'S VOICE: Lu Dingyi is a military secret agent. We have only learned of this now; perhaps there are further complications [i.e., more accusations]. . . .

JUDGE: Jiang Qing, did you hear that clearly?

JIANG: Yes— Oh! Let me think back. Yes, it's my voice.

JUDGE: It's your voice. I ask you now, did you ever say that Xü Xiangqian's wife, Huang Jie, was a "renegade"? [Xü Xiangqian is one of the original Ten Marshals of the People's Liberation Army created in 1955. He disappeared in the Cultural Revolution but was later rehabilitated and served as minister of defense from 1979 to 1981.]

JIANG: That was Old Kang! [Kang Sheng. It is common in China to use the appellations "young" and "old" with the surname to signify respect or consideration, while the given name is less often used outside the family circle.]

JUDGE: Nie Rongzhen's wife, Zhang Ruihua, was a "secret agent"—did you say that? [Nie is another of the Ten Marshals.]

JIANG: Old Kang said it!

JUDGE: I'm asking whether *you* said it or not!

JIANG: Old Kang said it!

JUDGE: Did you?

JIANG: Yes, yes.

JUDGE: So you also said it! Did you ever say that Wang Kunlun and Liao Mosha were very dangerous secret agents? Did you say those things or not?

JIANG: I can't remember. But such problems [of alleged political deviance] were associated with those people.

Wang Kunlun, who briefly gave testimony at this point, is a leading member of the Guomindang (Nationalist party) rump faction, which stayed behind when Chiang Kai-shek and his armies fled to Taiwan in 1949. He was active in the sphere of foreign relations before being purged in 1966, and was rehabilitated in 1979. In his testimony, which his daughter gave on his behalf because of his physical weakness, he accused Jiang Qing of unjustly persecuting him. A more interesting figure is Liao Mosha, a journalist who was victimized early in the Cultural Revolution because of his thinly veiled criticism of Mao in a series of articles called "Three-Family Village."

Wang Kunlun takes the stand.

WANG: Because my health is not good, I have asked my daughter, Wang Jinling, to speak for me.

JUDGE: Very well.

WANG: I was slandered and called a "secret agent" by Jiang Qing, Kang Sheng and Xie Fuzhi—all that bunch. Jiang Qing also said there was "cast-iron proof" that I was a secret agent. As a result I suffered very cruel persecution. They only said a word or two before arresting me and shutting me up in prison for seven whole years. In prison Jiang Qing, Kang Sheng, Xie Fuzhi, and all that bunch sent a special case expert to force me to confess that I was a "secret agent" and "a counterrevolutionary." They did this not because they had any special enmity toward such and such a person but as part of their conspiracy to subvert the authority of the party and the state. So they were compiling lots of name lists, struggling against, arresting, and killing many people.

Liao Mosha takes the stand.

LIAO: Jiang Qing slandered me as a "very dangerous special agent"; without any evidence or proof, she spat blood at people. It was pure fabrication and invention. From my teens, when I was at school in Hunan Province, I took part in revolutionary work, and grew up entirely under the party's leadership and instruction. Not for a single day did I fail to work for the party and the people. In 1933, when I was with the "United Left"[3] in Shanghai, Jiang Qing had just turned up there, and she knew me; after a while she agreed to put up at Comrade Tian Han's place. [Tian Han was a prominent writer, the vice-mayor of Peking, and among the first victims of the Cultural Revolution.] She also used to come to my place a lot to chat. In 1955, in the autumn, I got sick and was in the hospital in Peking. Jiang Qing even came to the ward. She loved to talk about the old days in Shanghai. But later she deliberately slandered me, trumped up a case against me, and I was unfortunate enough to be locked up for eight years. Then I was transferred to labor reform camp for another three years. I underwent "struggle-and-criticism" several hundred times. On top of that [begins sobbing], in the prison they carried out cruel physical maltreatment [weeping]. All my teeth have been knocked out and I have to use false ones. It wasn't only I who suffered this cruel persecution; the first secretary of the Peking Municipal Committee, Comrade Liu Ren [a veteran revolutionary purged in 1966], had the label of "secret agent" stuck on him, was arrested and imprisoned, and was made to wear manacles for five years in prison—

JIANG: Don't pretend! Weren't you in on the "Three-Family Village" business? Why—

JUDGE: [shouting] You're not allowed to speak!

JIANG: I had the right to expose you to the Chairman!

JUDGE: [hammering the table and shouting] You're not allowed to speak! Accused Jiang Qing, you're not allowed to speak!

JIANG: If I do, what will you do?

JUDGE: If you go on committing crimes—

JIANG: You're the one who's committing crimes! [Laughs.] You call these renegades and rotten eggs here to speak, and I want to make it quite clear that—

JUDGE: To go on slandering people is to go on committing crimes!

JIANG: What crimes? You—

JUDGE: Take her away!

Jiang Qing is escorted from the court.

JUDGE: Witness Liao Mosha, please go on with your testimony.

LIAO: Comrade Liu Ren was sent to prison with manacles on, so that when the weather was cold just before the New Year, he couldn't even put his clothes on and had to just drape them over himself. When he was fourteen or fifteen, he joined the Revolution; he went through fire and water all his life for the cause of the party, utterly loyal. An old revolutionary like that, to be so cruelly treated—he died tragically in prison [weeping].

Deputy Mayor Comrade Wu Han[4] was a famous historian and professor; throughout his life he was never separated from his books, he never put down his pen, but taught and wrote most diligently. He was an honest and straightforward scholar. As long ago as the resistance war against Japan, he accepted the party's program, and under the party's leadership he carried on the people's democratic fight, united with the broad patriotic and intellectual elements, with youths and students, and made big contributions to the cause of the people's liberation. That an old scholar like this, a good comrade, could also be called a "secret agent" and "renegade" by them, that they could arrest and imprison him, and that he should die tragically in jail! His wife, Comrade Yuan Zhen, and his daughter, Wu Xiaoyan, were also persecuted to death, their home was broken up and the family scattered.

Then there was the famous author Lao She [considered to rank with

Lu Xün as one of the finest twentieth-century Chinese writers—author of *Rickshaw Boy* and *Teahouse*]. He warmly loved the people and his motherland, warmly loved our party. When the country was liberated, he immediately came home from far across the seas, came back to his old home in Peking to answer the motherland's call, and created many fine works singing the praises of the new China. He, too, was framed and persecuted and died.

Numerous cadres and ordinary people of Peking were repeatedly persecuted, or persecuted to death. The total number was 10,289. Jiang Qing! Look what evils your bunch are guilty of—too numerous to count! The people of Peking really hate this bunch with all their might! I now demand that the Special Court judge the Lin Biao and Jiang Qing counterrevolutionary cliques with all the severity of the law!

JUDGE: The court is adjourned.

It will be plain by now that the personal feuds and bitter rivalries that underlay the Cultural Revolution—and its result, the trial—went back a long way, to the 1930s and even the 1920s.

The Chinese Communist party was founded in 1921, and there are no longer any survivors of the twelve men (including Mao) who met on a boat on a lake to hold the party's First Congress. They had chosen that difficult site to escape the attention of the police.

At that time China was in a state of disintegration and near-collapse unrivaled in her millennia-long history. The impact of Western technology, commerce, and ideas (introduced partially through Japan) had proved almost fatal to her medieval political and social systems. The decadent Manchu (Ching) dynasty had been overthrown in 1911; and after a chaotic interregnum, Dr. Sun Yat-sen had been summoned back from exile abroad to lead the new republic into the twentieth century with some semblance of progress and social change. Sun, a foreign-educated Cantonese, has often been called "the father of the Chinese Revolution."

In those days, communism and socialism were attractive only to a small number of educated Chinese, who saw them not only as a means of hauling the country out of its backwardness but also as a way of expelling or subduing the foreigners who dominated its commerce and industry, trained its navy, once even commanded its army, and collected China's customs dues for her. The presence of these foreigners was undermining basic Chinese assumptions about life in general, and if their modern ways could not be successfully copied, many Chinese patriots felt, the foreigners must be driven out before they ended up ruling the whole country.

The Communist party was born in the aftermath of the May Fourth movement of 1919, when patriotic Chinese of all social classes angrily demonstrated against the results of the Versailles conference, which redrew the map of the globe after World War I. Territories in Shandong Province that had been extorted from China by Germany were not returned to her but awarded to Japan—even though China, since 1917, had been at least a nominal combatant on the side of Britain, France, the United States, Russia, and Japan against Germany and Austro-Hungary.

Marx and Lenin foresaw socialism and communism as primarily urban movements, mobilizing the oppressed working masses against the bourgeois capitalists and exploiters. But China had relatively little modern industry in 1921, and the recognizable industrial proletariat was small in a nation of her huge size (about 350 million souls at the time). Mao rewrote Marx by taking the struggle first into the countryside, where a dispossessed and often starving peasantry was squeezed for its last drops of blood and sweat by landlords, small and great.

Mao spent years traveling in the rural areas and picking up some education here, some there, reading voraciously and forming his ideas of what was wrong with his country. He was the son of a well-to-do peasant, but had quarreled with his father and left home while still in his teens. In these early years, he admired from afar the leftist writer/scholar Chen Duxiu at the University of Peking, who became the first secretary-general of the party. (Later Mao denounced Chen as a deviant and had him expelled from the party.)

In the mid-1920s, Mao drew around him an armed band of revolutionaries in the rugged mountain areas of southeastern China. By this time the young Christian-convert General Chiang Kai-shek had become dictator of China following his defeat of the warlords who had been dominant in the northern part of the country after the collapse of the Manchu dynasty. Chiang saw himself as something of a revolutionary and a modernizer, and he presided over the growth of a parliamentary system (which never worked well), modernization of the armed forces, anti-illiteracy drives, dissemination of Western medicine, and all the other trappings of the modern state.

Chiang was obsessed with the need to wipe out the Communists, which he tried several times to do, but failed. Though greatly depleted in strength and undergoing severe privations, the Communists survived to make the epic Long March of 1935. This stirring page in the annals of the Revolution brought them in a tortuously circuitous route through west China and the fringes of Tibet to the province of Shanxi in the northwest, where they established a new base area in the vicinity of Yan'an.

The Yan'an period was not just one of rest and shelter for Mao and his followers; it provided the opportunity for Mao to experiment more thoroughly than before with the basic elements of his social and political thinking. (In the 1920s and early 1930s, he had defeated attempts by Moscow to gain control of the Chinese Communist party through agents of the Communist International, one of whom, Otto Braun, a German, actually took part in the Long March. The Soviets had also tried to use Chinese students who had been trained and indoctrinated in the Soviet Union, to make the Chinese party subservient to their own international aims. Mao, already experienced in guerrilla warfare and political maneuvering, successfully resisted their attempts to take over, and by 1935, was the acknowledged leader of the battle-hardened party and its armed forces.) Many of Mao's most important and characteristic writings came from this period, including his lectures on the role of literature and art in society—a role he saw as functional, educational, and inspirational, rather than as revealing any deeper truths about the human spirit. From the Yan'an period, too, came his important writings on the anti-Japanese struggle, collaboration with Chiang Kai-shek and the Guomindang, and on party organization.

As World War II, for China, turned into the Civil War against the American-backed armies of Chiang Kai-shek, Mao and his top commanders perfected that blend of main-force unit and guerrilla fighting which later influenced their global strategic thinking. Among his right-hand men at the time were Lin Biao, Zhu De, Peng Dehuai, and Deng Xiaoping.

When they finally marched into Peking in 1949 and spread their rule southward to embrace Shanghai, central and western China, and the coastal provinces, the Communists came more as military conquerors than as revolutionaries—though without the land reforms and other measures to improve the lot of the peasants in the areas under their rule, they would not have been able to recruit many soldiers at all.

Their political thinking, and particularly Mao's, was affected by a kind of military romanticism in which the Red Armies (renamed the People's Liberation Army) were held up as the model for all true socialists to copy. Its bravery, self-sacrifice, and idealism set it apart from the Chinese military tradition of cowardice, massacre, rapine, plunder, and mutiny. A military style of government was also appropriate for the reconstruction of the economy and the building of the heavy industries and massive hydraulic schemes that were to speed China's entry into the second half of the twentieth century.

American support of Chiang Kai-shek—who had taken refuge with his supporters on the island of Taiwan—forced the Chinese Communist leaders to accept technical aid from the Soviet Union, with whom their relations for the past thirty years had been touchy at best. But in 1956 Mao disagreed strongly with Khrushchev's decision to denounce Stalin for the cruel dictator he was; perhaps Mao feared this might bring a similar fate to the dictatorial style he himself was later to adopt. At this time the Chinese leadership was still largely a collective one. Social policies were still mild (except toward oppressive landlords and presumed counterrevolutionaries), and the Chinese cultural tradition was being fostered and preserved.

This mildness came to an end in 1957, when Mao launched a vigorous campaign against "rightists"—mainly academics, writers, and artists who had been bold or foolish enough to believe his assurances of the previous year that, in culture and the arts, "a hundred flowers should bloom and a hundred schools of thought contend." Either Mao overrated the progress made in spreading socialist ideology since 1949 or he cynically encouraged liberals and conservatives among the intelligentsia to stick their necks out so that he could metaphorically lop off their heads. Some of China's best writers and scholars disappeared from view, exiled to remote areas, imprisoned, or sent to labor camps.

Painful though it was, the antirightist campaign was soon submerged in the foundation of the people's communes in 1958 and the almost simultaneous launching of the Great Leap Forward. Mao believed the communes would boost agricultural production; actually they did the opposite, by merging villages and families into huge, amorphous work units and crushing individual decision-making in favor of centralized instructions that even determined such questions as when and how deeply to plough. The Great Leap was intended to push industrial production forward at unheard-of speeds, but took little notice of quality, maintenance of equipment, observance of tolerances, etc. By 1961 the country faced starvation and economic chaos. The Great Leap was terminated. The more moderate leaders succeeded in modifying the structure of the people's communes so that they no longer made the peasant so sullen and uncooperative, and there was a mild easing-up in cultural affairs.

Not for long would Mao leave China in peace, however. In 1966, after several years of relative seclusion, he launched the Cultural Revolution—a stormy leftist upsurge that broke over the heads of writers, provincial governors, city mayors, industrial managers, teachers and professors, actors and musicians. Millions of frenzied young people, styling themselves Red Guards, pulled top officials from behind their desks and made them stand on tables or platforms to be reviled and howled at, spat on, jostled, slapped, bent forward in a painful position called "jet plane," crowned with paper dunce caps, paraded through the streets, injured, and sometimes killed or driven to suicide. It was as though China's youth were taking its revenge for millennia of subjugation to older people, the traditional Chinese picture of a correct society.

The Red Guards were constantly fed with hysterical propaganda about the need to "defend Chairman Mao," whose portrait was hung everywhere and whose statues sprang up in public places. For hours on end, Red Guards would chant the political aphorisms of Mao contained in the famous *Little Red Book*, edited by the brilliant wartime commander who would later be accused of plotting to assassinate the demigod Mao—Marshal Lin Biao.

Thus began the extraordinary phase of Chinese history that this book sets out to describe, at least in part, through the mouths of those who planned it and those who fell victim to it. Oddly enough, the main figure in the drama was not a seasoned revolutionary or a veteran general, but a movie actress. The histrionic, baleful, self-indulgent Jiang Qing took it upon herself to issue orders for the arrest of this person, the public disgrace of that one. A good part of the trial proceedings is aimed at showing her leading role in the conspiratorial dealings of 1966–76.

Jiang Qing's hatred was directed especially against Wang Guangmei, the wife of Head of State Liu Shaoqi. (Chinese women often keep their own names after marriage, especially in the People's Republic.) Beautiful, accomplished, and stylish, Mme. Liu bore the brunt of Mme. Mao's revenge on the party for forbidding her to meddle in politics. And Mao, it seemed, indulged Jiang in her vengeance. She appeared by his side at rallies, wearing a military cap and brandishing the "Little Red Book." She helped supervise the "revolutionization" of Chinese stage works and music.

Almost till Mao's death in 1976, the Chinese media were still trying to whip up popular feeling against the imprisoned Mme. Liu, whose husband had died in jail of medical neglect in 1969. What had evidently riled Mme. Mao had been Mme. Liu's habit of dressing elegantly in a cheongsam, wearing jewelry and a smart hairdo—especially noticeable during a visit she paid to Indonesia in the company of her husband in 1964. Mme. Liu was mocked for this during the series of violent "struggle and criticism" sessions staged against her and her husband in 1967, when a necklace of Ping-Pong balls was hung on her. Thousands of vicious cartoons were stuck up on walls all over China's cities, ridiculing her finery. (Satirical cartoons became popular in China in the late nineteenth century, the concept having been introduced from Europe.) Ten years after the persecution of Mme. Liu, Jiang Qing herself faced a similar barrage of pictorial satirization. An exhibition of cartoons was even held in Peking's Palace of Minorities, concentrating on her attempts to suppress the customs and dress of non-Chinese ethnic communities such as the Mongols, Tibetans, and Muslim Uighurs.

Liu and his wife were allowed to continue living for several months at their house in the Zhongnanhai complex of buildings and lakeside parklands in central Peking, where many of the leaders then resided (and still do today). There the Red Guards—whom, it seems, army sentries and security men dared not refuse admission—subjected them to the classic treatment for hours on end, over a period of months. Shouting, abuse, spitting, slapping, "jet plane," and all the other humiliations the Red Guard loved to inflict did not, so far as is known, spill over into serious violence or result in bad injury to Liu or Liu's wife, but its effect on the physical and mental health of the couple can easily be imagined.

The court also indicted Jiang Qing and her friends for having the Lius' home searched while they were undergoing a struggle-and-criticism session. This was done on the pretext of smashing the "four olds" (old ideas, old culture, old customs, and old habits)—one of the chief slogans of the Red Guards. They used it to justify breaking into the homes of "bourgeois" elements or people considered to be "revisionists," smashing or stealing their antiques and furniture, letters, photographs, Gramophone records, money and valuables, diaries, notebooks, and clothing. Sometimes the entire contents of a house were tossed through a window onto the street.

Jiang Qing engineered the denunciation of Mme. Liu as "an American spy and secret agent"—by any standards a fantastic allegation. Mme. Mao worked through the "special case group" set up for the sole purpose of drafting accusations against Mme. Liu. But even members of the case group were flabbergasted by the baldness of Mme. Mao's concoctions, as Xiao Meng's testimony will illustrate later on. When confronted at the trial with evidence of her own activity in persecuting her rival, she claimed she could remember nothing about the events in question. Much of her testimony was impossibly rambling, tangential, or incomprehensible.

As the Cultural Revolution got under way, it became clear that certain figures in the leadership were playing prominent roles in guiding it. Much of its reputed spontaneity was illusory, for it was strongly influenced by agents of the top leftists and even by their Red Guard children.

One of the new group of extreme-left leaders was Zhang Chunqiao (pronounced "Jang Chin-chow"). As the new party leader in Shanghai, this former columnist and literary censor was in a position to manipulate the tide of popular unrest surging through the biggest city in China. With its 10–11-million population, its past history as a foreign concession where every kind of luxurious living, every vice and addiction, flourished under the protection of the Western powers and Japan, Shanghai was both the most inventive and modern of Chinese cities—and the least amenable to control from Peking.

After the Communists cleaned up its bars and brothels in the early 1950s, imprisoned or expelled the foreign priests and missionaries, but let some of the capitalists stay on to manage their businesses expropriated by the state, Shanghai continued to be a headache for the leaders in Peking. Its workers knew about strike tactics (although they did not use them until 1967); its intellectuals were better read than the sometimes nearly illiterate Communist cadres. It was also a great center of industry and technology, and knowledge of things foreign. The Communists needed Shanghai, but they never broke its unique spirit or the haughty way Shanghai people looked down on the country-bumpkin soldiers from the hinterlands. In 1971, so it is claimed, a plot was hatched to assassinate Mao in Shanghai. And in 1976 Shanghai teetered on the brink of armed mutiny against Peking.

Zhang showed brilliance in his handling of the mass movements and street fighting that marked the passage of the Cultural Revolution through Shanghai. He was aided by Wang Hongwen, then in his late thirties. A security officer at a cotton mill, Wang was a Korean War veteran who had evidently caught Zhang's eye in some political maneuver. Wang was entrusted with the command of the rowdier Red Guard elements, who were locked in an imbroglio with another faction calling themselves Scarlet Guards. The Scarlet Guards were originally a militia organization charged with guarding important installations such as factories and mines. They were on the whole older than the Red Guards, and were of mainly working-class background, while the latter took in more cadres' children and secondary-school and university students. The two groups became hostile to each other in the early stages of the Cultural Revolution and the Scarlet Guards' organization was destroyed. At one stage, Wang supervised the movement of tens of thousands of armed Red Guards across a river, with vehicles and fire engines, to attack a large group of Scarlet Guards who had staged a sit-in at a diesel-engine plant. Attacking with fire hoses, iron bars, cudgels, knives, and anything that came to hand, the Red Guards stormed the building from above and below and took all the Scarlet Guards captive. Some 700 people were injured, many of them seriously. Probably some died.

In 1973, when the Communist party held its first Congress since 1969, Wang—whom Zhang had doubtless recommended to the aging Mao as a potential symbol of youth in a position of leadership—was appointed a member of the Politburo. He was frequently shown by the media in the company of Mao, and took an active role in the training and organization of the nationwide People's Militia (irregular troops)—which in the end was his undoing.

Prominent in the management of the leftist propaganda campaign to denounce those overthrown in the Cultural Revolution and to glorify Mao and Jiang Qing was the Shanghai-born journalist Yao Wenyuan. Son of a prewar littérateur, he had also caught Zhang's eye as a useful type. Yao wrote some of the main newspaper editorials proclaiming the Cultural Revolution and viciously denouncing those who fell victim to it. By the mid-1970s, he was a sort of media czar, ordering this or that leader to be blotted out of a photograph showing him or her in the company of Mao; slashing television coverage of the funeral of the popular Premier Zhou Enlai in 1976; maneuvering Jiang Qing into more prominent places in formal, posed shots of leadership appearances, and so on.

These three men—Zhang Chunqiao, Wang Hongwen, and Yao Wenyuan—together with Jiang Qing, made up the "Gang of Four" and went on trial with her on November 20, 1980. The indictment, without which they could not even know the charges against them, had been served by a white-gloved policeman in full view of the cameras of Peking Central Television a mere ten days before.

Asked whether she wished to have defense counsel, Jiang Qing asked, "Will he be able to answer questions on my behalf?" Told that he could not, she declined counsel.

Zhang Chunqiao refused to accept the indictment and sat through the trial under an Iago-like vow of silence.

The group's nickname is said to have been coined by Mao in the early 1970s, when he warned them "not to operate like a gang of four." In the last years of his life, it is now officially stated, Mao was estranged from Jiang Qing—who nevertheless missed no opportunity to pursue her own ends under the mantle of authority that he never specifically lifted from her. However, less than a month after Mao's death on September 9, 1976, the other members of the Politburo sent security agents at night to arrest all four of them in their respective residences.

But it is time to return to the courtroom where Jiang Qing is being interrogated about her activities aimed at bringing about the disgrace and fall from power of Liu Shaoqi, Chairman of the People's Republic of China, the equivalent of a Western president or other head of state. (Mao was Chairman of the Party.)

JUDGE: Accused Jiang Qing, I now ask you: Was it on your decision and that of Kang Sheng and Chen Boda that on July 18, 1967, Qi Benyü organized the convening of the big struggle-and-criticism session against Liu Shaoqi and the search of his house?

JIANG: I seem to recall there were two issues here. One was the struggle-and-criticism in the limited context of the party center. I saw something about this, but I can't remember whether it was signed by Chen Boda or by Old Kang [Sheng] to show their agreement. They gave this document to me, yes, they did, and I marked it. And it was legal.

JUDGE: Slow down.

JIANG: Can't you hear me clearly? The second point concerned the support the three of us gave Qi Benyü[5] for the house search. Perhaps I participated directly—I don't know.

JUDGE: Your answer is in two parts. One is about the struggle-and-criticism in Zhongnanhai. You can remember that you marked [the document].

JIANG: It's not that I remember, it's this evidence they gave me [holding up the indictment].

JUDGE: Did it happen?

JIANG: I did make that mark.

JUDGE: Don't you remember about the house search, the other point?

JIANG: No!

JUDGE: Now show and read out the memo from Jiang Qing, Kang Sheng, and Chen Boda to Qi Benyü.

[Court reader reads out testimony similar to that in interrogation of Chen Boda—see Chapter 5.]

JUDGE: Is this what you say you saw?

JIANG: It doesn't look like it—I can't bring it to mind. Maybe that's it.

JUDGE: Read out Qi Benyü's confession of September 10, 1980.

COURT READER: "On July 18, 1967, the masses in the organs of Zhongnanhai carried out struggle-and-criticism against Liu Shaoqi and Wang Guangmei at a meeting that I organized. Jiang Qing suggested that while the meeting was going on, a small special case group should go through Liu Shaoqi's papers . . . and report back to her."

JUDGE: Now show and read out the report by the Wang Guangmei special-case group on the search of Liu Shaoqi's house, which Jiang Qing approved, dated October 24, 1967.

TV COMMENTATOR: The report says that the search turned up one hundred and eighty-eight notebooks of Liu Shaoqi's and Wang Guangmei's, of which Liu had written sixty-one and Wang Guangmei had written one hundred and twenty-seven, as well as the secretary's records of Liu's activities—in all, eight notebooks. There was also one diary of Liu Ping-ping [Liu's daughter] from 1965 and 1966.

JUDGE: Accused Jiang Qing, did you hear that clearly? Do you wish to say anything?

JIANG: The interrogators I had contact with—I think there were seven or eight groups of them—only wanted to talk about this point. As far as the Red Guards' "smashing the four olds" and searching houses was concerned, that was illegal, but at that time it had a historical background. The Party Center was putting out documents acknowledging the Red Guards' [right] to "smash the four olds." House searches were a deviation from the main current, but if you "smash the four olds," of course you have to search houses—that's revolutionary behavior! [The "four olds" are defined as "old ideas, old cultures, old customs and old habits."]

JUDGE: You, Kang Sheng, and Chen Boda approved the struggle-and-criticism against Liu Shaoqi, and carried out physical persecution of him. That was violating the Constitution. You took it upon yourself to arrest and abduct him, an act of gross violation of human rights and criminal behavior. You say this was "smashing the four olds," and of course that meant house searches. How did "smashing the four olds" come about? It was started by a reactionary article written by Chen Boda called "Sweep Away All Ghosts and Monsters"[6]—you must know that!

JIANG: I remember the headline.

JUDGE: Whipped up by that reactionary article, the young Red Guards carried out house searches all over the place. You can't say that was legal—

JIANG: No! The material you gave to me . . .

JUDGE: Listen to me! In the decision of the Eleventh Plenum of the Eighth Central Committee in 1966 to begin the Cultural Revolution, none of the sixteen points gives authorization for struggle-and-criticism against the Head of State or for the search of his house. In the Cultural Revolution, your bunch trampled and sabotaged our country's Constitution and laws, and committed many serious crimes. Now you're still making out that your campaign at that time was legal and not criminal, which explains your counterrevolutionary stand. Right up till now you still have not changed an iota. For this reason your legal responsibility for carrying out struggle-and-criticism against Liu Shaoqi and searching his house cannot be shuffled off. That's all. The defendant is accused of conspiring with Kang Sheng, Chen Boda, and others to take it upon themselves to convene the big meeting to apply struggle-and-criticism to Liu Shaoqi, and to carry out a search of his house, physically persecuting the Head of State of the People's Republic of China. The court concludes its investigation of these facts. Was it your decision to detain and imprison Yang Chengzuo[7] and his wife, Yuan Shaoying?

JIANG: I can't remember such a thing!

COURT READER: The original text of the report is as follows: "Comrade Qi Benyü's report on Yang Chengzuo and Yuan Shaoying's intelligence relationship with American strategic organs is an important clue in unmasking Wang Guangmei's relations with American secret agents. We agree with the Peking Public Security Bureau's Committee on Criminal Affairs that they should detain Yang and Yuan for investigation. Wang Guangmei Special Case Group, July 18, 1967." Qi Benyü noted on July 25: "This is an important matter; it should be sent to Jiang Qing for approval of implementation."

JUDGE: Accused Jiang Qing, did you hear clearly? I ask you again, when Yang Chengzuo was seriously ill, did you tell the special-case-group people to carry out blitz interrogation[8] of him?

JIANG: I don't recall.

JUDGE: You don't? Huh, I ask you again: Did you tell the special-case-group people, "You must get the things we need out of Yang before he dies"? Did you say that or didn't you?

JIANG: I don't recall.

JUDGE: You don't know? . . . Jiang Qing! Jiang Qing personally gave instructions for "blitz" interrogation and indeed gave most specific instructions. Yang Chengzuo was ill, very seriously ill, and she was afraid he would die before they had got to the heart of the matter—the materials on Wang Guangmei that Jiang Qing wanted. So she instructed the special case group to be sure to get what they wanted before he died. The special case group carried out many blitz interrogations [of the dying man].

TV COMMENTATOR: The court has made a judicial investigation of the facts of Jiang Qing's slander and persecution of the chairman of the Chinese People's Republic and vice-chairman of the Chinese Communist party, Liu Shaoqi. The indictment accuses her of directly controlling and instructing the special case group dealing with the case of Liu Shaoqi and [his wife] Wang Guangmei, to fabricate false testimony to slander and persecute Liu Shaoqi and illegally arrest innocent people. She conspired with Kang Sheng to slander Wang Guangmei as "an American secret agent" and persecute her. In the course of the judicial investigation, the accused Jiang Qing could not dispute or deny these facts or disclaim criminal responsibility. The court has adduced relevant evidence.

JUDGE: Now play the recordings of Jiang Qing's speech on September 18, 1968.

JIANG QING'S VOICE: "I am now responsible for the first major case. I've been working on it for five or six hours a day, and though I have read all the materials more than once, I've still had to evaluate them again, and I can tell you now that Liu Shaoqi is a 'five poisons' type of [screaming] big counterrevolutionary, traitor, renegade, secret agent, and villain . . . and sacrificed who knows how many good comrades! Who knows how many he sold out, that big traitor? [yelling] I think he should die the death of a thousand little cuts—ten thousand!"

JUDGE: Did you hear that, Jiang Qing?

JIANG: No, perhaps the voice—or—this—it seems to be—

JUDGE: Speak up!

JIANG: What does it matter? I can't hear clearly, but I can make out that it's my voice.

JUDGE: [shouting her down] You can make out that it's your voice!

JIANG: But I can't hear clearly. It's a bit like a letter I was given to read.

JUDGE: Now let the court reader read out the [other] contents of her speech. You made this speech on September 18, 1968, while receiving a Chinese economic delegation and representatives of other units.

COURT READER: [Reads out verbatim the passage quoted above.]

TV COMMENTATOR: The court's investigation also proves that Jiang Qing arrested innocent people at random and falsified evidence in order to frame and persecute Liu Shaoqi.

Xiao Meng, former head of the special case group for Wang Guang-mei, is called to testify.

XIAO: From May till November 1967, I took part in the special case work on Liu Shaoqi and Wang Guangmei, serving as head of the group and as its secretary. . . .

TV COMMENTATOR: Jiang Qing wanted Xiao Meng to write a report on Wang Guangmei's arrest.

XIAO: . . . Then Jiang Qing said, "This evening your whole group must write a report on the arrest of Wang Guangmei, and give it to me tomorrow morning." Kang Sheng said, "We can settle the question of Wang Guang-mei being a secret agent. The report on her arrest must be written as quickly as possible." We all thought this move was very sudden and were very alarmed. There was a lot of investigative work we still hadn't done, and we had no solid material with which to clarify this question. . . .

TV COMMENTATOR: Jiang Qing was dissatisfied with the report of the special case group, and got Kang Sheng to write one in person.

XIAO: . . . Later on, we saw Kang Sheng's slanderous report dated September 8, in which he said Wang Guangmei should be arrested. It named her as "an American strategic spy and secret agent, a secret agent of Japan and of the Guomindang bandits." Jiang Qing's signature was on the report. So you see the slander and persecution of Wang Guangmei was plotted by Jiang Qing and Kang Sheng in person.

The Head of State was not the only person whose home was searched on Jiang Qing's instructions. Her career in the Shanghai movie world of the 1930s had evidently been somewhat colorful. Rumors of promiscuity attached to her, as they will to any pretty and headstrong starlet. In the leftist Shanghai intellectual world of the day, free love was looked on as progressive, but there is no firm evidence that Jiang Qing was any more or less promiscuous than others. For a short while she was married to a Chinese scenarist who later emigrated to France and ran a small Chinese restaurant in Paris. When the Cultural Revolution got under way, Jiang Qing recalled some letters, photographs, and notebooks, even old movie journals, which she thought were in the possession of a well-known film director, Zheng Jünli, and other former acquaintances. She gave orders for a search of their houses, which was carried out by squads under the command of Jiang Tengjiao, then air-force political commissar of the Nanjing Military Region. Ye Qün, Lin Biao's wife, helped Jiang Qing to recover the compromising materials and burn them secretly.

It has never been publicly disclosed why Jiang Qing was so worried about the documentation of her past. If her compromising behavior was not sexual, or was only partly sexual, what else could it have been? It has been broadly hinted that she became a turncoat when she was arrested and detained by the Guomindang secret police, but no firm evidence of this has been proffered, except allegations that she took part in a stage performance to raise money for a plane to help fight the Japanese, and that she vied for the role of Sai Jinhua, a Qing dynasty courtesan who is regarded by some Chinese as a patriot, by others as an immoral traitor.

At any rate, whatever secrets Jiang Qing had from these years, she went to extraordinary lengths to guard them.

JUDGE: What about the house searches in October 1966?

JIANG QING: I don't know anything about house searches.

JUDGE: Call Jiang Tengjiao. [Jiang Tengjiao takes the stand.] Jiang Tengjiao, in October of 1966 did you organize certain people to make illegal searches at the homes of Zheng Jünli, Zhao Dan, Tong Ziling, Chen Liping, and Gu Eryi [formerly well-known figures in the Shanghai movie world of the 1930s]?

JIANG TENGJIAO: Yes.

JUDGE: Who instigated you?

JIANG TENGJIAO: In early October, Wu Faxian phoned me and told me to come to Peking to be briefed on a certain matter. I got there on the afternoon of the next day. In the evening Wu Faxian came to the place where I was staying and took me to an underground office. After less than ten minutes, Ye Qün [Lin Biao's wife] turned up. She told me Jiang Qing said a letter of hers had fallen into the hands of Zheng Jünli and Gu Eryi, but she wasn't sure who had it now. When I got back to Shanghai, I was to search the homes of those people and take any letters, diaries, notebooks, and other relevant material. This affair must be kept absolutely secret, Ye Qün said.

I went back to Shanghai the next day. On the day of the operation, Situ Xian [an officer] got some personnel together—there were about forty of them. On October 9, in the small hours of the morning, we mounted a surprise attack to search those people's homes. We carried all the stuff we took on a truck to the [air force] reception center. . . . I gave a brief report on the searches. Wu Faxian phoned me and told me to bring the stuff to Peking the next day, which I did. In the evening, before supper, Wu Faxian phoned me and said Ye Qün in person wanted to have a look at the material. At about nine P.M. Ye Qün arrived by car and took the notebooks. The next day she phoned me and said Jiang Qing was very pleased. She told me to look after all the other material very carefully after I got back to Shanghai. Shortly after my return to Shanghai, Ye Qün phoned again and asked me to send all the stuff to Peking, which I did.

JUDGE: Bring in Liu Shi'en [an air-force officer]. . . . Liu Shi'en, in October of 1966, did you conduct an illegal search at the homes of writers and artists in Shanghai?

LIU: Yes, I took part in that.

JUDGE: Sit down. Give an accurate account of this matter.

LIU: Very well. Jiang Tengjiao received verbal orders from Ye Qün to assist Jiang Qing in destroying evidence of her counterrevolutionary past in Shanghai—

JIANG QING: What evidence of counterrevolutionary—

JUDGE: Jiang Qing, don't speak, just listen. This is a court investigation, isn't it? It's an investigation of the facts, isn't it?

JIANG QING: Your "facts" are a real puzzle. Why should I go stealing into other people's homes? I only met the person once.

JUDGE: You just listen! Listen carefully!

LIU: What I'm telling you is all eyewitness accounts, things I personally heard about or personally experienced—important facts. Jiang Tengjiao got together a group of people including me at the Red Fourth Army reception center on Zhulu Road. I was given a "most important, glorious, and special political task." I was to organize a group of politically reliable cadres to search the homes of some "black gang" types who were following the "black line" in literature and art [i.e., had rightist leanings]. Jiang Tengjiao . . . said that we were to wear plain clothes with Red Guard armbands, and the most important thing was to bring all letters, note-books, and diaries back to the reception center and then report to Peking.

I led a group to search Zheng Jünli's home. Situ Xian took a group to search Zhao Dan's place. . . . Jiang Tengjiao particularly stressed that all this activity was to be kept absolutely secret, and at all times in any circumstances it must be kept to ourselves and not spoken about to any-body. Red Guards searching other homes should be told that these people were a "black gang." We should say that the air force had lost a top-secret document a few years ago and it apparently had something to do with them, so they were being searched. And we were to tell them to keep it a strict secret and not to mention it to their schoolmates or in front of their fathers or mothers.

While we were preparing for the searches, Jiang Tengjiao kept in close contact with Ye Qün in Peking by a personal secret telephone he had brought back from Peking. After all problems, big and small, had been settled and plotted through Ye Qün's instructions and conspiratorial plan-ning, the specific measures we should take were settled. Till the evening of the day of the searches, Jiang Tengjiao assumed personal unified com-mand of the five house searches. At the same time, he made preparations to deal with any accidental occurrences that could not be foreseen. In the interests of total secrecy, because he was afraid of his Mah-Jongg board [equivalent to English applecart] being upset, . . . we secretly assembled and stayed all day at another Red Fourth Army reception center. Then we split up, each group taking two or three sacks to use in the searches. Then we got onto five Red Fourth Army medium trucks, which had their five-digit air-force registration numbers deleted and replaced with the words *Red Guards* to conceal their identity.

Before midnight, the five groups went to the addresses of the five people to be searched, and concealed themselves in quiet, dark places. They waited till nobody was watching, then quickly and secretly rushed into the people's homes and carried out the searches straight away. In order to win time, we were to carry out "a short and decisive battle," and not be caught up in a protracted action. While we were searching we must confiscate any correspondence or notebooks and take them away imme-diately, before daybreak, to the gathering place, and go home se-cretly. . . . Later, on Jiang Tengjiao's orders, we went through all the confiscated material looking for anything connected with Jiang Qing, and gave it to him. This material was sent to Peking in two batches.

JUDGE: Call the witness Huang Chen [widow of Zheng Jünli]. . . . Sit down, Huang Chen. In the summer of 1966, did Zheng Jünli come home and tell you to look for all photographs and letters concerning Jiang Qing?

HUANG: Yes.

JUDGE: In October of 1966, was your home searched?

HUANG: Yes.

JUDGE: The court wishes to have your testimony.

HUANG: [to Jiang Qing] Don't you recognize me? You are Lan Ping [Jiang Qing's screen name], I am Huang Chen. I'm telling you, I know about your history in the 1930s. In the autumn of 1966, the Guomindang special agent Zhang Chunqiao—

JUDGE: Slow down a bit.

HUANG: All right. He sent for my husband, Comrade Jünli, and told him to hand over all literary materials on Jiang Qing. When Jünli had handed them over, Zhang Chunqiao again personally sent for him twice. The first time, Comrade Jünli came back after seeing Zhang and told me Zhang had threatened him and told him that he must hand over all letters, photographs, stage shots, and similar materials. We put all that kind of stuff together in a big package and got somebody to take it to Zhang Chunqiao. . . . Zhang summoned Jünli. I could feel there was great pressure on him. He was distraught; I could see he was afraid our family would be burdened. Early the next day he went to work and at five P.M. he was supposed to go and take part in labor. Before he left—I went a bit after him—he said, "Huang Chen, one day I may not come home." These unexpected words made me worry day and night. All the time I was anxious that something might happen to Jünli.

One evening soon afterward, around midnight, a number of people whose identity we didn't know rushed into our home and began searching it. . . . One of them was dressed entirely in blue, very tall and thin. His face was on the dark side, and he had a Shandong accent. They locked up our whole building and nobody was allowed in or out. From midnight they searched till past five A.M. They all had big face masks, especially designed so that only the eyes could be seen. They searched everything— our clothes, collars, hair, even our shoes, and our bodies. The leader warned us to bring out all written materials in our home. We told him we had nothing like that, but they didn't believe us.

When they began to search, they overturned all our furniture and all our wardrobes, threw all our books on the floor. They were very practiced. I saw they had special training. Over a hundred literary and art books that Jünli had been collecting over a period of decades, manuscripts, and other materials—[turning to Jiang Qing] his heart's blood, you carried them all off! Even all my study notes, my report cards from kindergarten to high school graduation, were swept away; not a scrap of paper was left! At the end, he threatened us, saying, "If any written things are left in your home, you will be responsible for all the consequences!" When they were ready to leave, he told us maliciously, "If you'd been in Peking, we'd have shot you ages ago!"

Not long after the search, in September of 1967, you—Jiang Qing, Lan Ping—used the procurator's office, which you controlled, to put my husband, who was already a wreck, into so-called protective custody, which in fact was secret arrest! In prison, Comrade Jünli received inhumane, severe maltreatment, he was cruelly persecuted. For the whole of two years, you persecuted him to death. You—

JIANG QING: I don't know anything about that!

HUANG: You're not allowed to speak. I don't allow you to speak. What sort of creature are you?

JIANG QING: I don't know anything at all about that.

HUANG: I won't speak to you, you have no right to speak to me!

JIANG QING: Why haven't I the right to?

JUDGE: You haven't the right.

HUANG: I'll go on. After Comrade Jünli died, the little sons he left me . . . [break in the recording]

JUDGE: Read out the testimony given before his death by Zhao Dan [a well-known film actor] on October 7, and that of Wang Zhongying [his wife].

COURT READER: "At midnight one night in October 1966, a gang of people— we reckon there were thirteen of them—suddenly rushed into our home, making barely a sound. They were wearing Red Guard armbands, but were quite unlike the Red Guard rebel faction chiefs. They acted very secretly and quickly, as though they had specialist training.[9] First they searched our bodies, then they turned out all the wardrobes and cupboards and searched every corner of the house, and between the leaves of all the books. To cut a long story short, they took away all manuscripts, notebooks and diaries, books, photo albums, negatives, old movie magazines from before Liberation, a notice of the convening of a meeting signed by Zhang Chunqiao—in short, anything that had writing on it— not a scrap of paper remained. When it was getting light, they put the stuff into two sacks and made off in a big truck. The Lin Biao and Jiang Qing counterrevolutionary cliques wrought havoc for ten years; their towering crimes are too numerous to record! They are public enemies whose crimes no indictment can encompass. . . . Our home was searched many times and there was barely a thing left in it. The incident I described had an obviously political goal. We strongly condemn this kind of fascist behavior and urgently demand that the culprits be severely punished according to the law."

JUDGE: Read out the document number ninety-nine published by the Shanghai Municipal Committee office on October 20, 1966.[10]

COURT READER: "On October 9, toward dawn, Wang Zhongying, Zhao Dan, Zheng Jünli, Tong Ziling, Gu Eryi and others had their homes searched at almost exactly the same time by unidentified Red Guards. The special characteristic of all these people was that they were only interested in articles and literary materials, nothing else. Their manner was secretive. Zheng Jünli's house was searched for important confidential materials. In the small hours of the morning, around one A.M., over ten people wearing Red Guard armbands, aged between about twenty-five and thirty, entered Wukang Buildings, barred the front door, restrained the lift operator, and prevented anyone from using the telephone, while the rest of them went upstairs and entered Zheng Jünli's apartment. They moved and spoke very softly, and told Zheng straight out that they wanted to search his apartment for articles and top-secret documents. They made a very thorough search, not only in every corner of the flat but also of Zheng's body, clothes, and shoes."

JUDGE: Read out the testimony given on February 26, 1977, by Zhang Chunqiao's wife, Li Wenjing.

COURT READER: "In May of 1967, when I was helping out the interdepartmental documentary group, the rebel faction at the Haiyan Factory reported that on the night of October 8, 1966, Zhao Dan and Zheng Jünli had had their homes searched. At the time we felt that those movie personalities from the 1930s had had intimate relations with Jiang Qing, and the idea of the house searches was to confiscate material concerning her. So we mounted an investigation and discovered as a result that these searches were carried out by the Red Fourth Army. We realized then that this was a very important matter and we didn't dare investigate it any further. I wrote a letter to Zhang Chunqiao and Yao Wenyuan and gave it to Zhang's secretary, He Xiuwen, who sent a security guard to Nanjing. Zhang and Yao wrote back saying we shouldn't get involved in this. When Zhang and Yao returned to Shanghai, they said they knew about this matter, and the materials had all been sent to Jiang Qing in Peking. Looking at it now, those house searches were a conspiracy by the Lin Biao counterrevolutionary clique and the Gang of Four. When the Cultural Revolution started, they used means to protect Jiang Qing, as they were afraid the materials on her dirty history might fall into the wrong hands."

JUDGE: Accused Jiang Qing, I'm asking you whether in January 1967 you went to Ye Qün's residence.

JIANG: I don't remember.

JUDGE: You don't remember. I'm warning you again, was it under your personal supervision that Ye Qün and Xie Fuzhi burned the materials about you in Ye Qün's residence?

JIANG: I know of nothing like that.

JUDGE: You don't know. Chief Judge, on July 1, 1967, under the personal supervision of the accused Jiang Qing, at the former residence of Lin Biao and Ye Qün, Xie Fuzhi and Ye Qün burned the photographs, letters, and other materials that Jiang Tengjiao had collected in Shanghai. Concerning this crime of Jiang Qing's, the service personnel who were around when the materials were burned are important witnesses. First bring in the witness Zhao Gensheng.

[to Zhao] Were you working as a secretary in Lin Biao's office in 1967?

ZHAO: Yes.

JUDGE: This court advises you as a witness that according to the Code of Criminal Procedure, Article 115, you must give truthful testimony. If you intentionally give false testimony or cover up criminal evidence, you will bear responsibility under the law. Do you understand?

ZHAO: Yes.

JUDGE: Now, according to what has been uncovered concerning Jiang Qing's burning of the materials from the house searches, you will truthfully give testimony to the court. Let's hear it.

ZHAO: It was one day in October of 1966. I was in the office reading documents when Ye Qün called me to the Air Force Reception Center.

JUDGE: To go where?

ZHAO: To go to the Air Force Reception Center to pick up some materials. I didn't know what they were, but when I got there I found it was just a lot of old books, magazines, letters, notebooks, photographs—that sort of thing. They were stuffed any old way into a big bag. By looking at the books on the top, you could see it was all private materials belonging to Shanghai literary and art figures like Chen Liping, Zhao Dan, and other comrades. Ye Qün told me to take the lot back to a little office adjacent to her bedroom at her residence. After a few days, Ye Qün selected some of the material . . . and stuffed it into a bag, which she told me and Secretary Zhang to take to the Air Force Headquarters security office. We were quite in the dark and didn't know what she intended to do. She said, "These materials are very important. . . . Jiang Qing has given instructions for them to be taken to the safest place possible. . . . The air force has a command center in an air-raid shelter and one can go in when, necessary. I have already fixed things up with the air force. Don't worry about anything else. Take it there and don't let anyone else withdraw it except you—tell the air-force office." Thereupon Secretary Zhang and I took the package of materials to the security office of the air force, and told them only to give it to us when we came to get it. We asked for a receipt and left.

After about two months, in January of 1967, I was on duty one afternoon when Ye Qün phoned me from the Fishing Platform Guesthouse and told me to bring her the materials straight away, but not to open the seal. I got the materials from the section commander at the Air Force HQ security office. I took a car to Ye Qün's place and she soon appeared. When she saw the bag, she checked it to see the seal hadn't been broken. She said, "Wait a moment while we deal with this stuff. Go straight away to the furnace room in the back courtyard and open the furnace." I did so. After a short while, I saw Ye Qün, Xie Fuzhi, and Jiang Qing coming—they didn't say anything in my presence, and I left the room. Just as I was leaving, I saw Xie Fuzhi tear open the package and he and Ye Qün put the material bit by bit into the furnace. Jiang Qing went to a distance of about three meters from the furnace and paced back and forth, sometimes glancing across. Soon all the stuff was burned. . . .

JUDGE: Accused Jiang Qing, earlier you said you knew nothing of Ye Qün's searching of houses. . . . According to the testimony we have just heard, the confession of a criminal in front of the court, we can clearly see that she did know about it. While Ye Qün was making preparations to carry out this task, she said—did she not?—that a letter of Jiang Qing's had fallen into the hands of Gu Eryi and Zheng Jünli. . . . Then why, one may ask, did Ye Qün, who did not know Jiang Qing in the 1930s, and did not know Zheng Jünli or the others, and if Jiang Qing had not raised it, would not have known about Jiang Qing's letter falling into their hands, [know about this]?

As for the material Jiang Tengjiao found in the searches—if Ye Qün saw it and then indicated she was not satisfied with it . . . and she still had it put in the safest place possible, and it was burned under her [Jiang Qing's] personal supervision in January 1967—can this be taken to mean that this crime had nothing to do with her [Jiang Qing]—that she knew nothing about it?

Her denial absolutely cannot stand up. Today the court's investigation has made it clear that Jiang Qing schemed with Ye Qün to conduct illegal searches and to persecute close acquaintances from the literary and art world of the 1930s, and this had a goal she would not disclose. What must be especially pointed out here is that this crime had extremely serious consequences. The five literary and art figures mentioned above, after having had their homes illegally searched, all met vicious physical persecution. Zheng Jünli and Gu Eryi were persecuted to death. Zhao Dan was convicted and cruelly maltreated in prison for years on end. Chen Li was imprisoned, falsely accused of being a renegade and secret agent; Tong Ziling was "put in the cowpen."[11]

Jiang Qing cannot evade her criminal responsibility. It must also be pointed out that the illegal searches of those people's homes, and the physical maltreatment of them, were crimes committed jointly by Jiang Qing, Zhang Chunqiao, Ye Qün, Wu Faxian, Jiang Tengjiao, and Xie Fuzhi. They were a clear example of the scheming and collusion between Lin Biao and Jiang Qing in the Cultural Revolution.

Call Wu Faxian. . . . [to Wu] In October of 1966, did you have Jiang Tengjiao transferred from Shanghai to Peking?

WU: Yes.

JUDGE: Relate this matter truthfully.

WU: In October 1966, Ye Qün called me personally one evening and told me to have Jiang Tengjiao summoned to Peking immediately, on the grounds that she had an important task for him, but to maintain absolute secrecy. A few days later, Jiang Tengjiao suddenly arrived in Peking and at eight P.M. phoned me and asked me to come to the Air Force Reception Center at Dongjiaominxiang. He told me, "I've come to Peking because Ye Qün wants me to organize some Red Guards in Shanghai—that is, some people disguised as Red Guards—to search the homes of some people in literary and art circles and find some documents Jiang Qing wants and bring them back." Then Jiang Tengjiao opened a sack [he was carrying] and let me see the leather case inside it. Inside the case there were diaries, photographs, letters from Jiang Qing. Before I'd finished looking through them, Ye Qün arrived and said, "You're not to look at that, I'm taking it." And she hurried off with it. There's one other thing I want to say.

JUDGE: Go ahead.

WU: . . . I want to say what Jiang Qing's counterrevolutionary acts were. Toward the end of 1968, Jiang Qing summoned me in Shanghai and committed three big counterrevolutionary acts. One was that on February 22, 1968, in the evening, she said she had received a letter from Shanghai telling her that the Shanghai Public Security had spread around materials concerning her. So she told me to go straight away to Shanghai, make some arrests, and collect some materials. She ordered me to arrest Liang Guobin, Huang Chibo [senior public-security officers] and some other people concerned, and send back all materials picked up in Shanghai. I said I didn't know the situation in Shanghai and there were no people there who would obey me. Chen Boda said, "It doesn't matter, we'll give you a letter of authorization." He immediately took out some paper and wrote a letter of authorization for me. . . . When I got to Shanghai, I took the letter to Zhang Chunqiao, who promised me all assistance. . . . Then we arrested the people Jiang Qing had named, and took them back to Peking, where she had them locked up. . . .

As we have seen, Jiang Qing was particularly assiduous in suppressing facts about her life as a film actress in Shanghai in the 1930s. Her treatment of her former domestic servant and of the deputy secretary of the Shanghai Writers' Association showed the lengths to which she was prepared to go in silencing such people. She used her contacts in the Chinese Air Force to bring them to Peking and lock them up. Wu Faxian went on to tell the court of these incidents.

On the evening of February 23, 1968, the day before I was due to go to Shanghai, Jiang Qing sat down beside me at a meeting in the East Hall of the Great Hall of the People. She brought out a book, a novel; the author's name was Sun Jünqing [deputy secretary of the Shanghai Writers' Association]. He had written to Jiang Qing, and she asked me if I could look him up at my own convenience and send him to Peking. I should see him and have a chat with him, she said. I said I didn't know the man but I'd ask around after him. Jiang Qing said, "You're not to ask Zhang Chunqiao or any member of the Shanghai Municipal Revolutionary Committee. You can go to the [publishing] company and ask after him."

When I got to Shanghai, I looked up Jiang Tengjiao and another person, and after a couple of days asking around, I heard there really was such a person as Sun Jünqing. I had him brought round for a talk, face-to-face. I asked him, "Did you write to Jiang Qing in Peking?" He said he had. I said, "Jiang Qing wants you to take a trip to Peking so she can talk to you." Sun Jünqing said, "When shall I go?" I said, "In a couple of days I'll get an aircraft to take you to Peking." Later I looked up Zhang Shao-zhuan, head of a special case group, and Sun was taken to Peking by him.

On March 1, in the evening, Jiang Qing phoned me and asked me round to the Fishing Platform Guesthouse, to an apartment in Building Sixteen. She gave me some things to read, and told me that Sun Jünqing had intimate, "black" relations with some people in the General Political Department [of the armed forces] and in the air force, so the Peking Garrison should be asked to put him under guard. Jiang Qing wanted me to write a report for her and for Chen Boda and Kang Sheng. She told me to let her have it the next day, and when I did, she marked it "approved" and Sun Jünqing was arrested.

I had got back from Shanghai on February 28. On March 2, in the evening, Jiang Qing said that in the Thirties she had had a servant who knew a lot about her affairs. She wanted me to send someone to Shanghai to bring this person back to Peking. She was to be told that Jiang Qing wanted to have a chat with her. So I sent Zhang Shaozhuan and an assistant to fly to Shanghai and find her. As in the other case, Jiang Qing said they shouldn't tell Zhang Chunqiao or the Shanghai Municipal Committee, not even the Red Fourth Army, but should make inquiries secretly.

They asked around in Shanghai for three days. When they got back, they asked me, "What shall we do with this old woman we've brought?"— her name was Qin Guizhen. I told them to send her to the north building of the Dongjiaominxiang Air Force Reception Center and treat her as an honored guest. Then I told Zhang Shaozhuan to report back to me. He said, "Qin Guizhen's not badly off. The Shanghai Public Security Bureau has been looking after her for a long time; the Municipal Committee also takes care of her, and she's got contacts with Hongkong."

I reported this to Jiang Qing, and asked her when she wanted to see

Qin Guizhen. Jiang Qing said, "I won't see her. Write me a report saying that she has 'black' relations with the Shanghai Public Security Bureau and the Municipal Committee, and contacts with Hongkong. I want her arrested so that she won't bother me, and I'm not going to see her." She took out a notepad and told me to write a report then and there. So I followed her instructions and wrote a report, which she approved.

Toward evening, she sent Ye Qün and me and three other people to speak to Qin Guizhen. Qin took out Jiang Qing's photo and wept. Ye Qün said, "I can't speak Shanghai dialect." I asked Qin how she was, and told her that Jiang Qing couldn't see her because she wasn't well. In less than half an hour, Jiang Qing sent two jeeps to take her away, and she was arrested.

The accusations against Jiang Qing at the trial were damaging enough, though she was not implicated in the military plot to assassinate Mao. She acted mainly in her own interest, intriguing against people she hated or envied and using the Cultural Revolution group as the agent for her vendettas. She also had personal influence in the top air-force command. The role ascribed to her in the "revolutionization" of the Chinese stage and other cultural activities has been exaggerated, if one believes the testimony of people involved in these matters, as printed in the party media between late 1976 and the summer of 1977. (This is discussed in detail in chapter 9.)

Jiang Qing's main crimes, as laid out in the indictment, were her attempt to poison Mao's mind against Zhou Enlai and Deng Xiaoping; her involvement in the framing of Liu Shaoqi and her archrival, his wife, Wang Guangmei; her role as kingpin of the Gang of Four, purporting to serve as a direct channel to Mao (though it is now claimed that she and Mao were estranged from about 1971 on); her ordering of illegal house searches and the destruction of compromising material about herself; and her persecution of old friends and acquaintances, right down to her former housemaid.

There was undoubtedly sympathy for Jiang Qing when she claimed that everything she did was with Mao's authorization. The sly indication that the Gang of Four was actually a gang of five (including Mao) was popular in Peking at the time. It makes no sense to believe that as long ago as 1966 Mao simply was not aware of the activities of his wife and other top leftists; though, as time went on and he grew feebler, she may have misled him and distorted his instructions. Certainly Mao had no reason to be ignorant of the persecution of Liu Shaoqi, even if he did not personally organize its details.

Unofficial reports in Peking during and after the trial said Jiang

Qing made great play with Mao's alleged support of her activities, and also claimed she was in league with Hua Guofeng[12]—something that probably led to his political tumble in 1981, when he was replaced as party chairman by Deng's ally Hu Yaobang.[13]

To the Chinese people, these political accusations against Jiang Qing are perhaps less interesting than the exposés published in 1976–77 concerning her life-style. Many of these might have been dismissed as biased or exaggerated were it not for the coincidence that a few years earlier she had granted a series of lengthy interviews to an American historian, Dr. Roxane Witke.[14] Dr. Witke, with certain reservations, seemed genuinely to admire Jiang Qing—there was some meeting of minds between two feminists. The other top leaders were reportedly angry at Jiang Qing for giving the interviews to a foreigner and tried to have them suppressed. But once they were published, they were to damn her in the eyes of ordinary people the world over. Dr. Witke was certainly not trying to denigrate Mao's wife when she published her book on the interviews in 1977. However, her descriptions of Jiang Qing's personal life-style—her elaborate meals, the luxury of her private jet—could not fail to confirm subsequent accusations that she lived in a state of intense self-indulgence and dilettante amusements. According to Dr. Witke, the aircraft's forward cabin "was equipped with writing and dining tables, electronic fittings, and a full-sized bed covered with delicately embroidered silk sheets with a matching pillow of pink and white . . . two spectacularly pretty PLA girls delivered plates of roast duck, various sweet-meats, freshly steamed buns, exquisite fruits, ice cream, liquors, beers and wines."

"Take a photograph of me at work," Jiang Qing is quoted as saying in the caption to a photograph of her pressing dead flowers in a book—an activity more suited to a bored Victorian miss than to a self-styled revolutionary.

Jiang Qing aroused "male-chauvinist" feelings of dislike inherent in the Chinese tradition of oppression of women. Cartoons after her arrest showed her variously as a fox and as a snake—symbols of crafty women. One showed her embracing the Empress Dowager, who did so much to ruin China in the nineteenth century and on her deathbed reputedly warned against ever again letting a woman ascend the throne. Others concentrated on the black head scarves she affected, regarding them as a Western fashion unsuited to attendance at the funerals of Zhou Enlai and Mao himself. There were also persistent but not necessarily reliable rumors that she wore a wig, that the wig came off when she struggled while being arrested, that she tried to undress in the courtroom, etc., etc.

Jiang Qing's attitude toward Western culture is an odd mixture of hostility and appreciation. She adores Greta Garbo films. She may have been behind the purchase of *Last Tango in Paris* by a Chinese government organ in 1972. But she and Mao evidently thought nothing of banning all foreign dramatists from the Chinese stage, and all foreign novels. She is alleged to have suggested the design for the first Western-style frock to go on sale in Peking in the mid-1970s (it did not catch on). She ate large Western-style meals from time to time, and used an expensive Hasselblad camera. Yet in her public persona she was fiercely chauvinistic about foreign things. The mass-criticism group of the Department of Light Industry has offered the following anecdote:

> Jiang Qing once asked an arts-and-crafts factory in Tianjin [Tientsin] to make an embroidered handbag for her. In accordance with her requirements, the embroidery worker designed a peony pattern for her approval, but she angrily denounced it, saying: "This is not a Chinese flower, but a foreign peony! You are so accustomed to fawning on foreigners and worshiping things foreign!" In order to show her "expertise," she immediately asked the attendants to pluck a real peony for contrast. The result showed it looked exactly like the one embroidered. So she was embarrassed in front of everybody.

Her taste in literature also drew a great deal of criticism. One of the more bizarre attacks on Jiang Qing concerned her liking for Alexandre Dumas's *Count of Monte Cristo*. She was once indiscreet enough to say that "the characters are good" in the French novel. Her detractors in 1977 proclaimed that the book glorified the power of wealth and the rule of the aristocracy:

> By playing up Monte Cristo and publicizing the reactionary decadent bourgeois ideology, Jiang Qing played the disgusting role of corrupting the masses [who had no access to the book]. But this also illustrated her filthy soul and further bore out that she was an out-and-out typical representative of the bourgeoisie, as well as a fierce archenemy of the dictatorship of the proletariat. Although she was on the rampage for a long time, she was extremely feeble in essence. Just look at today's Jiang Qing. Hasn't

she eventually become dogshit spurned by mankind? This is really good![15]

Jiang Qing was fond of Margaret Mitchell's novel *Gone With the Wind*, and after her overthrow she was accused of admiring Scarlett O'Hara, whom the post-1976 media called Jiang's "foreign sister." Her critics found it easy to point out that Scarlett O'Hara was a member of the landlord slave-owning class. Jiang was said to have "lavished praises on her" in a talk she gave in 1972.

(When she met Witke in 1972, she is recorded only as having said, "It is not that it [*Gone With the Wind*] has any great literary merit. Rather the novel has enabled me to understand the American civil war in a graphic way. . . . In my youth I studied some American history, but I don't recall it clearly.")

During her movie career, Jiang Qing allegedly wanted to play the title role in *Sai Jinhua*, a play written by the 1930s author Xia Yan (an early victim of the Cultural Revolution). It portrayed the life of a courtesan of the late Qing (Manchu) dynasty who married a German general and accompanied him during the relief of the besieged foreign community in the Legation Quarter in 1901; as a result, the play was highly controversial, both for its historical content and its favorable evaluation of the female protagonist. Zhou Yang—who was later to become China's top literary bureaucrat—said in 1936 that it "opened a new vista for national-defense drama." But some patriotic Chinese were enraged by the sympathetic portrayal of a person they saw as a traitor. Jiang told Witke that there were threats on her life because she denounced the play. Witke notes Jiang's extreme vehemence in her dislike of the work in which she failed to star.

If Jiang's detractors are truthful in saying she herself wanted to play the role of Sai Jinhua, it is understandable that she should be so indignant about any suggestion that she liked the play, once it had been denounced by the Communist party.

One of Jiang Qing's most eloquent detractors was Guo Fenglian, a young woman member of the Central Committee, a member of the Standing Committee of the National People's Congress, and previously chairwoman of the Shanxi Province Revolutionary Committee. Two months after the overthrow of the Gang, she published her account of Jiang's visit to Dazhai Model Production Brigade. Guo claimed that Mao's widow arrived for a visit on September 8, 1975, in a special train with a retinue of over 100 people, several carloads of personal belongings, and four horses. She alone occupied a guesthouse that could accommodate over 100 foreign visitors, Guo claimed. Hating to have her peace and quiet disturbed, Jiang Qing banned the use of dynamite for farmland construction projects, and also banned wired broadcasts, driving of motor vehicles in the village, kitchen bellows, loud talk, and "any noise made while walking." She posed for photographs in front of vines and fruit trees, holding a basket, and insisted that an air-raid shelter be built on top of a nearby mountain, where millet fields would have to be destroyed to accommodate it. The brigade leaders compromised by digging up a tobacco patch, as the millet was nearly ripe, and she posed with a shovel in her hands to be photographed. She censored two-thirds of the items in a cultural show that had been planned for her entertainment, and instead sent out for old-style opera singers, and people to chant ancient poems to her. She demanded that a series of interlinking caves be joined together to make a villa for her, according to Guo."

On her next visit, Jiang Qing was furious that the people of Dazhai had filled in her "air-raid shelter" and erected a pigsty on the site. She said this had been done on orders from Vice-Chairman Deng Xiaoping, whom she detested. She criticized the way the peasants had planted some oil-bearing beans that she had donated, and began hoeing the patch until she complained that she was "tired and sweaty." She broke off wheat and maize stalks, complaining about their condition; accused the local leaders of arrogance; and said too many apple trees had been planted. Talking to the sales staff in the local store, she extolled women above men, claiming that Chinese society was originally matriarchal and making her notorious claim that even under communism there could be an empress. She donated color enlargements of photos of herself, but on her next visit found mainly pictures of Zhou Enlai on the wall. Guo Fenglian cleverly sidestepped her criticism of this by pointing out that as Guo herself, a relatively junior figure, was also shown in the enlargements, it would not be fitting to hang them on the wall.

"She had to be lifted out of bed, and to be dressed by others. She forced the service workers to fall on their knees to put on stockings and shoes for her. Once, as a comrade squatted on the floor and helped her put on the shoes, she turned on her with a scream of abuse: 'Go to hell!' With a kick, she caused this comrade to fall on her knees. What was more hateful was that she often incited her pet monkeys to chase and tease the women service workers. She burst into fits of laughter amid their cries."[16]

Xinhua quoted a VIP air crew as saying that when flying in a special plane she would use the bed and let the older and frailer Premier Zhou Enlai sit in the rear cabin for hours at a stretch. "In the eyes of Jiang Qing," this report said, "Premier Zhou was not worthy of respect. Flying the plane for Jiang Qing was a most difficult job. The temperature, light, and ventilation in the cabin had to be controlled strictly according to her standards, and even the slightest bumping on takeoff and landing was not allowed. Once when the plane landed with a slight bump, she flew into a rage and compelled the pilot to make a self-criticism."

She demanded that whenever she watched an indoor sporting contest the air conditioning be turned on—a very expensive procedure in a large hall due to the shortage of electric power in China.

Jiang Qing was accused of having opposed the posthumous cult of Dr. Sun Yat-sen, "father of the Chinese revolution." During a visit to the Biyun Si (Azure Clouds Temple) in the Western Hills near Peking in 1971, she ordered the removal of Mao's picture and quotations from the small museum there devoted to Sun, and shortly afterward ordered the museum closed. It was reopened, together with the temple itself, in 1979.

There are other stories of ways in which Jiang Qing tried to rewrite history. One such incident has to do with the Xisha Islands battle. In 1974 the Chinese Navy was involved in a battle with South Vietnamese naval vessels over the sovereignty of the Paracel (Xisha) Islands in the South China Sea. The Chinese won, and established garrisons and settlers on the islands, which are thought to be located near big deposits of offshore oil. They are now a bone of contention between Peking and Hanoi.

After the battle of the Xisha Islands, Jiang Qing sent an unnamed writer to the area to write up the incident. After a brief visit to the South China Sea, the writer went to Canton and wrote a poem that took the dual form of a description of the battle and a report on it to senior leaders. Jiang Qing was delighted with this work and ordered its early publication. Her detractors say that she wanted the poem to eulogize her as the inspiration to the navy men who expelled South Vietnamese occupation forces from the islands. This is indicated by a passage describing how the captain of one of the Chinese vessels, at the very point of engagement, rested his eyes on a photograph of Mt. Lu taken by Jiang Qing.

It was not the first time Jiang Qing had shown an interest in the South China Sea arena. Between 1964 and 1971, it is alleged, she visited the region three times, "indulging herself all the time in gluttony and pleasure-seeking." She made a fool of herself by asking why she could not see the Xisha Islands from Hainan Island, some 300 miles away, and she belittled the military difficulties of capturing and holding the Xisha, saying it could be done simply by "sending some militiamen."

Jiang Qing was evidently heartily disliked by many ordinary Chinese people who came in contact with her, and her reputation was lurid. It is rumored that when she was finally arrested, her female attendants spat in her face and said the equivalent of "Now you'll get yours, you old bitch!"

2
YAO WENYUAN: "THE WAY I SAW IT THEN"

The clown of the trial—and such grim events often provide moments of light relief—was Yao Wenyuan, the Shanghai-bred journalist and propagandist whose 1965 article attacking a play by Peking's Vice-Mayor Wu Han was the prelude for the Cultural Revolution. With his popping, fishlike eyes, his stammer, and his general air of immaturity, it is almost impossible to believe that he masterminded the ideology of a movement in which millions of people died or were severely maltreated.

Yao Wenyuan, who was fifty at the time of the trial, is a native of the picturesque town of Shaoxing in the lush province of Zhejiang. In the 1950s he was prominent in the Communist youth movement and began to write articles on Maoist theory. His writing became increasingly polemical until in 1965 he published an article in the Shanghai daily *Wenhui Bao* attacking Peking Vice-Mayor Wu Han for his play *Hai Rui Dismissed from Office,* which allegedly criticized Mao's demotion of former defense minister Marshal Peng Dehuai.[1] Some believe the article was instigated by Zhang Chunqiao, on the instructions of Mao. Yao joined the Central Cultural Revolution Group in Peking in the following year, and in 1967 became Zhang Chunqiao's deputy as leader of the Shanghai Revolutionary Committee. However, he spent most of his time in Peking, writing many of the keynote articles guiding the progress of the Cultural Revolution. Rumor had it that he married one of Mao's daughters. In 1969, at the Tenth Congress of the Communist party, he was appointed a member of the Central Committee and Politburo, positions he held until his purge in 1976.

Yao's testimony made clear that even during the trial he was still thinking in Marxist—or rather Maoist—terms. His chief line of defense was that, before his disgrace, he supported a leftist political line, and all his "mistakes" could be seen in the light of that basic position. This defense was not very effective since it had been declared at the outset that the court would try the accused only for actual crimes, as defined in the 1980 Criminal Code, and not for political "errors" or mistaken positions adopted in the "line struggle" that has dominated Chinese politics to this day.

Yao was tried principally for his part in the conspiracy to denounce Premier Zhou Enlai and Vice-Chairman Deng Xiaoping to Chairman Mao while the latter was resting in Changsha in 1974; and for his whipping up of the antirightist campaign of 1975–76, which aimed to discredit Deng in the eyes of the party and nation. Yao was blamed for using his influence in the party media—especially the *People's Daily* and *Red Flag*—to gather discreditable material on veteran cadres (particularly those who had been disgraced in the early Cultural Revolution, returned from 1973 on, and been given responsible jobs again by Deng). Yao was also accused of suppressing media coverage of the funeral of Zhou Enlai in January 1976, and of manipulating press photographs to falsify the relative status of individual leaders. He was blamed, too, for producing in 1974 the slogan "There's an atmosphere like at the Lushan Plenum"—and having Wang Hongwen repeat it to Mao in Changsha.

The Lushan Plenum to which he referred should not be confused with the one at which Marshal Peng Dehuai met his nemesis in 1959. Yao's slogan referred to the Second Plenary Session of the Ninth Party Congress, held in August 1970, when Lin Biao attempted to go against Mao's wishes by restoring the position of Head of State previously held by Liu Shaoqi. Lin wanted to "kick Mao upstairs" by again making him Head of State, a post he had held in the Fifties, and which, as shown by the overthrow of Liu Shaoqi, bestowed no real power on the incumbent, but would tie him up in a lot of formal functions and meetings with visiting foreign dignitaries.

In the interrogation of Yao Wenyuan, it is clear how much importance the court attached to pinning down his responsibility as a manipulator of the media—taking it upon himself to send out press reporters as political spies, changing the texts and headlines of articles, dictating their content, and planning their use in the campaign against Deng in 1975–76, as well as in the early Cultural Revolution. Deng seems to have been viewed by Yao Wenyuan as "public enemy number one" throughout the course of the Cultural Revolution decade of 1966–76.

The interrogation of Yao shows how important the media are and were in Chinese political campaigns. The tiniest change in the text can mean a major difference of political line, and a cursory nod of approval could lead to the arrest and maltreatment of anyone so much as suspected of disloyalty to the Maoist banner.

YAO'S CONFESSION OF AUGUST 30, 1979

COURT READER: "In October 1974, about eight o'clock one evening, at a Politburo meeting chaired by Wang Hongwen, Deng Xiaoping had a violent quarrel with Jiang Qing. After the meeting, Jiang Qing told me to come to the Fishing Platform Guesthouse cinema. Wang Hongwen and Zhang Chunqiao were there too. We had already heard that Chairman Mao had decided to make Comrade Deng Xiaoping first vice-premier. To tell Chairman Mao things about Comrade Xiaoping and denounce him again was just trying to alter a decision Chairman Mao had already taken."

EXTRACT FROM YAO WENYUAN'S DIARY FOR OCTOBER 18, 1974

COURT READER: "The struggle has undergone a rapid change of character. There's already a feeling like at the Lushan Plenum. The development of the situation will not be governed by our will."

TESTIMONY GIVEN BY ZHANG YÜFENG[2] ON JULY 18, 1980

COURT READER: "In October 1974, Chairman Mao was convalescing in Changsha. On October 18, at about 1400 hours, Chairman Mao received Wang Hongwen at his residence, and I was also present. Wang Hongwen said, 'With your approval, I came immediately. I've come at some risk.' Then Wang Hongwen brought out some documents about the M.V. *Feng Qing*.[3] He said that at a Politburo meeting Jiang Qing had a blazing row with Deng Xiaoping over this matter, and he repeated some of the things Jiang Qing and Deng Xiaoping had said. He also said, 'You see, Deng is still pushing his previous line that buying ships is better than building them, and chartering them is better than buying them.' He said speculatively that such hard feelings were connected with the issue of the appointment of a chief of the general staff, which had been brewing up lately. . . . Wang Hongwen gave puffs to [praised] Zhang Chunqiao, Yao Wenyuan, and Jiang Qing. He said Yao Wenyuan liked reading so much, while Zhang Chunqiao was good at analyzing problems. He praised Jiang Qing, too.

"When they had finished talking, Chairman Mao asked Wang Hongwen how many days he was staying, since he could get out and about and take a look around. Wang Hongwen said he had to rush back to Peking that day because he wanted to tell the others what the Chairman had said. The Chairman said, 'All right, go back and see more of the premier and Comrade Ye Jianying. Don't work with Jiang Qing. Be careful of her.' "

JUDGE: Whose idea was it to send Wang Hongwen to Changsha to slander Deng Xiaoping and other party and state leaders?

YAO: It was Jiang Qing who at the very beginning suggested that Deng Xiaoping—oops!—I mean Wang Hongwen—that Wang Hongwen should go to Changsha.

JUDGE: So this business was Jiang Qing's idea?

YAO: Yes.

JUDGE: What were you aiming at with this plan?

YAO: By [sending Wang Hongwen] to Changsha [we hoped to] give Chairman Mao a distorted picture of the situation. As far as I personally am concerned, my thinking at the time was that I objected to Deng Xiaoping being made first vice-premier. But now I think of it, I didn't raise any objection to his appointment, none at all. So this business of someone going to Changsha to object to Deng Xiaoping being made first vice-premier was really trying to influence Chairman Mao over a decision he had already taken.

JUDGE: I now ask you: When, in your conspiracy and secret plan, you said that Peking at that time had something of the flavor of the Lushan Plenum, and you had a similar thing written in your diary—

YAO: Some people were saying, "Deng Xiaoping has jumped out again [i.e., become politically active again]."

JUDGE: Did somebody say these words?

YAO: I can only say truthfully that I really can't remember now, I can't confirm or deny it.

JUDGE: Huh! Jiang Qing was a member of the Politburo. How could she so easily convene a meeting of a party vice-chairman [Wang Hongwen], a full member of the Politburo [Zhang Chunqiao], and you, a Politburo member, at Building Seventeen? Was that normal?

YAO: I acknowledge that it was not normal. This—

JUDGE: This question exposes the fact that Jiang Qing was the head of the counterrevolutionary clique, the Gang of Four.

The *People's Daily* (June 18, 1977) compared Yao, in a saying of Mao's, to "an ant coming out of a hole before a storm." It alleged, without quoting references, that Yao had followed Khrushchev in denigrating personality cults, "thus pointing the spearhead straight at the great leader Chairman Mao."

This makes bizarre reading in the 1980s, when the party, under Deng Xiaoping's effective leadership, has roundly condemned Mao's personality cult as one of the worst aspects of his rule. Yao was also credited with attacking party leaders as "having only mechanical dogmas and a vision as narrow as the eye of a needle," and "knowing only about machines and slogans, not about people." This is similar to the standard critique of the post-Mao bureaucracy frequently voiced in Peking by the Deng group.

Equally ironic, in view of Yao's supposed orientation toward Maoist leftism, is the accusation to the effect that Yao had said, "The presence of leaders in [formation of] ideology is liable to make some young people who dislike using their brains become simpleminded. They are not accustomed to thinking independently and are not accustomed to judging things independently on the complicated tide of thought. They parrot what others say and follow blindly like a swarm of bees." This is almost identical with the Dengist right-moderates' strictures on the Cultural Revolution and the cult of Mao. In other words, the supposed prototypical extreme leftist identified some of the same problem areas in the Communist system of government as do the Deng group and their propagandists of the current day.

Yao was supported and promoted by Zhang Chunqiao, who was more of an organizer than theorist or writer, and wanted Yao's pungent, polemical style to be used in the leftist cause. In the mid-Sixties, Jiang Qing visited Shanghai, her old stamping ground, and Zhang introduced Yao to her. The journalist had already set his sights high by publicly attacking the Shanghai Public Security Bureau for "secret-police methods." By coincidence, Jiang Qing was furious with the Shanghai police for holding on to the dossier compiled on her by the former Guomindang security police. Eventually she had three top public-security officials sent to Peking and imprisoned, and one of them was "persecuted to death."

Like most top polemicists in China, Yao Wenyuan resorted to historical allegory to make his points in the party press. He recalled that the legendary emperor Shun was followed by his people wherever he went and was quoted as saying, "We [the Gang of Four] are like this." He also quoted the ancient Legalist philosopher Han Fei to commend the practice of conspiracy and lying for political goals.

Himself a strict dogmatist, Yao understood the objections to dogmatism. He once wrote: "Dogmatic ideas are the stumbling blocks to 'let a hundred flowers bloom and a hundred schools of thought contend,' " and he called on the country's literary critics to "liberate themselves from the rigid formula of dogmatism." He called dogmatists "people with the mentality of Buddha-worshipers." It would be fanciful to pigeonhole Yao as a secret opponent of Mao, but it is instructive to note that political alliance with the extreme left does not necessarily mean the surrender of all independent thought.

Yao suffered from a Maoist policy that in theory he would have supported—the visiting of political sins on the heads of their perpetrators' offspring. Yao is the son of Yao Pengzi, a left-leaning littérateur active in Shanghai in the 1930s. Most unfortunately for his son, Yao Pengzi fell out with the great writer Lu Xün and was denounced by him. He did indeed renounce communism in May 1934, and declared his allegiance to the democratic ideas of Sun Yat-sen. This was used to smear Yao Wenyuan's name after Mao's death.

Yao Wenyuan backed up his opinions from widely disparate literary and artistic sources. In reviewing a volume of poetry, he expounded his ideas on the dignity of labor, drawing on the classic Chinese novel *Shui Hu Zhuan* (the Oriental equivalent of England's Robin Hood legend, but much richer and more extensive). He praised the sculptor Rodin's idea of constructing a pillar glorifying labor, and he extolled the writings of a Tang dynasty author, Li Shen, who had written about the sufferings of the peasantry.

One of the most specific accusations against Yao—not gone into in the trial transcripts—was that he misused newspaper photographs to play down the importance of Hua Guofeng, Premier Zhou Enlai, and Marshal Zhu De, who was chairman of the Chinese People's Political Consultative Conference (CPPCC) and who died in 1976 shortly before Mao.

Yao allegedly restricted newspapers to a single page of commemorative photographs of Zhou Enlai's funeral, when four pages had been originally proposed. He banned pictures of Zhou and Mao standing together, and ordered that Mao be cut out of a picture showing the leaders welcoming Zhou on his return from negotiations in Moscow in 1964. He proscribed sets of photos prepared by Xinhua on the life of Zhou. Yao also ordered that photos of the faces of mourners at Zhou's funeral be touched up to remove traces of tears! He had Wang Hongwen inserted into a picture of Mao talking to Zhou in 1973 at the Tenth Party Congress, and interfered with later pictures of leaders to play down the position of the fast-rising Hua Guofeng. A Shanghai newspaper was ordered by Yao to print photos of the Tenth Congress that showed Wang Hongwen "1.45 cm. taller and broader than Zhou." Jiang Qing insisted on having Zhang Chunqiao stand next to her in a photograph and refused to be shown standing next to General Xü Shiyou, at that time commander of the Nanking Military Region, which includes Shanghai.

(It is a matter of satisfaction for China watchers that these allegations, printed by Xinhua on March 29, 1977, officially confirm the importance of photo-doctoring in Chinese power struggles. They have often been accused of blowing the significance of official photographs out of proportion, but the Xinhua report shows that, far from doing that, they missed important angles that Chinese politicians would have spotted.)

On the evening of April 30, 1976, Mao wrote out his famous instructions to his chosen successor, Hua Guofeng: "With you in charge I am at ease." Turned into an oil painting, this event was widely publicized after Mao's death as evidence of Hua's moral authority. But Yao Wenyuan, according to the current-day version, suppressed a selection of other pictures showing Mao and Hua together, which had been specifically ordered by the old Chairman.

Yao has also been accused of having suppressed press photos showing Hua visiting Tianjin and the earthquake-stricken city of Tangshan in 1976, one of the worst such disasters in world history. Instead he published a picture of Jiang Qing and Wang Hongwen presiding over a meeting of rescue workers—relegating to the background Premier Hua Guofeng, who was giving a speech at the meeting.

Yao's manipulation of the Chinese media was his real specialty, which he carried out from 1966 until the fall of the Gang in 1976. Besides the photo-doctoring described above, he sent teams of news reporters out to the provinces with instructions to send back accounts of the progress of the campaign against the disgraced Deng, and by implication those of his associates who were still in power.

FURTHER INTERROGATION OF YAO WENYUAN

JUDGE: In 1976, you ganged up with the former editor of the *People's Daily*, Lu Ying, to send people into various departments of the Party Central Committee, and to certain provinces and cities, to collect material to be used to frame and persecute leading cadres of the party, state and armed forces. Answer!

YAO: Very well! . . . It is a fact, I admit it, that in 1976 we sent people out to get a better understanding of the campaign to "Counterattack the Rightist Wind of Reversing Verdicts."[4] At first we didn't send out any reporters, but after Wang Hongwen returned to Peking,[5] the Politburo was just having a meeting. I hadn't told Lu Ying about this meeting, because I respected the party statutes [concerning secrecy of high-level proceedings]. Without telling me, Wang Hongwen called Lu Ying and a responsible person from Xinhua News Agency to go to his place for a talk. The talk was pretty frank; he told them, "It's not enough just to have Xinhua reflecting what's going on; it should be matched up with the *People's*

Daily so that the [Party] Center will be able to understand what's up."
Lu Ying later reported to me on what Wang Hongwen had said. He
told me, "Vice-Chairman Wang has issued an important directive with a
new spirit." Lu Ying told me what Wang Hongwen had said. At that time
my thinking was that I really didn't want to send reporters out, because
in the former part of the campaign against Lin Biao and Confucius, the
reporters had raised many problems, and it wasn't long since we'd tight-
ened up.[6] I didn't know whether I ought to approve Wang Hongwen's
opinion, so I just gave it tacit consent and let Lu Ying send the reporters
out.

JUDGE: Did you give tacit consent or did you agree to it?

YAO: I should say that in the beginning I was just giving tacit consent . . . but later I must say I agreed with it.

JUDGE: Tell me, what did you send those people out to do?

YAO: To collect information on the so-called Counterattack Against the
Rightist Wind of Reversing Verdicts. At that time the "counterattack" was
aimed at a number of cadres who had come out [of detention or disgrace]
and had been working for a while. I admit that. The campaign tended to
use [leftist] phrases like "the home-going contingent."[7] . . .

JUDGE: You ought to realize that the campaign at that time was conducted
according to extremely clear regulations laid down by the Party Center
to every leader of a party committee. Do you understand? Do you?

YAO: I know.

JUDGE: If you knew that, why did you send those people out?

YAO: Wang Hongwen was a vice-chairman! He had already spoken to Lu
Ying, and very specifically.

JUDGE: *You* sent the reporters out. Don't try to make out it was Wang
Hongwen! Wang Hongwen had his own sphere of activity. *You* looked
after the reporters!

YAO: Yes.

JUDGE: Read out Wang Jingzhong's testimony.

COURT READER: "At the time I was a responsible person on the news desk
at the *People's Daily*. I was a witness to the sending out of reporters by
Lu Ying and Liu Zhiping. I recall that in 1976, from January till September, Lu Ying sent out altogether four teams, about a hundred people in
all. The first three teams were mostly sent to Jiangsu, Fujian, Jiangxi,
Zhejiang, and other provinces. They pointed their spearheads at the responsible comrades of those places; for instance in Fujian they pointed it
at Comrade Liao Zhiqao, in Jiangxi at Comrade Jiang Weiqing, and in
Jiangsu at Comrade Peng Chong."[8]

[The witness Wu Lun, a former journalist, takes the stand.]

WU: One afternoon in May of 1976, Wang Hongwen summoned me to the
Fishing Platform Guesthouse and we met in a conference room. He talked

a lot and I took notes, which I've already handed over to the government. He spoke mostly about collecting materials on old cadres. He also instructed me to go to the Party Center and to the State Council, as well as to Fujian, Zhejiang, and some other provinces and cities to collect such materials. He said, "Go and see Yao Wenyuan again and discuss it with him."

In the evening I phoned Yao's secretary and said I had something to report to him. The secretary phoned me back and I got a car to his residence. In a conference room at his house, I sat and waited for a while, then he appeared. I first told him about my talk with Wang Hongwen, and told him Wang had ordered me to send a reporter from the *Wenhui Bao*[9] to certain departments of the Party Center, the state, and the armed forces, and to Fujian, Zhejiang, and other provinces and cities, to collect data. "Wang Hongwen told me to come and discuss it with you."

Yao said, "I know about it. I agree." He also gave me instructions to the general effect that it was important that the reporters go to the provincial party committees to find out what was going on. . . . Unrepentant people following the capitalist road weren't just one person, they were a stratum—not only in the Party Center but in the provinces, too. People who were sent down [to investigate] should pay much attention to the new cadres' opinions. They should be good at going against the tide[10] and have a high level of line consciousness, their [ideological] banner should be bright, and they should not fear difficulties. Then he told me, "When you go back to pass out these instructions, don't say they come from me. Say what I said in your own style—that'll be fine."

Apart from this occasion, Yao Wenyuan many times instructed me to send out reporters to the Party Center and other places to gather materials. . . . Toward the end of June 1976, he phoned me one day and said, "Come to the Fishing Platform Guesthouse and revise the July 1 editorial."[11] When I got there, [we met in] a big conference room, and Zhang Chunqiao was there, too. After we'd revised the July 1 editorial, Zhang Chunqiao said, "The Ministry of Foreign Trade is taking the things the workers have sweated blood to produce and is selling them off cheaply in foreign countries while importing things from abroad at high prices. This is nation-selling capitulationism!" He spoke with great emotion. "You can send some reporters to investigate!" Yao Wenyuan immediately said, "I hear that a policy research group of the State Council is preparing an article or something. I don't know what. Send some people to find out."

JUDGE: Read out the situation report given to Yao Wenyuan on July 29, 1976.

COURT READER: "In July last year, Deng Xiaoping used the Political Research Bureau to get control of an academic department, and sent Lin Lide, Liu Yangqiao, and Song Yiping to organize a temporary leadership group and seize power of the academic department and push his revisionist

line in it. He is conducting restorationism on a big scale, and has turned
the department into part of his opinion-forming territory for restoration
of capitalism."

YAO: [interrupting] I'd like to say a few words about that. As regards the
letter I received from him,[12] I didn't want to—he—I didn't tell him to
go and find out what was going on in the department. I was concerned
about it. It wasn't a leadership matter, it was another matter. . . . It's
only after I read [the indictment] that I realized, because on December
5—as regards the bit about the department, attacking leaders and cadres!
My notes reflected my own views—but you see, telling him to slip in to
find out what was going on, well, it's true, I take responsibility.

One summary of the charges against Yao gives some sense of the
scope and variety of his activities:

TV COMMENTATOR: Yao Wenyuan is accused of the following crimes. First,
he slandered Chen Pixian and Cao Diqiu [respectively mayor and vice-
mayor of Shanghai, overthrown in 1967]. . . . Second, in 1967 he supported the Shandong Revolutionary Committee chairman, Wang Shaoyü,
in using armed force to suppress the masses' struggle. Third, he created
a climate of opinion and propaganda that enabled him personally to revise
and approve articles slandering old leading cadres in the party and government by calling them "bourgeois democrats" and "followers of the
capitalist road," whipping up [the movement to] persecute them.

JUDGE: On March 3, 1976, the *People's Daily* published the article "Criticize
the Unrepentant Follower of the Capitalist Road in the Party," slandering
old cadres. . . . This was an organized, planned movement with its own
theory and program. Did you revise this article?

YAO: There were a lot of articles. I can't remember now.

JUDGE: You can think about it.

YAO: I believe the court undoubtedly has a factual basis [for the accusation].
Since I revised and checked the article, and it exists, we can take it as a
factual basis.

JUDGE: Very well. Now show Yao Wenyuan the article. [to Yao] Take a look
and see if it was revised by you.

YAO: Yes, it was. The headline originally was "Rectify the Unrepentant
Follower of the Capitalist Road in the Party."

JUDGE: Did you incite the writing and revise and check the article entitled
"From Bourgeois Democrat to Follower of the Capitalist Road," signed
with the pseudonym Chi Man [literally, "latecoming"], which was printed
in the number three issue of the journal *Red Flag* in 1976?

YAO: That article was revised and inspected by me.

[The witness Lin Wenmu takes the stand.]

LIN: I was one of the responsible persons in the editorial department of *Red Flag*, and I understood the way the writing of this article was organized and the circumstances of its revision. Now I truthfully testify to the court that throughout the writing of that article, and the process of its revision, Yao Wenyuan twice gave verbal instructions, gave written directions twice, and made two telephone calls about it. The verbal instructions were connected with the arrangement of the contents of the article. Yao Wenyuan also read it himself five times, and three of those times he made revisions in his own handwriting before approving it for publication.

YAO: What the witness has said about my revision of the article and my changing its headline is true, I admit it.

So the case against Yao rested on the views he had expressed orally or in writing—even down to the significance of the change of one word in the title of an article. To "criticize" someone in the Cultural Revolution would be an act of extreme hostility. Merely to "rectify" someone implies that he or she will be treated quite leniently provided a confession and self-criticism are submitted and accepted.

Even more controversial than Yao's changing of headlines, or using reporters to stir up the campaigns against Deng, or his manipulation of the press coverage of Zhou Enlai's funeral, was his reaction to the Tiananmen riots of April 5, 1976, a turning point in the Chinese public's responses to the leadership style of the Gang of Four. Premier Zhou Enlai, who died in January of that year, was genuinely mourned by the people, who knew that he had tried to soften the more callous acts of Mao's group of left-radicals in the Cultural Revolution. On Sunday, April 4, thousands of people, especially young people, thronged the huge square in the center of Peking, writing and pasting up emotional declarations and poems dedicated to Zhou, and making speeches. That night, however, the radicals sent people to clear away the wreaths. People on their way to work the next morning reacted with fury when they saw what had been done. Some tried to storm the huge bronze and glass doors of the Great Hall of the People. Others burned cars, trees, and even a small police station in a corner of the square. Young men who shouted criticisms of Zhou were beaten bloody. As night fell, militiamen—or police in disguise—fell upon the rioters with nightsticks. Some were taken into a nearby park, and—many people in Peking insist—they were shot there in batches.

Deng Xiaoping was blamed as the indirect cause of the riots—the intimation being that he had seduced the masses with his attempts to bring them a better material and cultural life. He was removed from his posts but allowed to keep his party membership "to see how he behaves." The public reaction to Deng's ousting was one of irritation and then apathy. People on the streets would turn their heads away when they saw a truck with drums and cymbals and red bunting celebrating his downfall.

With the suppression of the rioters, the Gang's position, bolstered by its association with Mao, grew temporarily stronger. But less than a month after Mao's death on September 9, other members of the Politburo—including Mao's former personal security chief and custodian of the party records, Wang Dongxing—turned on the Gang and arrested them. Yao Wenyuan was interrogated about his role in the publication of an article condemning the riots.

THE TIANANMEN SQUARE RIOTS

JUDGE: Let us investigate this matter. On April 3, 1976, was it you who revised and approved the proofs of a collection of reports of the people's demonstrations in front of the Monument to the Heroes [of the Revolution]? Show, project, and read out these proofs. [to Yao] Was that revised by you?

YAO: Yes.

COURT READER: The first part of the original text reads as follows: "On April 2, many people continued to arrive at the Monument to the People's Heroes to commemorate Premier Zhou. From April 1 till the afternoon of April 2, about two hundred thousand people came, bringing more than a thousand wreaths. All round the terrace of the monument, memorial poems have been stuck up, and at any given time there must be several tens of thousands of people on the square." Yao Wenyuan deleted the first sentence.

JUDGE: Further, did you add the word *extraordinary*?

YAO: Yes.

JUDGE: Now project the proofs! They contain a poem entitled "The River Is a Red Flood." Yao Wenyuan deleted part of this poem. Read it out.

COURT READER: *"The ancient Chinese earth*
Shrugs off a few buzzing flies . . .
They like their own sound.
The great man in his glory is here.
Why let the little insects lay their maggots?
My breast burns with rage,
I slap the table and stand up.
Oh, you of like mind,
Unite closely in our own defense.
Premier Zhou!
Take up the fire and iron,
Prepare for the decisive battle.

No matter how fierce the bear is,
We'll fight him blow for blow!
We'll pluck out the wicked wolf with his hidden tail!
Fight till the end!"

Yao Wenyuan deleted the first half of this poem, and left in only the passage beginning "Take up the fire and iron!" In his own handwriting, he added at the end: "This kind of counterrevolutionary, inflammatory talk shows that the planner behind the scenes [Deng Xiaoping] is hoping to act when the talking's done."

JUDGE: Yao Wenyuan, I ask you: Why did you delete the content [of the poem] that expressed the masses' defense of Premier Zhou?

YAO: The main reason was that I felt it was too sweeping! Too abusive—I mean that stuff about flies— Those—those words, those—those proofs, only a dozen or so people had seen them, but I, you see, at that time I deleted it. The main thing is— The bit about Premier Zhou, there's a lot of it! At the time I deleted this abusive stuff. Not only this, either! But I see now that I shouldn't have deleted anything but printed it as it stood!

JUDGE: Then how could you say that the people's defense of Premier Zhou was counterrevolutionary and inflammatory and constituted counterrevolutionary acts?

YAO: Be—because for those past ten years, the way I saw it then, it wasn't mourning for Premier Zhou, it was "taking up the fire and iron." In my thinking, my thinking, I felt—felt—at that time I'd never seen such slogans!

JUDGE: Further, on April 5, 1976, the "Report on the Situation" printed in the *People's Daily*, the text of the proofs—"Counterrevolutionary Political Incident on Tiananmen Square"—was it revised and approved by you?

YAO: Yes!

JUDGE: Now show and project the original proofs Yao Wenyuan approved.

COURT READER: The original text said: "There were about a dozen young fellows who were separately beaten up by rioters. The rioters said afterward that two of them were worker-peasant-soldier students from Qinghua University, and one of them was in the army. They had said publicly that Premier Zhou was the biggest capitalist-road follower in the party. Because of this their heads were covered with blood and their faces were swollen, with blood running off them. Many people shouted, 'Kill them! Kill them!' "

Yao Wenyuan deleted the bit about their saying Premier Zhou was a follower of the capitalist road, and the words *because of this*.

JUDGE: Yao Wenyuan, why did you delete the words insulting to Premier Zhou, which were said by the people who were beaten up?

YAO: Oh! I'll tell you truthfully. When I heard about this, it was a good long time later, on the day when things were particularly tense because of the Tiananmen Square incident. When I got this news, I'd been hearing many people's verbal reports on what was going on in the square. Some of them were told by [Vice-] Chairman Wang Dongxing [Mao's internal-security chief] and [Vice-] Chairman Wu Deh [mayor of Peking] and some responsible people from Qinghua University and from the Public Security Bureau, and lots of others. None of them said that such a slogan had been uttered. Naturally it would have been [considered] a counterreactionary slogan.

JUDGE: Yao Wenyuan's revisions were made entirely with an ulterior intention, to stand truth on its head and protect people who blackened and slandered Premier Zhou, turning them into good, innocent people.

Having established to its own satisfaction that Yao was firmly against the rioters, the court set out to demolish his contention that he was mainly guilty of political error and not guilty of any specific criminal act. (It had been stated at the outset of the trial that the defendants were not being tried for political error but for actual crimes.)

JUDGE: Now tell me, if the masses rise up to expose conspirators, and the conspirator Zhang Chunqiao was trying to seize power, how could you say this was counterrevolutionary activity?

YAO: All right, I'll answer that question. At the time, ideologically speaking, I thought that during the so-called Counterattack on the Rightist Wind of Reversal of Verdicts— Now I have revised my perception, and won't talk about the way I perceived things then. I felt that the wall posters which went up like that and the emergence of that kind of slogan was a counterblow against the Counterattack on the Rightist Wind of Reversal of Verdicts. According to directives from the Central Committee at that time, the Rightist Wind represented the bourgeoisie, didn't it? It was a counterrevolutionary adverse current—that's what my thinking was at the time.

JUDGE: Read out and project Yao Wenyuan's diary for April 3, 1976, the day he telephoned Lu Ying.

COURT READER: "On April 3, after reactionary slogans appeared in Jiangsu and Zhejiang provinces, they have begun to be seen in Peking. Yesterday crowds of people congregated on Tiananmen Square and used commemorations of the premier [Zhou Enlai] to hint at dissatisfaction with the [antirightist] movement, made counterrevolutionary speeches, and proclaimed counterrevolutionary slogans. Some are openly anti-Communist; those are the manifestation of the decadent forces' life-and-death struggle and their wild counterblows. Have they used up their behind-the-scenes source of strength? The capitalist class's intellectual elements, like the Number Seven Engineering Department of the Academy of Sciences, are their base, and this fully explains why the people in the party taking the capitalist road have got on the road. Not only may we lose the revolutionary achievements of socialism, and the democratic revolution, but it will also deeply educate the leftists and some of the centrists. It's a live lesson in class struggle, and the forces of reaction want to extol Premier Zhou Enlai."

JUDGE: At the end of March 1976, did you telephone to Lu Ying [editor of the *People's Daily* at the time] about big-character posters being put up by the masses in Nanking to mourn Premier Zhou and oppose Zhang Chunqiao?[13]

YAO: Yes, yes, I did.

JUDGE: What did you say to him?

YAO: At that time— There's something I'd like to explain. At that time I saw the Xinhua proof of [an article on] the big-character posters; I realized that it wasn't just a question of posters, but also things painted on the train—the train was going from Nanking direct to Peking. So I told Lu Ying, "Slogans attacking the masses of Nanking represent a reactionary adverse current; the bourgeoisie is fighting for its life," though I'm not sure what words I used specifically—I told him about this business on the phone, I remember.

JUDGE: Read out and project the record of Lu Ying's conversation with Yao Wenyuan on April 2, 1976, at 3:45 P.M.

COURT READER: Yao Wenyuan said, "We must analyze this counterrevolutionary adverse current and see if there is a headquarters. It's very rabid and is a manifestation of the decadent classes. It won't win any support. But because there is this bourgeoisie, it wants to jump out [become politically active]."

JUDGE: Read out and project the extract from Yao Wenyuan's diary of March 30 [1976].

COURT READER: "The posters aimed against Shanghai which have burst forth [are the work of] ambitious people who want to 'pull out Khrushchev' and [include] slogans like 'oppose seizure of power.' It seems they got a few students, children of high cadres, to go out on the streets. This is a sign of the sharpening of class struggle. Every time the movement gets to a certain stage, reactionary forces will always jump out and make a show of strength. That's all right! Let the revolutionary masses see better how obtuse the Politburo is! On April 1, big-character posters in Nanking named Zhang Chunqiao, [calling for] the overthrow of people with wild ambitions, conspirators, or Lin Biao's crowd at the Lushan Plenum. There is obviously an underground headquarters active in this. It may also serve to educate a few stupid idiots! The fierce struggle in China goes on; even if one solves one aspect of the contradiction, some aspects still aren't solved completely. Why can't we shoot a few counterrevolutionary elements? After all, dictatorship is not like embroidering flowers!"

JUDGE: Yao Wenyuan, listen! How could commemoration of Premier Zhou turn into the life-and-death struggle of the reactionary forces?

YAO: Because at that time I thought that some of the people who went to

Tiananmen Square to take part in the commemoration were not genuinely commemorating Premier Zhou, and the commemoration was really aimed at the Gang of Four—so, at that time, you see, I was one of those whom they were opposing and trying to overthrow.

JUDGE: So you thought that your last day had come!

YAO: At that time I didn't have such a strong feeling as that, but I felt I was being opposed! Because I could see those leaflets weren't phrased in a normal way—they were very sharp!

JUDGE: How could those intellectuals turn into the social base of reactionary forces? Why do you hate intellectuals so much?

YAO: I'll tell you. Nowadays I can see that intellectuals are not the social base of reactionary forces. The alliance of workers, peasants, and intellectuals is the strong base of our society's dictatorship of the proletariat—

JUDGE: We needn't go into that!

YAO: [protesting] I'd like to say a few things about that point, just a word or two!

JUDGE: Go on, then.

YAO: There were such a lot of people from those work units that were sending wreaths and passing out leaflets—so you see, I fell to thinking this way—

JUDGE: Yao Wenyuan's diary has exposed the fact that his counterrevolutionary schemes were the motive force behind his thinking.

YAO: [interrupting] What I just said, about shooting some people, that—

JUDGE: [shouting him down] *Whom* did you mean?

YAO: [arguing back] At that time I thought that way—with leaflets being passed out like that on Tiananmen Square—so, you see, I said some things attacking the masses and calling for their suppression.

JUDGE: You still haven't answered my question: Whom did you mean when you said "shoot a few people"? According to what you've just said, it was the revolutionary masses on Tiananmen Square!

YAO: Only some of them! Some of them! I mean, *some* of the masses! That was just my feeling, what flashed through my mind; it didn't become one of my concepts!

JUDGE: This thing that "flashed through your mind"—it was aimed at the masses on Tiananmen Square, wasn't it?

YAO: Yes, yes!

A VOICE: Chief Judge, I want to say something.

JUDGE: Uh!

VOICE: Yao Wenyuan, ever since the beginning of interrogation, in relation to every question, he says he made mistakes, serious mistakes, but that he wasn't a counterrevolutionary, or that he didn't deliberately perform counterrevolutionary acts. But the facts that have just been investigated clearly show that all revolutionary masses, revolutionary movements, revolutionary acts in his eyes were counterrevolutionary! In his eyes revolutionary cadres were "home-going contingents," people following the capitalist road, counterrevolutionaries, and renegades. . . . Looked at in this light, his counterrevolutionary posture is very, very clear. [He would like it to be believed that] his arguments here are not counterrevolutionary, he hasn't committed antirevolutionary acts or entertained counterrevolutionary ideology. It must be pointed out, and Yao Wenyuan given a warning, that in law he may not be permitted to use such sophist arguments.

Who said this? It was not clear in the television film. Though the attack on Yao seemed spontaneous, the judge would hardly have allowed such an interpolation if it had not been scripted in advance. Not even Chinese court procedure would explicitly permit such interruptions. On the other hand, it could have been one of the deputy prosecutors, or the judge's assessors (the closest thing to a jury in China), or even one of the spectators who had been given leave to interject the "opinion of the masses."

3
WANG HONGWEN:
"I SHOULD MAKE A SPEECH"

Wang Hongwen, who was forty-six at the time of the trial, is a native of Qilin (Kirin) Province in the former Manchuria. He served in Korea during the war there, but it has been publicly said that he was guilty of cowardice, could not get used to the hardships of a soldier's life, and stole food from Korean peasants. He used to go absent without leave to fish.[1]

From 1953 on, Wang was a worker at a textile mill in Shanghai. However, he managed to secure a transfer to the factory's security department, and was there until 1966 when he wrote a big-character poster attacking the management. Mao heard of this poster and praised it highly.

The Shanghai Municipal Party Committee attempted to quell the unrest at Wang's textile mill, but only succeeded in further inflaming tempers. Receiving the backing of the Cultural Revolution group in Peking, Wang denounced the party leadership in Shanghai and visited Peking at least twice to put his case. In January 1967 Wang and other leftists succeeded in toppling Chen Pixian, the top party official in East China, and Cao Diqiu, mayor of Shanghai. By March, Zhang Chunqiao had made Wang vice-chairman of the newly formed Shanghai Revolutionary Committee. In 1969 he joined the party's Central Committee in Peking while continuing to carry out extensive duties in Shanghai.[2]

Wang was appointed to the Party Politburo at the Tenth Party Congress in 1973, and seemed to become a confidant of Mao's. He sat in on several visits to Mao by foreign dignitaries. He seemed ideal as a symbol of youth in leadership, a favorite theme of elder statesman

Deng Xiaoping. But Wang was destined to quarrel with Deng—and to try to persuade Mao that Deng should not be vice-premier and vice-chairman of the party. Mao rebuffed him.

In the post-Mao period of late 1976 and early 1977, Wang was attacked in the media almost as fiercely as Jiang Qing. He was portrayed as a coward, a work-shirker, a bully, and a self-indulgent playboy who wasted large sums of the government's money buying imported goods for himself or having them specially produced in Shanghai factories.

The charges against Wang fall into three broad counts. First, it is alleged that he instigated two violent riots in Shanghai in the early stages of the Cultural Revolution—the affrays at Kangping Road and at the Shanghai Diesel Engine Plant, which between them left nearly 800 people badly injured or dead.

Second, he allegedly tried to poison Mao's mind against Zhou Enlai and Deng Xiaoping.

Third, Wang was accused of attempting to organize an armed mutiny in Shanghai after the death of Mao in 1976. The coup bid fizzled out, however.

Wang's chief ally and protector was Zhang Chunqiao, who was quoted as saying, "They [the leftists] all look on me as their venerable master. What I say counts."[3]

Wang's involvement in politics made his wife demand to know why he could not spend more time at home. Wang allegedly replied, "When I become a high official, you won't have to do any housework. Then you can enjoy yourself to your heart's content."[4]

Wang Hongwen and his allies worked through the Shanghai trade unions to gain political control of factories and other enterprises. "Many political movements were initiated and led by the trade unions, and a great deal of work was decided on by them and carried out by the party committees. [Normally, it would be the other way around.] In appointing or dismissing party and government cadres, it was necessary to have the recommendation and approval of the trade unions."[5]

Through his network of contacts and allies—colloquially called "little brothers"—Wang had high-class cameras, wristwatches, film projectors, cars, candies, and the best cigarettes delivered to him. He commissioned a factory to make large numbers of miniature submachine guns to be used by the Shanghai People's Militia in a coup attempt. Less sinister, he ordered spotlights installed on the roofs of vehicles he went hunting in at night. And he wanted special vacuum cups to keep his tea hot.

Wang's followers voted themselves and him special cash allowances; the sum of 4,364 yuan ($2,464) was paid to Wang in 1974 alone. (A worker's annual wages should be in the region of 900 yuan a year.) They wined and dined each other, according to the *People's Daily,* at reckless expense to the state.[6]

Wang was also indicted for interfering in political affairs in other provinces. He fomented trouble in Hunan, Fujian, and Yunnan (where race relations are a problem); and at the key central China railway junction of Zhengzhou, he allegedly incited bad elements to interfere with rail transport, seize weapons, and loot state granaries.[7]

When Premier Zhou Enlai died in January 1976, Wang assumed he would be in charge of the work of the Politburo, in which he already had experience in 1974 and probably 1975. He proposed to have a new standard portrait photograph of himself taken, and said, "I should make a speech."

Trivial though these accusations sound, they have symbolic importance in China, where appearances count for much more in politics than in the West. For instance, Wang once visited a department store and picked up a birdcage, striking a pose that he laughingly said made him look like an old-style Shanghai gangster. For this he was excoriated after his downfall.

To the Chinese spectator in court, these affectations would suggest more than mere vanity—rather Wang's assumption that he was about to move even further up the political scale, and therefore would require a fresh portrait for use in the press, posters, etc. Saying "I should make a speech" bolstered this impression, because most leadership changes or shifts in policy are explained to the public in speeches. To make a speech that will be published nationwide is an incomparable political cachet.

Wang was extremely vain, however, even if only a quarter of the accusations against him are justified. He had an account of the upheavals of the Cultural Revolution at his factory turned into a book called *Chronicle of Events at the Shanghai No. 17 Cotton Mill.* His own name appeared in it some 200 times.

In 1969 Wang demanded that certain places in the mill associated with the struggle of the early Cultural Revolution period should be preserved or commemorated—especially his own security office and the place where he put up his first wall poster. "Sure enough, everything in this office was kept intact as during the Great Proletarian Cultural Revolution, and even a voting card left by Wang Hongwen under the glass tabletop was not allowed to be moved."[8]

An intriguing glimpse into the politics of the early Cultural Revolution is given by one group of mill workers who recalled that the No. 17 mill was not, in fact, one of the earliest to join the leftist movement. This meant that when various political activists met in November 1966 to inaugurate a workers' general headquarters, Wang could not be seated in a prominent position. Therefore he conspired with the representative of another mill, which also had low precedence in the seating order, to argue that background, class origin, and work experience were more important criteria than the question of who had joined the leftist movement first. In this way he promoted himself as a demobilized soldier, a security cadre, and a party member. Having obtained the position of deputy commander of the Workers' General Headquarters, he boasted that Mill No. 17 could mobilize 3,000 people to attend the inaugural rally. "Wang Hongwen basically had no idea of how many people the mill could send. After having made his boast, he was nowhere to be found, and hardly ever did any work. On the day of the inauguration, only several hundred people from the mill attended, and both the mobilization work and the organization work had to be done by the comrades at the mill."[9]

In September 1975, Wang dropped hints to his followers that they should make a revolutionary shrine of his former house in Shanghai's Dinghai Road. This scheme, however, did not materialize before Wang's arrest the following year. Wang had moved into the Dinghai Road district in 1958, and apparently had made himself unpopular in the neighborhood, for in 1966 one of the early wall posters denounced him for "ten major crimes" (not further specified in this text). After he seized a key post on the Shanghai Municipal Party Committee, he sent his wife and supporters to investigate the person who had written this wall poster and examine his family background for three generations. The person concerned, who is identified only as a neighborhood group leader, was banned by Wang from party membership.

As far back as 1974, Wang and Zhang Chunqiao had been secretly compiling lists of people who would take positions as ministers, vice-ministers, and departmental directors. They even went so far as to groom people in Shanghai for posts abroad as ambassadors for the new ultraleftist China.

Wang and his followers seem to have only partially understood that without the support of some or all of the People's Liberation Army, their militia force would be hard pressed to stage a limited coup just in Shanghai, let alone in Peking or nationwide. Wang denounced the crucially important Military Affairs Commission of the Communist party, saying, "We'll take the lid off it, and smash it if it can be smashed, and blow it up with a grenade if it cannot be smashed." On another occasion he said, "Killing a few people and setting a few things on fire do not mean anything."

The interrogations of Wang Hongwen have an oddly matter-of-fact tone, and are much less colorful than those of his coconspirators.

JUDGE: Accused Wang Hongwen, with whom did you secretly plot to go to Changsha to see Chairman Mao?

WANG: Zhang Chunqiao, Jiang Qing, and Yao Wenyuan.

JUDGE: When and where?

WANG: On the evening of October 17, 1974, at the Fishing Platform Guesthouse, Building Seventeen.

JUDGE: Who summoned you?

WANG: Jiang Qing.

JUDGE: What did you secretly plot?

WANG: The important thing at that time was to denounce Comrade Deng Xiaoping to Chairman Mao.

JUDGE: What else was there? Think carefully.

WANG: There was some other stuff. Yao Wenyuan brought up the topic of the atmosphere in Peking being "similar to that at the Lushan Plenum."

JUDGE: When you went to Changsha, why did you do it behind the backs of Premier Zhou and the politburo?

WANG: Well, actually we were engaged in a conspiracy.

JUDGE: Why were you in such a hurry to see Chairman Mao before he received some foreign guests? Whose idea was that?

WANG: Jiang Qing's.

JUDGE: Why?

WANG: Well, actually it was because she was afraid Deng Xiaoping would go first, and while welcoming the guests tell Chairman Mao what the real situation was. Actually that's what it was all about.

JUDGE: Did you say something like this to Chairman Mao: "The Premier is sick and staying in the hospital. He still sends for people late into the night to talk to them. Almost every day there's someone. Deng Xiaoping, Ye Jianying, Li Xiannian are among those who often go to see him." Did you say that?

WANG: Yes. I've told you the outlines of what I said, but I can't vouch for the exact wording. . . .

JUDGE: When did you come back to Peking from Changsha?

WANG: On the evening of the eighteenth.

JUDGE: And then?

WANG: I went to the Guesthouse.

JUDGE: At what time?

WANG: Around six P.M. Five or six.

JUDGE: You came back on the same day you went. Why?

WANG: The reason was simply that I hadn't told Premier Zhou or the Politburo when I left.

JUDGE: So you went in a great hurry?

WANG: Yes.

JUDGE: What was your aim in going to Changsha to slander Deng Xiaoping?

WANG: Actually, we wanted to stop Deng Xiaoping from becoming first vice-premier.

JUDGE: Read out Zhang Yüfeng's testimony of July 18, 1980.

COURT READER: "On October 18, 1974, Chairman Mao saw Wang Hongwen in the guest room at the place where he was staying. I was present. Wang Hongwen sat down and asked how the Chairman's health had been lately. Then he said that in Peking there was 'an atmosphere like that of the Lushan Plenum.' He said, 'I've come to Hunan without telling the premier or the other members of the Politburo. The four of us had a night meeting to discuss the question of my going to Changsha to report to the Chairman. I've come at some risk. [Repeats the allegation about Zhou's activity in the hospital.]' He said those people were very busy with the choosing of delegates for the Fourth National People's Congress. Wang also gave individual puffs [praise] to the other three—Zhang, Yao, and Jiang—in front of Chairman Mao. When he had finished, Wang said he wanted to go back to Peking that day, as the others wanted him to bring back Chairman Mao's opinion. The Chairman said, 'All right, you go back and talk more to Premier Zhou and Comrade [Ye] Jianying. Don't work together with Jiang Qing. You should be careful of her.' "

WANG: . . . Actually, I didn't do as he said. Though I did talk to Premier Zhou about this matter, I did not distance myself from Jiang Qing.

JUDGE: I want to ask you a few questions. A short while ago, in the course of the proceedings against you, you pleaded guilty to the clause in the indictment that accuses you of trying to blacken Premier Zhou's name and that of Comrade Deng Xiaoping.

WANG: Yes.

JUDGE: There are two questions you must answer more clearly. The first is this: The chief [instigator] of your activity in slander and sabotage, and in the plans the four of you made together, was Jiang Qing, is that right?

WANG: Right.

JUDGE: And you were a zealous participant. You were acting directly on your own behalf, but made yourself extremely useful, right?

WANG: Right.

JUDGE: The second question is, this activity of yours did not arise by coincidence. At that time you used the case of M.V. *Feng Qing* as a pretext, but actually if you hadn't had the M.V. *Feng Qing* affair, you'd have found some other issue, wouldn't you?

WANG: Yes.

JUDGE: . . . In the context of the preparatory work for the Fourth National

People's Congress going on at that time, you were hampering the nomination of Deng Xiaoping as first vice-premier, weren't you?

WANG: Yes.

JUDGE: All right, that's all.

TV COMMENTATOR: The accused Wang Hongwen is summoned for interrogation for the second time. The court has examined the charges in the indictment as follows:

1. At Zhang Chunqiao's instructions, the accused conspired with Xü Jingxian and others to fabricate and collect slanderous materials against Chen Yi, Ye Jianying, Li Xiannian, Chen Yun, Nie Rongzhen, Li Fuchun, Tan Zhenlin, and other old-guard proletarian revolutionaries.

2. The accused in 1967 instructed Lu Ying [editor of the *People's Daily*] to send people to several departments of the Central Committee and to several provinces to collect materials slanderous of leading cadres of the party, government, and army.

3. Toward the end of 1966, the accused deputed people to organize and direct the Kangping Road incident in which the Shanghai workers' organization, the "Scarlet Guards," were attacked in military fashion.

4. On August 4, 1967, Wang Hongwen schemed to surround and attack with arms the Shanghai Diesel Engine Factory "revolutionary rebels" headquarters and masses' organizations.

JUDGE: Wang Hongwen, how did you plan and direct the Workers' General Headquarters [a mass organ favorable to the Red Guards] to attack the Shanghai Diesel Engine Factory?

WANG: Let me say simply that I assembled people . . . to discuss how to sort out some organizational problems.

JUDGE: What day was that?

WANG: . . . It was August 3, in the afternoon.

JUDGE: You convened this conference in order to work out how to proceed?

WANG: Yes. In the evening we decided to send some of our forces to surround and attack the trade unions.[10] At dawn on August 4, we sent in a hundred thousand people—we'd started off with only forty thousand.

[Wang and the judge sort out a disagreement about the figures, because 40,000 and 100,000 sound similar in Chinese. Wang insists that the final figure was 100,000.]

WANG: . . . In the afternoon we began the attack on the trade unions headquarters. By evening we'd smashed them.

[The witness Xü Panqing, a participant in the battle, takes the witness stand.]

XÜ: On the morning of August 4, 1967—after Wang Hongwen had called a meeting to put a top-secret plan into effect—he sent over a hundred thousand people and several thousand vehicles of every sort, and boats, to move on our factory by water and by land. Under Wang Hongwen's personal command, they surrounded us many ranks deep, cut off the water and electricity, and attacked us from all sides. They forced their way into the factory grounds, beating anyone they saw, and Wang Hong-wen had high-pressure fire hoses used to violently drench all the masses and cadres who were watching from upper-story windows. When they had occupied the roof of this building, they broke in, fought their way, and beat black and blue anyone they came across. They took all the male comrades' upper garments off and ripped the upper garments of the female comrades, as an example. Then they made them raise their hands and dragged them off to illegal imprisonment.

JUDGE: What did this armed clash result in? What responsibility should you bear?

WANG: In this incident, which resulted in the death or injury of seven hundred people, I bear the responsibility; it is mine. I must confess this to the people of the whole country.

4
ZHANG CHUNQIAO
"CHANGING DYNASTIES"

Throughout the trial proceedings, one of the defendants remained completely silent despite frequent rebukes by the judge.

The elderly defendant had a wedge-shaped, intelligent face and several days of grizzled stubble on his chin. This was Zhang Chunqiao, former vice-premier and member of the Politburo, journalist and Marxist theorist, effective ruler of Shanghai from the early Cultural Revolution till the mid-Seventies. He sat impassive, locked in his silence, barely even raising his bespectacled face to survey the proceedings.

Not much is known about Zhang's origins, except that he was a newspaper columnist in Shanghai in the 1930s, using the pseudonym "Dick." He crossed swords with Lu Xün in the interminable polemics about the war between the Communists and the Guomindang, and the correct way to resist the encroaching Japanese. Later, it is believed, he saw action as a guerrilla fighter.

Zhang surfaced as a Communist party official when he was named director of the east China branch of Xinhua News Agency in 1950, and was deputy director of the regional publishing committee—both of which posts would have involved him heavily in questions of ideology and censorship.

In 1954 he became managing director of the military newspaper *Liberation Army Daily*, thus beginning a long career as a political commissar responsible for morale and political correctness in the People's Liberation Army (PLA). In 1958 he became a secretary of the Shanghai Municipal Communist Party Committee. In 1960 his name was published among the members of the Central Cultural

Revolution Group in Peking, and he was frequently seen in the capital while holding high office in Shanghai. In early 1967 he became head of the "Shanghai Commune"—a latter-day attempt to imitate the 1870 Paris Commune, one of the great episodes in the history of Marxist revolution. In 1969 Zhang was elected to the Central Committee of the party, and at the Tenth Party Congress in 1973 he became a member of the politburo. In 1975 he was named a vice-premier and head of the General Political Department of the PLA, a very sensitive and important post. For three years, from 1973 on, he intrigued against the newly rehabilitated Deng Xiaoping, and was arrested, together with the other members of the Gang of Four, in October 1976.

The prosecution accused Zhang of having called for an all-round seizure of power by the leftists and a "change of dynasties." He was alleged to have said of veteran cadres, "All of them are bad" and "None shall be spared". He had supplied the program of action for the Gang of Four, and falsely accused and persecuted party and state leaders, including Liu Shaoqi, Zhu De, Chen Yi, Ye Jianying, Li Xiannian, Chen Yun, Nie Rongzhen, Li Fuchun, and Tan Zhenlin, and had made false charges against Deng Xiaoping (which were transmitted to Mao by Wang Hongwen). Zhang used the Peking riot of April 5, 1976, as an excuse to overthrow Deng, and instigated the persecution to death of Cao Diqiu. He operated a secret action group that kidnapped people and extracted confessions under torture, the prosecution claimed. He was partly responsible for armed clashes in Shanghai (on December 28, 1966) and Ji'nan (on May 7, 1967). The Shanghai incident caused ninety-one casualties, and in Ji'nan 388 people were unlawfully arrested. Together with Wang Hongwen and others, he is said to have plotted an armed uprising in Shanghai after Mao's death in September 1976. So the official version goes.

Most of the evidence against Zhang was presented at court sessions that were not publicly recorded. But two interrogations of the stubbornly silent defendant give insights into the way he and other top radicals manipulated younger activists to overthrow political rivals.

ZHANG CHUNQIAO DENOUNCES DENG

JUDGE: Zhang Chunqiao, the Special Procurator's Office accuses you, Jiang Qing, Yao Wenyuan, and Wang Hongwen of having plotted and schemed to send Wang Hongwen to Changsha [to see] Chairman Mao Zedong and slander Zhou Enlai, Deng Xiaoping, and others, and to prevent Deng Xiaoping from becoming first vice-premier of the State Council. . . . Now

I ask you: On the evening of April 17, 1974, what did you say while conspiring with Jiang Qing, Yao Wenyuan, and Wang Hongwen, at Building Seventeen in the Fishing Platform Guesthouse?

ZHANG: [silent]

JUDGE: Do you understand?

ZHANG: [silent]

JUDGE: [Repeats the question. Zhang remains silent.] I have asked you three times, now I am telling you that even if you have no reply, or refuse to reply, the court's judgment will not be affected. This court is conducted in accordance with the provisions of the Code of Criminal Procedure, of which Article Thirty-five specifically stipulates: "If there is only a confession by the accused, and no other evidence, the accused may not be found guilty or punished. If the accused makes no confession, but the evidence is completely solid, the accused may be found guilty and punished." Do you understand?

ZHANG: [silent]

JUDGE: Well, if you won't speak, the court will let the evidence speak. Read out Wang Hongwen's confession of June 17, 1980.

COURT READER: "On October 17, 1974, the Politburo was having a meeting, and Jiang Qing and Deng Xiaoping had a row. When the meeting ended, we went back to the Fishing Platform Guesthouse, and Jiang told me, Zhang Chunqiao, and Yao Wenyuan to come for a meeting at Building Seventeen to analyze and discuss the reasons for her quarrel with Deng. She said, 'Deng Xiaoping was determined to have a row because he's hostile to the Great Proletarian Cultural Revolution. . . .' Zhang Chunqiao said, 'Perhaps the reason why Deng Xiaoping has jumped out [become politically active] is because in discussing the Fourth National People's Congress [to be held early the next year] there've been nominations for chief of the General Staff. . . .' He also said, 'I have a feeling something's going to happen soon.' I realized that the idea of reporting to Chairman Mao was to cast aspersions on Comrade Deng Xiaoping and stop him from working, and certainly prevent him from becoming first vice-premier. The trip to Changsha to report to Chairman Mao was deliberately concocted to slander Comrade Deng behind the back of Premier Zhou and the politburo."

JUDGE: Zhang Chunqiao, did you hear that clearly?

ZHANG: [silent]

JUDGE: Show him Wang Hongwen's confession.

ZHANG: [silent]

JUDGE: Very well, you won't speak, so we shall let the evidence speak again. Read out the confession made by Zhang Yüfeng [one of Mao's entourage in Changsha].

COURT READER: "At about two P.M. on October 18, 1974, Chairman Mao was receiving guests at his residence and I was present and saw Wang

Hongwen. He sat down, and after asking about Chairman Mao's health, he said, 'In Peking just now the atmosphere is just like that of the Lushan Plenum. I've come to Hunan without telling Premier Zhou Enlai or the Politburo that we four people—Zhang Chunqiao, Jiang Qing, Yao Wenyuan, and I—had a late-night meeting and decided I should come to report to you. I've come at some risk.' "

JUDGE: Zhang Chunqiao, did you hear clearly? You won't talk, so you have tacitly admitted it. I ask you now: When Wang Hongwen came back [to Peking] and the four of you sent Wang Hairong and Tang Wensheng to go to Changsha and make another report to Chairman Mao, what did you say to them? Zhang Chunqiao!

ZHANG: [silent]

JUDGE: Very well, we'll let the evidence speak again. Read out Tang Wensheng's[1] testimony given on September 20, 1980.

COURT READER: "On October 18, 1974, Jiang Qing called me and Comrade Wang Hairong to Guesthouse Seventeen. The four of them were there. Jiang Qing first got Zhang Chunqiao to brief us on so-called problems of the situation. Turning truth on its head, he said that since the Campaign to Criticize Lin Biao and Confucius [had begun], the domestic budgetary imbalance and the adverse situation in foreign trade had come about because leading comrades worshiped foreign things. He said, with a malicious, sinister air, 'Comrade Xiaoping has made a big issue of the M.V. *Feng Qing* affair. This is no coincidence. Before the Great Proletarian Cultural Revolution, he took the stand that building ships was not as good as buying them, and buying ships wasn't as good as chartering them. Zhang Chunqiao said with a spiteful look, 'The Politburo meeting on the evening of October 17 was like the February Adverse Current.'[2] The four of them told us to report these views of theirs to Chairman Mao. In Changsha we told the Chairman. When he heard what we had to say, he was very angry and said, 'The question of M.V. *Feng Qing* is basically a small one, but Jiang Qing is still carrying on about it.' To counter the conspiratorial activity of Wang, Zhang, and Yao to subvert the party and seize power, the Chairman proposed that Comrade Deng Xiaoping be made vice-chairman and first vice-premier, vice-chairman of the party's Military Affairs Commission, and chief of the General Staff. . . ."

JUDGE: I now ask you: Did you instruct Wang Hongwen and Xü Jingxian to compile the so-called *Short Collection of Chen Yi's Reactionary Statements*? And did you give a copy of this pamphlet to every Shanghai delegate to the Ninth Party Congress [in 1969]?

ZHANG: [silent]

JUDGE: Apart from compiling this pamphlet, did you collect any other materials?

ZHANG: [silent]

JUDGE: Project Zhang Chunqiao's instructions to Wang Hongwen and Xü

Jingxian,[3] and have a court official give an introduction to them. Zhang Chunqiao, are these your instructions for the compilation?

ZHANG: [silent]

COURT READER: The main contents were records of speeches made by Chen Yi from 1953 until 1960, at conferences in Shanghai and Peking [Chen Yi was mayor of Shanghai], reports, and even talks with foreign visitors, made up of extracts taken out of context, divided altogether into nine parts—nine cooked-up charges to blacken his name. They were: "Viciously attacking the great leader Chairman Mao, opposing Mao's invincible thought, promoting the politics of the bourgeoisie stubbornly in all kinds of work, widely propagandizing the restoration of capitalism, strongly pushing the doctrine of the dying-out of class struggle, zealously recommending cooperation among classes, opposing the political line of the socialist revolution, the economic line and the ideological line, peddling Khrushchev's 'three unities line,' prettifying and surrendering to imperialism, repudiating the political movement of history, encouraging rightists to overturn verdicts, and assailing the party," and so on,[4] [by these means] carrying out framing and persecution of Chen Yi.

JUDGE: Zhang Chunqiao, did you hear clearly? . . . That pamphlet underwent your inspection and examination. . . .

ZHANG: [silent]

JUDGE: If you won't speak, we'll go on letting the evidence speak.

COURT READER: Testimony given by Xü Jingxian on September 16, 1980: "One day Zhang Chunqiao and Yao Wenyuan convened a conference of leading members of the Shanghai Municipal Revolutionary Committee in a small auditorium on Kangping Road, and discussed the preparatory work for the Congress. Zhang Chunqiao told the meeting: 'We are about to do the Shanghai preparatory work for the Ninth Party Congress, which will shortly be convened. We must form a documentary small group.' He also clearly stated: 'We must assemble materials on the black cadres and generals Ye Jianying, Chen Yi, Li Xiannian, Li Fuchun, Tan Zhenlin, and Nie Rongzhen, and prepare to continue criticizing them at the Ninth Congress.' Subsequently the Ninth Congress Documentation Small Group drew up black materials on them. In January of 1969, the Central Committee decided that Comrade Chen Yi should be elected to represent Shanghai, and Zhang Chunqiao again ordered the assembly of Chen Yi's 'counterrevolutionary statements' as a single volume and its issue to the delegates from Shanghai so that they could go on criticizing [Chen Yi]. After I'd looked it over and corrected it, I sent it to Zhang Chunqiao, who personally revised and approved it. On January 21 it was issued to the Shanghai delegates. At the Ninth Congress, the Shanghai delegates held several meetings at which they attacked Chen Yi according to the specifications of Zhang Chunqiao and Yao Wenyuan."

JUDGE: Zhang Chunqiao, did you hear that? You must answer: Was it you who approved [the pamphlet]?

ZHANG: [silent]

JUDGE: [to Zhang Chunqiao] I now ask you: During the meeting of all members of the Shanghai Revolutionary Committee at the Workers' General Headquarters on Kangping Road, did you talk about a "change of dynasties," and what did you mean by that? What "dynasty" was to be "changed"?

ZHANG: [silent]

JUDGE: Read out Xü Jingxian's testimony of July 11, 1980.

COURT READER: "In September 1967, one day Zhang Chunqiao received a full meeting of the committee members of the Workers' General Headquarters, and I attended it. Before he turned up, we all sat in the small conference room at Kangping Road waiting for him. When he arrived, he glanced at the people who were attending the meeting, and said, 'Today, except for Xü Jingxian, there's not a single member of the old Municipal Committee present—this looks like [a meeting to] change dynasties!' "

JUDGE: Zhang Chunqiao, did you say similar things to Ma Tianshui[5] in March 1968?

ZHANG: [silent]

JUDGE: Read out Ma Tianshui's testimony of January 26, 1978.

COURT READER: "Around the middle of March 1968, I went to Zhang Chunqiao's residence on Xing Guo Road to report on economic matters. Before I'd had a chance to make my report, he told me: 'This afternoon . . . some people are coming here to discuss some things.' He said what they were going to discuss was all about before the Cultural Revolution and after the Cultural Revolution, mixed up together. They were going to look at before-and-after as one affair. They basically didn't understand that the Cultural Revolution is a change of dynasties. He said their ideology was full of problems [i.e., faulty]."

JUDGE: Zhang Chunqiao, did you say that to Ma Tianshui?

ZHANG: [silent]

JUDGE: I'm asking you again, aside from what you said to Ma Tianshui, did you say the same thing to Huang Tao[6] in Peking in 1976?

ZHANG: [silent]

JUDGE: Bring in Huang Tao. . . . [to Huang] I want you today to tell the court about Zhang Chunqiao's having said to you that the Cultural Revolution was "a change of dynasties." How did he say it to you?

HUANG: In November of 1975, I was in Peking attending the national planning conference when I went to Zhang Chunqiao's residence at the Fishing Platform Guesthouse. I reported to him how everything was being adjusted and rectified. Enterprise management especially needed serious rectification . . . even restoring some of the rules from before the Cultural Revolution.[7] Zhang Chunqiao interrupted me and said, "I'm also in favor of rectification. After all, what did the Cultural Revolution destroy, and what did it create? Shanghai alone stands firm. From the seizure of power in the January Storm [of 1967], it has advanced under the slogan of grasping revolution and boosting production." Then he said, "The Cultural Revolution is a change of dynasties." . . .

JUDGE: Accused Zhang Chunqiao, have you anything to say about Huang Tao's testimony?

ZHANG: [silent]

JUDGE: Huang Tao, when you leave the courtroom, read through the record of your testimony, and if there are any omissions or errors, you can have it corrected or amplified, then sign it. The court will now investigate the facts in the indictment concerning Zhang Chunqiao's instructions conveyed at the West Gate of Zhongnanhai to the Qinghua University student Kuai Dafu, his instructions concerning demonstrations and parades in Peking and overt whipping up of feeling in favor of the overthrow of Liu Shaoqi and Deng Xiaoping. I now ask you, Zhang Chunqiao: Is it a fact that on December 18, 1966, at the West Gate of Zhongnanhai, you gave instructions to Kuai Dafu?

ZHANG: [silent]

JUDGE: . . . Read out and project the letter Kuai Dafu wrote to the Qinghua University Party Committee on January 15, 1971, during the movement to ferret out the May 16 [group].[8]

COURT READER: "Throughout the Cultural Revolution, I had only one private contact with a responsible person of the Party Center (including the bad people at that time hiding there). . . . I met with Zhang Chunqiao for over an hour in a room at the West Gate of Zhongnanhai. Comrade Chunqiao told us to [struggle] to the last with Liu Shaoqi."

JUDGE: Zhang Chunqiao, have you listened to the [two] statements by Kuai Dafu? One was written in December of 1971, the other in January of that year. One of them is an outline of instructions, the other is a letter to the Party Committee at Qinghua University. At that time you were still on the stage [politically prominent and active], so it was impossible for him to slander you. It even calls you "comrade." You must answer truthfully about this. Did this happen? Was the organization of the "Jinggangshan Regiment"[9] by you and Kuai Dafu a result of this talk?

ZHANG: [silent]

JUDGE: If you won't answer, we'll let a witness speak. Bring in Kuai Dafu.[10] . . . [to Kuai] I want you to give truthful testimony about the time Zhang Chunqiao received you at the West Gate of Zhongnanhai, what you spoke about and what you did. Answer!

KUAI: As regards Zhang Chunqiao's illegal incitement of me to oppose the former Head of State of the People's Republic of China, Comrade Liu Shaoqi, it was like this. Around the middle of December in 1966, I had come back a short while before from a liaison trip to Shanghai. In the afternoon of—I think it was December 18—the Cultural Revolution Office of the Party Center telephoned the Jinggangshan Red Guards general headquarters at Qinghua University and said I was to go to the West Gate of Zhongnanhai at two P.M. because someone wanted to talk to me. Somebody at the headquarters took the call for me. Incidentally, I was head of the Qinghua students and the Jinggangshan Red Guards.

Before two P.M. I got a car from the university and arrived at the West Gate of Zhongnanhai. I said to the PLA sentry at the gate, "Let me in!" At that moment a car came out of Zhongnanhai and stopped at the gate. A man got out wearing a military greatcoat and I saw at once that it was Zhang Chunqiao. We had met before. He barked at the sentry, "I told him to come. Let him in!" . . . He led me into the north-facing janitor's room at the gate and into a small room opening off it. I talked with him for about an hour. Nobody else was present. I didn't take notes, either, though later I wrote a simple memo. I have handed this memo and the original notebook over to the court.

The conversation began with the situation since I had returned from Shanghai. Zhang Chunqiao asked me something about my liaison work in Shanghai, and I told him about it. I did most of the talking and he would occasionally interrupt. Then I reported to him concisely on the state of the movement at Qinghua. When I asked him to tell us how to proceed, he said some things to me that were roughly as follows: "As far as the country as a whole is concerned, the reactionary bourgeois line is still fairly rabid [and] we must go on criticizing it. The two people in the Party Center who continue to promote the bourgeois reactionary line will still not surrender. Although they've been investigated, their attitude is still bad! You little revolutionary generals must get united and show a revolutionary spirit, beat the dogs in the water,[11] blacken them—no half measures!" I immediately realized that Zhang Chunqiao wanted us to resist [Liu Shaoqi]. Zhang had another meeting, so I took my leave.

Zhang used our meeting to tell us to blacken the bourgeois reactionary line of the so-called "two people in the Party Center." It was a clear instruction. It meant that Zhang had put his cards on the table before me by using his position as deputy head of the Cultural Revolution Small Group to set up a private meeting with me like this. It was as though he were expressing his future trust in me. At the time, this put me much in awe of him. Because of this I put his instructions about blackening the names of Liu and Deng into effect very vigorously and thoroughly at the university. When I got back there, I repeatedly mobilized and organized the teachers and staff of the entire university to concentrate the spearhead of attack against Comrade Liu Shaoqi and Comrade Deng Xiaoping, especially at Comrade Liu Shaoqi.

5

CHEN BODA: "JUST THINGS I'D HEARD"

Chen Boda, who was tried by the First (civilian) Tribunal along with the Gang of Four, was the leading interpreter of Mao's Thought, on which he wrote numerous books and articles. He was considered Mao's confidant until his arrest at the time of the Lin Biao coup bid in 1971. He was sometimes called "Mao's private secretary," and therefore his personal role in the persecution of Liu Shaoqi and others implicated Mao rather clearly. Working closely with another organizer of the anti-"revisionist" witch-hunt, Qi Benyü, Chen was to a large extent responsible for putting Liu and his wife on public trial—or rather exposing them to unending struggle-and-criticism sessions by the Red Guards in 1967. He personally called for the persecution of Deng Xiaoping, Tao Zhu, and their wives. Another prominent victim of Chen's was propaganda chief Lu Dingyi, who, together with his wife, was ordered to write day-by-day accounts of their activities for the past year. When Lu was eventually jailed, Chen had him permanently manacled. Chen initially tried to deny recollection of actions attributed to him by witnesses, but the evidence was weighted against him.

JUDGE: Accused Chen Boda, you are accused of colluding with Jiang Qing and Kang Sheng in taking it upon yourselves to subject Liu Shaoqi to struggle-and-criticism and convening a big meeting for this purpose organized by Qi Benyü, at the same time carrying out a search of his house. You inflicted physical maltreatment on Liu Shaoqi and [his wife] Wang Guangmei on July 18, 1967. Is this true? Answer!

CHEN: I can't remember.

JUDGE: You can't remember. Then I ask you again: Around the middle of July 1967, did you or did you not receive a report from Qi Benyü about the struggle-and-criticism to which Liu Shaoqi and Wang Guangmei were to be exposed?

CHEN: I really can't remember that. Excuse me, I'm very old. At that time there were lots of matters, many important matters. I really can't remember.

JUDGE: You still can't remember?

CHEN: I can't. I've thought about it for a long time, many days.

JUDGE: Show and read out the report of the struggle-and-criticism to be inflicted on Liu Shaoqi with the approval of Jiang Qing, Kang Sheng, and Chen Boda on July 15, 1967.

COURT READER: "Comrade Qi Benyü, below is the report written by all the revolutionary comrades to [Vice-] Premier [Wang] Dongxing, demanding that Liu Shaoqi's false confession be subjected to struggle-and-criticism by them and be dealt counterblows, and that he be forced to hear their criticism. Please consider this matter and report to the higher level asking for a decision." This report was not sent to Premier Zhou. It was looked over by Wang Dongxing; Qi Benyü made a note on it requesting that Chen Boda, Jiang Qing, and Kang Sheng make a decision. Kang Sheng and Jiang Qing signed and approved it. Chen Boda crossed out "Shaoqi" [Liu's given name] and wrote in the names Deng [Xiaoping] and Tao [Zhu] and the words "and their wives." [Deleting the given names was a way of insulting the three.]

JUDGE: Have you read this? Was it written personally by you?

CHEN: It's my addition. I recognize my handwriting.

JUDGE: You colluded with Jiang Qing and Kang Sheng to take it upon yourselves to subject Liu Shaoqi to struggle-and-criticism and to expose him and Wang Guangmei to physical maltreatment?

CHEN: I remember now, that is true.

JUDGE: A short while ago you admitted that you signed the report and added some words. Now, according to your testimony, you not only looked it over and approved it, you turned it from a report on struggle-and-criticism against Liu Shaoqi into one of struggle-and-criticism against Liu, Deng, Tao, and their wives—six people in all. . . . In accordance with your decision, Qi Benyü made firm arrangements for the big struggle-and-criticism meeting of July 18, at which Comrade Liu Shaoqi was to be physically maltreated.

[At the judge's request, a court official reads out the testimony of Shao Meng, a former official who worked on the case of Liu Shaoqi.] "On July 17, 1967, Qi Benyü called an urgent meeting in the Great Hall of the people to organize and mobilize people for struggle-and-criticism of Liu, Deng, and Tao. Qi Benyü gave us a pep talk, saying we could make them bow their heads and bend their waists and prostrate themselves."

JUDGE: Following speeches made by Chen Boda, Xie Fuzhi, and Wu Faxian, they drew up a plan of campaign, in which the most emphasis was laid on "going backstage" [to unmask alleged revisionists in the leadership]. In the process they manufactured the phony case of the "Marxist-Leninist party of China,"[1] slanderously claiming that Zhu De was its secretary general, Chen Yi was deputy secretary and minister of defense, Li Fuchun was premier, and that other participants were Dong Biwu, Ye Jianying, Li Xiannian, Wang Zhen, Liao Chengzhi, He Long, Liu Bocheng, Xü Xiangqian, Nie Rongzhen, Tan Zhenlin, Yü Qiuli, and others, slandering them as having illicit relations with foreign countries and planning to stage an armed uprising and coup d'état. All these things were done on the orders of Chen Boda, Xie Fuzhi, and Wu Faxian. Accused Chen Boda, the Special Court indicts you for criminally slandering and persecuting Lu Dingyi [now aged seventy-nine, formerly minister of culture and top party propagandist]. In May 1968, a special case group sent you a report suggesting that Lu Dingyi be arrested. What did you decide?

CHEN: I don't remember it.

JUDGE: Show the report on the arrest of Lu Dingyi, which was approved by Chen Boda, Xie Fuzhi, and Wu Faxian.

COURT READER: "Dear Comrades Boda, Fuzhi, and Faxian. The big traitor Lu Dingyi was a turncoat from the outset, and carried out a series of counterrevolutionary conspiratorial activities. For this reason we propose that he should be arrested and imprisoned in order to intensify the dictatorship [of the proletariat] and to investigate his towering crimes. Please comment on our report. [signed] Lu Dingyi Special Case Group, May 23, 1968." Chen Boda, Xie Fuzhi, and Wu Faxian read the report and approved it.

JUDGE: Is it true that you handed over Lu Dingyi to the Red Guards for trial?

CHEN: I was in charge of the Lu Dingyi case.

JUDGE: Show and read out Chen Boda's instructions for the Lu Dingyi case.

COURT READER: "One, lower his living standard. Do not let him have more than twelve yuan [$6]. Take away his sofa, soft bed, desk, etc. Two, get him and his wife to write a day-by-day account of their activity from October last year until their arrest. Three, examine the question of handing him over to the Red Guards for trial, or dealing with the matter internally."

JUDGE: I now ask you: Did you have manacles put on Vice-Premier Lu Dingyi, and have blitz-style interrogation of him carried out?

CHEN: I can't remember.

JUDGE: Call the witness Xiao Wengwen. . . . [to Xiao] You previously worked on the Lu Dingyi special case group, didn't you?

XIAO: Yes.

JUDGE: During the period when Chen Boda was in charge of the Lu Dingyi case, did he ever say Lu Dingyi should be manacled or blitz-interrogated?

XIAO: He did say that. It was in December 1967. Chen Boda, Xie Fuzhi, and Wu Faxian called some responsible persons on the Lu Dingyi case to the Great Hall of the People to be given special instructions for the interrogation of Comrade Lu. Chen Boda said Lu was extremely evil and should wear manacles. Xie Fuzhi said, "Keep attacking him continuously!" Wu Faxian said no leniency should be shown and he should be made to bow his head and bend at the waist.

JUDGE: Did Chen Boda say Lu Dingyi should be handed over to the Red Guards for trial?

XIAO: Yes. You may ask: What was the idea of handing Lu Dingyi over to the Red Guards for trial? It was aimed at getting the masses to take part in struggle-and-criticism. This wasn't an isolated case. In 1966, when Chen Boda took over the handling of the Lu Dingyi special case, on October 10, he came for the first time to visit our group and recommended mass struggle-and-criticism. He said that in the case of Lu Dingyi and Yang Huiping,[2] a mass meeting would be very intimidating. Yang should be tried first, and then her younger sister. After that the Central Propaganda Department often organized mass-criticism meetings for Comrade Lu Dingyi and Comrade Yang Huiping at the East Peking Sports Stadium.

JUDGE: You have just said that the word "manacles" was brought up by Chen Boda, and it was Xie Fuzhi who mentioned "continuous interrogation," right?

XIAO: Right.

JUDGE: From October 10, 1966, when Chen commenced work on the Lu Dingyi case, until December 27, a period of over two months, he saw the special case people eight times. Only two of those times were when the special case people called on him to report; on the other six occasions, he himself took the initiative to go to the special case group and frame and persecute Lu Dingyi. His conduct of this case was not passive but zealous and active. He thought up every imaginable way to portray Lu Dingyi as a counterrevolutionary, traitor, and renegade. His motive was to slander and persecute cadres on behalf of the Lin Biao and Jiang Qing counterrevolutionary cliques. . . .

It was also on Chen's orders that the *People's Daily* printed the most famous of all articles initiating the Cultural Revolution—entitled by him "Sweep Away All Ghosts and Monsters"—or, more literally translated, "ox heads and snake bodies."

JUDGE: The facts of the accused Chen Boda's slander and persecution of Lu Dingyi have now been fully investigated. [to Chen] Did you organize and check the writing of the editorial in the *People's Daily* on June 1 [1966] entitled "Sweep Away All Ghosts and Monsters"?

CHEN: I checked it and approved it.

JUDGE: Show and project the first draft of the editorial with Chen Boda's alterations and approval. . . . Chen Boda, did you choose this headline?

CHEN: Yes.

[The court hears testimony given on August 12, 1980, by Zhu Yuepeng, a journalist.]

"On May 31, 1966, Chen Boda and Kang Sheng had seen the principal content of the next day's editorial at the Fishing Platform Guesthouse. He [Chen Boda] said, 'The editorial is a newspaper's banner and spirit. Today we want to write a good one, and publish it tomorrow.' So that evening we got up an editorial. . . . After ten P.M. Chen Boda corrected it at the *People's Daily* and gave it the headline 'Sweep Away All Ghosts and Monsters,' which was published on June 1. The editorial was not submitted to the Party Center or to Chairman Mao for inspection."

An important aspect of the Cultural Revolution was the series of localized purges in different provinces and cities, some of them going back to the revolutionary movement of the Civil War period, from 1945 till the Communist victory in 1949.

Chen Boda was clearly a specialist in organizing political purges at all levels. One such was the purge in East Hebei.[3]

Hebei, the province surrounding the municipality of Peking, stretches from the Gulf of Bohai in the North and East to the frontiers of Henan and Shanxi provinces in the South and West. The principal city of East Hebei is the coal-mining center of Tangshan, where mines were originally excavated by British investors. The Japanese occupied it in World War II. The city was developed further by the Communists until it became one of China's principal coal-mining centers. There was also a flourishing porcelain industry.

According to official reports, the factional fighting of the Cultural Revolution—stirred up by an inflammatory speech made by Chen Boda on December 26, 1967—resulted in the persecution of 84,000 people, of whom 2,955 died in one way or another. The first party secretary of the municipality was "dragged from one party institution to another, from school to school, to all the factories and villages throughout Tangshan Prefecture. He was reviled, abused, manhandled, and made to stand bent down, with his arms pinned behind him, for hours on end. He was savagely beaten. Condemned as an 'active counterrevolutionary and a diehard follower of the capitalist road,' he was expelled from the party and made to do forced labor under surveillance.[4] His home was searched and many of his relatives were also persecuted."

Tangshan was destroyed almost completely by a force-eleven earthquake in the early morning of July 28, 1976. An estimated 500,000 people in the city and surrounding region died or were seriously injured.

JUDGE: Accused Chen Boda, the indictment accuses you of having said at Tangshan, on October 26, 1967, that the East Hebei party organization was probably a part of Guomindang-Communist cooperation, and, in fact, it might be Guomindang members and renegades who played the dominant role.

CHEN: I can't remember about the Tangshan problem. I've never talked about it. I haven't seen this stuff before.

JUDGE: Read out the record of Chen Boda's speech to the big meeting of all county and municipality officials, reform teams and military delegations.

COURT READER: [Repeats the quotation used by the judge, and continues.] "The first party secretary of the Tangshan Municipal Committee, Yang Huan, has admitted that he was originally a member of the Guomindang County Committee. There's a woman, too, Bai Yun, the mayor of Tangshan. I know her husband. He's a big lord of the manor. [Bai Yun's husband, Zhang Da, was party secretary of a state-owned orchard.] After Liberation he built up a big manor here in your city of Tangshan. You should know a little history. The big feudal landlord has a manor of more than 50,000 acres set up after Liberation. The Cultural Revolution is supposed to raise your ideological level a bit. Here in this place you've got Japanese [agents] and members of the Guomindang. You should be careful and learn to spot them. They want to restore the Guomindang paradise, the Japanese paradise, the British paradise. . . ."

JUDGE: Accused Chen Boda, did you say those things?

CHEN: Those were my words.

JUDGE: Did you have any basis for them?

CHEN: Absolutely none. I was just going by things I'd heard.

JUDGE: By things you'd heard. When you slandered Comrade Zhang as a "big feudal lord of the manor," had you ever visited the orchard?

CHEN: No, I saw Comrade Bai Yun, but I don't recall what her old man said. . . .

TV COMMENTATOR: The prosecution has given a detailed account of the accusations in the indictment concerning Chen Boda's creation of a climate of counterrevolutionary opinion, his taking it upon himself to subject Chairman Liu Shaoqi to struggle-and-criticism, and conducting the East Hebei frame-up.

CHIEF JUDGE: The facts recounted again elucidate the accused Chen Boda's zealous participation in the conspiracy by the Lin Biao and Jiang Qing counterrevolutionary cliques' crimes in conspiring to subvert the party and seize power, bring ruin on the country and people, overthrow the People's Republic of China, the dictatorship of the proletariat, and the socialist order. He was one of the main culprits in the Lin Biao and Jiang Qing counterrevolutionary cliques. He violated Articles 90, 92, 98, and 102 of the Criminal Code of the People's Republic of China. His crimes are serious, and we propose to the Special Court to punish the accused Chen Boda for these crimes in an appropriate manner.

JUDGE: Accused Chen Boda, do you wish to make any statement or plea?

CHEN: I . . . I do not wish to plead for myself.

JUDGE: Do you wish to make any submission, statement, or plea with regard to the accusations of the Special Procurator's Office?

CHEN: As far as that's concerned, I think the indictment is excellent teaching material in my case.

DEFENSE COUNSEL: According to the Code of Criminal Procedure, we have accepted the responsibility [of speaking in Chen's defense]. We have since carried out serious research, examined the material concerning this case, and had frequent meetings with Chen Boda. In the process of the court's investigation, the court has examined a large amount of evidence, while Chen Boda has been given ample opportunity to make statements or pleas. Now that the court's investigation is concluded, we have a clear understanding of the case. We wish to present the following opinions.

TV COMMENTATOR: Chen Boda's Defense Counsel Gan Yüpei puts forward his defense with regard to the accusations of the prosecution. He points out that Chen Boda's position and function at the time must be distinguished from those of Lin Biao and Jiang Qing. The several frame-ups that Chen Boda engineered are a responsibility he cannot shirk. But there were other factors in his engineering of frame-ups and their consequences. . . .

DEFENSE COUNSEL: The principal defendants in this case all had different positions and functions in the cliques. Concerning the accused Chen Boda's attitude, during the process of interrogation in court he has acknowledged his entire responsibility for the criminal events concerned and the consequences that ensued. He has acknowledged that "his crimes are grievous." . . . Furthermore, he has several times admitted before the court his criminal liability, and expressed his willingness to accept the appropriate punishment—so his attitude has been fairly good. Accordingly . . . I request that the court in its deliberations on the sentence should consider leniency. That is the conclusion of the defense.

CHEN: May I say something?

JUDGE: You may, you may.

CHEN: I bear heavy responsibility for the struggle-and-criticism against Liu

Shaoqi. I just want to say the following: I wrote three things on the report of the special case group for Lu Dingyi. That was also a crime, a crime! The third thing was the East Hebei affair. I said those words and that was a crime.

JUDGE: I declare the defense concluded. Chen Boda, do you have any final statement to make?

CHEN: I ask the party to handle my case with leniency.

JUDGE: Accused Chen Boda, await the verdict. The court must deliberate. . . . Take the accused Chen Boda away.

PART TWO

INTRODUCTION

The Gang of Four were not just conspirators; they were active political figures with a platform and a system of ideas and policies that went beyond their secret campaign to promote themselves to the absolute leadership of China.

Call them what one will—Trotskyites, left-radicals, anarchists—they shared, with varying degrees of lucidity, a vision of China and the world that in its official form was considered rational and progressive by left-inclined people in many countries of the globe, and by millions of Chinese people in the party, the government, and the armed forces—indeed in all walks of life. The influence of those ideas, on the wane for the present, cannot be discounted as a factor in post-Mao China. One of the reasons why Deng Xiaoping and his leadership group have been able to discredit the Gang of Four is precisely because they did not thoroughly carry out the ideas they professed, but succumbed to what in Marxist jargon is called "left opportunism."

Left opportunism is a political line in which high-sounding radical principles are used to justify shady dealings, plots, and coups without reference to the real strength of the party among the masses. "Right opportunism" means allying the party with conservative or moderate elements in society, even with some right-wingers, in the interest of gaining backing, funds, places in a coalition government, etc.

Some surprising things emerge when one studies more closely the political platform of the Gang of Four. For instance, that Jiang Qing, while providing the guiding impetus for the modernization of Peking opera, actually did little work on it. Or that some of Yao Wenyuan's ideas were not dissimilar to those of the Deng group. Or that the courtly, academic-looking Zhang Chunqiao was behind some of the most violent acts of the Cultural Revolution.

The victors are always in the right. After all the misery and suffering the Gang of Four caused, one would hardly expect them to be handled dispassionately in the post-Mao media. Some charges against them are implausible, others ludicrous. But in the months following their downfall, reams of information on their aims and political style came to light, presented here in a condensed form.

6

POLITICAL TACTICS

The Gang of Four's most important aim in the short or medium term was to ensure that they monopolized leading posts after or shortly before Mao's death.

Jiang Qing, it has been frequently alleged, saw herself as the future party chairman and effective ruler of China. Wang Hongwen, despite his youth, was to be chairman of the Standing Committee of the National People's Congress—the highest constitutional position in the People's Republic while there was no Head of State.[1] Zhang Chunqiao would almost certainly have been appointed premier if the Gang's program had succeeded, while Yao Wenyuan would have exercised control over the media, propaganda and culture, education, and intellectual affairs.

To seize power, they had to accomplish two main tasks: discredit the policies of the leadership group around Deng Xiaoping, which enjoyed the patronage of Premier Zhou Enlai as long as he was alive; and push their own supporters into influential positions while squeezing out the followers of the Zhou-Deng line.

The basic difference between the political line of the Zhou-Deng tendency and the Gang's followers concerned the issue of class struggle. The Zhou-Deng group's philosophy inclined toward the theory of the "dying out of class struggle," which is closely linked to the strategy of a united front.[2] The Gang, while also strongly anti-Soviet, were suspicious of the policy of closer links with the West, as they thought it would be accompanied by the spread of "bourgeois" cultural influences such as pop music and pornography. They propounded the adage of Mao: "Never forget class struggle." In practice, this meant that the Gang and their supporters sought to discredit and overthrow elderly party and government leaders who had survived the Cultural Revolution and been reinstated from 1973 on, under the aegis of Zhou and Deng. (Deng himself reappeared for the first time in 1973, after seven years' disgrace.) This they did by accusing the old leaders of "bourgeois" tendencies, "capitulationism," "restorationism," "opportunism," "economism," failure to attend to class struggle, "spontaneous" tendencies toward capitalism and revisionism, etc. They discredited the theory of a united front by saying it favored Guomindang agents, bourgeois infiltrators of the party and state, links with overseas capitalists, subservience to foreign tastes and luxuries, and sell-out to the international enemies of Chinese socialism.

The Gang pursued an active program of promoting their followers to party membership. According to the mass-criticism group of the Henan Provincial Party Committee, they lauded "rebellion" as an important criterion for admission of new members to the party. In half a year—from the end of 1973 to early 1974—they made use of their power, behind the back of the Provincial Party Committee, to rush people into the party and promote cadres by shock tactics: "They either wantonly trampled upon the party's organizational principles, or prepared name lists for party membership and for promotion, or bypassed the party branch and let certain people at a higher level examine and approve applications, or made a unit in another place fix things for them when approval was denied by the local unit, or put together a so-called temporary party branch to increase party membership."[3]

Jiang Qing allegedly called for the freeing of convicts to join the Gang's faction in Henan. (It is not stated whether the people concerned were political prisoners or common criminals.) In the summer of 1976, their followers mobilized leftist elements in Henan for a big push to expel senior party officials from their posts. The leftists are quoted as saying, "If they can't be toppled, they must be attacked and driven away; and if they can't be driven away, they must be discredited. . . . We must drive the old fellows mad. Only so can problems be solved." Some wanted the older cadres to be criticized, attacked, and shot.[4]

The magnitude of these "helicopter promotions" of leftists in the party, during the Cultural Revolution and the anti-Deng campaign, was made clear in 1982 when Premier Zhao Ziyang announced the impending purge of all unreformed leftists from the party, and measures to "reeducate" some 20 million party members—out of a total nationwide membership of 39 million. Wang Hongwen is quoted as having said, "After all, what is meant by the centralized leadership of the party? It is to set a trap for the first secretaries of all provinces so as to let them make mistakes, and then give them a hard time." Provincial first secretaries are the party's topmost leaders outside of Peking, ruling provinces the size of big European countries. The Red Guards achieved the astonishing feat of toppling most of them in 1967, weakening the party's nationwide control to the extent that the army had to be called in to impose a semblance of order. During Zhou's fatal illness, Wang allegedly egged people on to "write letters, issue bulletins, and put up posters . . . calling for the elevation of the vicious mastermind Zhang Chunqiao to form a cabinet as premier."[5]

As soon as Mao died, Wang infiltrated his own agents into the leadership complex at Zhongnanhai and telephoned to all provinces asking them to report to him directly and take his instructions in all matters "in a vain attempt to sever contacts between the Party Central Committee headed by Chairman Hua Guofeng and the local party committees, so that the Gang of Four could give orders to the whole country."[6]

To assist their attempt at seizure of national power, the Gang allegedly tried to move all Shanghai-based members of the Party Central Committee to Peking, where they could wield more direct influence and attend emergency sessions if required. Wang Hongwen ordered the assignment of officials loyal to the Gang to government ministries in the capital, and prepared a list of candidate ministers and ministries they wanted to control. The Gang demanded that more Shanghai workers be elected to party membership, as the city is such an important industrial center.[7]

Shanghai was the Gang of Four's base area. Yao, Zhang, and Wang had spent their youth there, and Zhang in particular played an important role in the struggles of the early Cultural Revolution in the city. Jiang Qing, though born in Shandong Province, made her career as an actress in Shanghai before moving to Yan'an and marrying Mao. In the prewar period the International Settlement, ruled jointly by Britain and other powers, was a relatively safe haven for political activists opposed to the Guomindang.

The sophistication and deviousness that are acknowledged traits of the Shanghainese character kept Shanghai politically lively while many people in other parts of the country merely accepted Communist rule

as yet another change of dynasty. In addition, the municipal party
and government officials had the Gang of Four and their hangers-on
as a direct channel to Mao. The Gang gave instructions for the compilation in Shanghai of a new version of the party's history, and allegedly ordered that the names of such revolutionary giants as Zhou
Enlai, Zhu De, Ye Jianying, and Chen Yi be omitted. Minions of the
Gang—probably new party members elected from the ranks of Red
Guard leaders—wrote flattering letters to Jiang Qing encouraging her
in her ambition to become a new empress of China.[8]

> On the pretext of studying the history of the struggle between
> the Legalist and Confucian schools [of ancient Chinese thought],
> in December of 1975 they prepared twenty items in print and
> four in manuscript. They collected speeches by twelve leading
> comrades, including vice-chairmen of the Central Committee
> and vice-premiers, on various occasions, classified them into eight
> categories, and compiled extracts on them to be issued as material
> for criticism throughout the city. Such material was distributed
> to other provinces and cities as well. . . .
> They clamored: "Only two-and-a-half ministries under the State
> Council are reliable, all the bigwigs in the rest of the ministries
> are no good." In some ministries they placed their faithful fol-
> lowers, while in others they pitted people against each other.
> They spread rumors to vilify some ministries, while looking upon
> other ministries as places where they could make "breaches" and
> proceed to usurp supreme party and state leadership. One of
> their faithful followers in Shanghai stated explicitly: "The struggle
> around the question of foreign trade does not concern only that
> ministry—it concerns the Politburo."[9]

The criticism of Deng Xiaoping first became explicit in Shanghai
in February 1976, and the Gang planned to oust at least five provincial
first secretaries through their campaign:

> The Gang was overjoyed early this year [1976] when they re-
> ceived an anonymous letter from Jiangxi, viciously attacking the
> Jiangxi Provincial Party Committee. Jiang Qing herself arranged
> to find out who the writer of the letter was and incited him to
> stir up trouble in Jiangxi. The Gang's faithful followers in Shang-
> hai sent people to collect information in other provinces and
> municipalities. In addition, they invited people from other places
> to Shanghai, to read big-character posters that vilify leading com-

rades at central and local levels, and instigated them to attack the Party Committee in their own provinces.[10]

Most especially the Gang wanted to build up Shanghai as an armed base of support. Wang Hongwen is reported as having said, "The army is not in our hands. We've no men in the army. That's my greatest worry." Zhang Chunqiao is quoted as saying, "The army is not reliable. It is most dangerous. If the army turns the gun against us, what do we do then?" While training the Shanghai People's Militia, they refused to do the usual thing and put them under the control of the Shanghai Garrison Command, instead forcing the PLA to supply them with firearms. Wang Hongwen conducted an experiment in merging the rural militia of the surrounding area with the Shanghai Militia, and the Gang's plans even extended to setting up a nationwide militia command structure, which would have virtually turned the irregulars into a second standing army.[11]

The tactics of the Gang of Four were described as "hitting, kicking, and ferreting out." "Hitting" consists of "indiscriminately bludgeoning you, accusing you of putting production above revolution, and saying that 'the greater your output is, the bigger your mistakes will be, and the farther away from Chairman Mao's revolutionary line you will be.'" "Kicking" was the term for smashing the power of party committees at all levels, on the basis that "it won't do just to make a dent or hole in them—they must be smashed in pieces so that they can never be assembled again." "Ferreting out" consisted of "struggling against and toppling leaders at all levels . . . who did not follow them [the Gang]."[12]

Two agents of the Gang of Four—identified only as "a man and a woman"—set up an office at Qinghua University, apparently not to deal with the university's affairs but to provide an alternative reception center for letters and visitors from various parts of China, to rival that of the Party Central Committee. "They went so far as surreptitiously withholding and making extracts from letters sent to Chairman Mao or the Party Central Committee through them, so as to gather blacklist information for incrimination of central and local leading cadres, and to send special reports to the Gang of Four."[13]

Wang Hongwen, according to the People's Daily, "smuggled out minutes of meetings, and documents of the State Council and the party's Military Affairs Commission, for use as material for concocting antiparty shells.

"By means of letters and visitors from all parts of the country and

other subversive methods, this clandestine liaison point secretly compiled a lot of blacklist information for incriminating large numbers of
responsible comrades of the party, the government and the army, at
the central and local levels, including *some comrades of the Politburo,*
the responsible comrades of certain ministries and committees of the
State Council, the responsible comrades of some headquarters and
certain services and arms of the PLA, as well as the first secretaries,
deputy secretaries, etc., of certain provincial committees and party
committees of autonomous regions [italics added]."[14]

Zhang Tiesheng, the notorious student who turned in a blank examination paper to express his scorn for formal academic criteria
(discussed in detail on p. 144), was recruited to come from Liaoning
Province to encourage leftist radicals at Beijing University and at
Qinghua, where he is quoted as having declared, "The veteran cadres
are mostly bourgeois democrats." Later he was sent to carry out
similar missions in Shanxi Province.[15]

What has been made abundantly clear by the retrospective analysis
of political tactics in the Cultural Revolution decade is that the violent
poster wars on the streets of China's cities and towns were rarely as
spontaneous as they seemed. The general orientation of a political
conflict was determined from above, even down to the terminology
deemed appropriate. The poster debates were essentially a spillover
of factional struggle at the Politburo, Central Committee, provincial,
and municipal levels. As the poster wars not infrequently turned into
scuffles, fights, and even pitched battles involving firearms, spears,
clubs, and, in the case of Qinghua University, deadly catapults made
from the inner tubes of bicycles, it is fair to say that the top-level
intriguers used the masses as their cannon fodder. Just about everybody in China now understands this, which will make it harder for
any ambitious person to launch a new mass movement in the future.
And mass movements have been specifically ruled out of the program
of the Communist party. The new party statutes adopted at the Twelfth
Congress in 1982, as well as the state constitution promulgated in the
same year, have been shorn of the leftist rights of political agitation
and struggle that were built into the documents during the Cultural
Revolution.

7

PROPAGANDA AND ALLUSION

In 1974 a dramatic scene occurred at the editorial office of the new Shanghai political journal *Study and Criticism*. One of the Gang of Four's followers burst into a conference, shouting, "We are going to write an article about Empress Lü. Anyone volunteer? Swallow the bait if you can! The article will be strongly realistic, but it will entail some risk."[1]

The Empress Lü, who lived in the third to the second centuries B.C., is a notorious figure in Chinese history as it has been recorded by generations of Confucian scholars. Ruthless and ambitious, she murdered anyone—from concubine to minister—who stood between her and the throne.

Jiang Qing admired Empress Lü as a personification of her idea that women should be equal to men in politics—an unimpeachable notion by modern standards, but not one that has found implementation in China even today.

In 1974–75 the party press was strewn with articles extolling the Empress Lü and making veiled attacks on Premier Zhou Enlai and Vice-Premier Deng Xiaoping. Mao's wife also admired Wu Zetian, the Empress Wu of the Tang dynasty, who set aside the legitimate heir to the throne and acceded herself in A.D. 684. Jiang Qing probably admired the Empress Dowager Ci Xi (Tz'u Hsi), who presided over the decline of the Manchu Qing (Ch'ing) dynasty in the nineteenth century. But Ci Xi's name was reviled by the Communists, who considered her to have sold out China to foreigners.

Seemingly innocent historical analysis was used regularly in this period of the Cultural Revolution's aftermath. The *pi Lin pi Kong*

(Criticize Lin Biao and Confucius) campaign was kicked off in the autumn of 1973. Yao Wenyuan telephoned from Shanghai to his followers in Peking to tell them to write an article that would make the movement serve the Gang's purposes—principally the attack on Premier Zhou Enlai. The writing group entrusted with this task began turning out numerous articles attacking prime ministers in China's imperial past. Meanwhile Zhang Chunqiao and Wang Hongwen masterminded an article on reform of the People's Militia. Using the 1870 Paris Commune as an example, it advocated the separation of the militia from the party leadership. Published in *Study and Criticism*, this article was followed up by attacks on the veteran cadres, saying that they were "revolutionary in the first half of their lives but no longer revolutionary in the second half." After Zhou's death in 1976, it is alleged, the attack was turned against Hua Guofeng.

In the Campaign to Criticize Lin Biao and Confucius, the Gang laid great stress on the "progressive" historical role of the Legalists, the ancient school of political thought that provided the ideological base for the first Qin emperor when he united most of China toward the end of the third century B.C. The Gang particularly lauded the works of the semilegendary Shang Yang and the philosopher Han Fei, whose theories, somewhat akin to Machiavellianism, exempted the ruler from all moral responsibility for his acts, provided they contributed to the strength and stability of the state. Jiang Qing "talked nonsense to the effect that the Legalists were the spokesmen of the peasants, and believed that a peasant uprising could clear the way for the accession of the Legalist ruler [i.e., one of the Gang]."[2] Since the Legalists (like the leftists) hated and despised book learning and Confucianism—having buried Confucian scholars alive and burned many of the ancient books—the praise of the Legalists was a corollary of the covert attack on Zhou Enlai, indirectly represented as the arch-Confucianist of modern China.

The Gang's admiration for the Legalists was attacked soon after their fall, and the qualified reverence for Confucius, as a figure whose thought encapsulates some of the best qualities of the Chinese nation, was restored to favor. *Historical Research* observed that while both Confucianism and legalism were used to suppress the common people of China, and while legalism had certain progressive features, its conception of history was nonetheless "idealistic and metaphysical." It concluded: "Their [the Gang's] eulogy of the Legalists, as well as their upholding of the statecraft, schemes and contrivances used to defend the feudal autocracy, was a component part of the Gang's intrigue to prepare public opinion for usurping top party and state power."[3]

Study and Criticism was set up by the leftists as a rival source of political authority to *Red Flag*, the official theoretical organ of the party. Throughout the period 1974–76, it could be relied upon to support the ideas of the Gang of Four, covertly attack Zhou, and in 1976 openly denounce Deng. Although diplomats and journalists in Peking at the time, as well as most China watchers outside the country, were unwilling to see its existence as evidence of a straight two-line power struggle, in point of fact a mere count of the recurrence of leftist political slogans in *Study and Criticism* by comparison with those in *Red Flag* could show their difference of line. *Study and Criticism* was closed down permanently soon after the downfall of the Gang of Four.

An important ideological struggle was waged from 1973 on for control of the academic journal *Historical Research*, originally an organ of Shanghai's Fudan University. History has long been of great importance to the Chinese in the formulation of current policy. More than any other nation, they have taken to heart the adage that "he who does not study history is doomed to repeat it." Starting from the premise of a prehistoric Golden Age (shared by Confucianists and Communists, though in different forms), their scholars debated problems of government in terms of historical fact and the good and bad examples set by historical figures, especially rulers.

Whereas to the Confucianists this was simply a matter of intellectual principle, for the Communists it has served another purpose: the disguising of political attacks on others and the leaving open of escape routes in the event of defeat. Having attempted to smear an opponent through historical allusion, and having failed, the Chinese politician can innocently claim that he or she was only discussing a topic of academic interest. And foreigners can be discouraged from prying into the ebb and flow of internal political struggle by bland assertions that no contemporary allusion is intended in the discussion of a historical topic.

Historical Research, whose publication was suspended during the Cultural Revolution, was revived in 1974, but Zhang Chunqiao and Jiang Qing tried to prevent its editorial department from exercising full control over the contents.[4] The selection of titles and the editing were controlled by "Liang Xiao," the ultraleft writing group that penned much of the propaganda of the mid-1970s before the Gang's overthrow. (Their name is a pun on the words for "two schools"—

meaning Peking University and Qinghua University.) Other writing groups—Luo Siding and Chu Lan (meaning respectively "screw" and "first wave")—were also involved.

In October 1975, allegedly because of Mao's denunciation of the Gang's attempts to gain supreme power, the control of *Historical Research* was restored to the Department of Philosophy and Social Sciences—a rare example of the Gang suffering an ideological setback in the period before their overthrow.[5]

Peking's two main universities—Beida and Qinghua—were used by the Gang to propagate their leftist line in the 1970s through the Liang Xiao writing group. From 1973 to 1976, this group and others like it put together 219 articles, of which, it was subsequently stated, 181 were published. They dominated such prestigious organs as the *People's Daily*, to say nothing of the small forest of university and teachers'-college writing groups that sprang up, especially in Peking, Shenyang, and Shanghai, to propagate leftist views. The Gang of Four personally chose or specified the titles of thirty-six of the articles published by the main writing groups. Principal targets in 1975 were three reports that had been compiled at the request of Vice-Chairman Deng Xiaoping, referred to by the leftists as "the three big poisonous weeds." These were "On the General Program for All Work of the Party and Government," "Outline Report on the Work of the Academy of Sciences," and "Some Problems in Accelerating Industrial Development." We will look at "On the General Program" on page 110.

The text of Deng's last two papers has not been officially released, but it appears that the report on the Academy of Sciences complained of inactivity among scientists and researchers who were afraid of being dubbed "bourgeois experts" in the anti-Confucius campaign. Laboratories were underequipped and access to foreign scientific literature was restricted. China was falling far behind the developed world in scientific research, whereas previously her scientists were of world standard. Scientists were particularly vulnerable to leftist pressure because many of them had been educated abroad, which made them automatically suspect as having "subversive" links with the outside world.

"Some Problems in Accelerating Industrial Development" is thought to have contained proposals for introducing bonus payments and other material incentives in industry, which the Gang outlawed; reducing investment in heavy industry and increasing it in light industry to obtain more consumer goods; and modernizing old industrial plants rather than buying new equipment.

Besides relying on written historical allusions to disseminate propaganda, Jiang Qing was not above echoing more recent symbolic actions. For example, in 1966 Mao had made a symbolic gesture of sending a basket of mangoes to the left-wing activists at Qinghua University to show his approval of their activities. In imitation, Jiang in 1974–75 sent mangoes, melons, tomatoes, millet, pastries, and candies to her propagandists in the two main universities. She told her agents there to make a point of eating millet gruel as a symbol of their loyalty to her.[6]

A large part of 1975 was dominated by the leftist campaign against "bourgeois rights." These were defined as differences in income, such as characterize the socialist period in Marxist theory—but this was not the essence of the Gang's attack, which was led with press articles by Zhang Chunqiao and Yao Wenyuan.

They advanced the proposition that "bourgeois rights" are inevitable under any form of socialism that is not yet far advanced toward communism, and are reflected in the eight grades of wages of Chinese workers—governed mainly by seniority, to some extent by political attitude, and least of all by output. (This system had not fundamentally altered six years after the Gang's overthrow; the bonuses they decried are routinely being paid to industrial workers across the board, thus defeating a bonus's main purpose, and creating inflation.) Building on the theory of bourgeois rights, Zhang and Yao proclaimed that its existence inevitably engendered bourgeois attitudes, special privileges, and class distinctions—even in the bosom of the Communist party. The real target of their covert attack on "bourgeois" attitudes was Deng Xiaoping himself, the effective leader of the government at the time.

Among the Gang's favorite slogans regarding bourgeois attitudes was one dealing with "old democrats"—people who went along with the Communist party for patriotic reasons or because they opposed the Guomindang. Such people were reasonably well treated in the early 1950s, mid-1960s, and again from 1977 on. During periods of left-wing upheaval, however, they were easy targets for left-wing activists. The Gang is credited with these two maxims: "Over 75 percent of the old cadres are bourgeois democrats," and "As a rule, democrats end up by turning into people who follow the capitalist road."[7]

A favorite policy of the Gang was to denigrate veteran revolutionaries on the grounds that they began their careers as "democrats," thus rendering their subsequent sympathies to the Communist party suspect. According to the *People's Daily*, the Gang threatened to "carry out major surgical operations" on so-called democrats, "without retaining any remnants."

> They wanted to give these old cadres a bad name and hang them. Should you grasp production, they would accuse you of practicing "the theory of the dying out of class struggle" and "the theory of productive forces." Should you grasp class struggle, they would accuse you of "pointing the spearhead downward and opposing corrupt officials only, not the emperor." In short, they abused without exception all old cadres who adhered to Chairman Mao's revolutionary line as "democrats" so that they could exclude and topple them.[8]

Even Hua Guofeng, whom the Gang accepted as a compromise candidate for the post of acting premier after the death of Zhou (the choice would otherwise have been between Deng Xiaoping and Zhang Chunqiao), was subjected to their veiled attacks. They ceased equating Confucius with Zhou or Deng and instead transferred the analogy to Hua.[9] They wrote critically of the sage's promotion in the twelfth year of the reign of Duke Ding of Lu from minister of crime to acting prime minister. The fact that Confucius was fifty-six in that year was censored out, as it would have been "too bare-faced"—Hua Guofeng was also fifty-six when he was promoted from the post of minister of public security to be acting premier.

Yao Wenyuan allegedly thought this symbolic allusion was too obvious, and telephoned the *People's Daily* to advise them: "Don't be artificial, like comparing the minister of crime to the minister of public security. . . . If it is inadvisable to establish links for the time being, don't do it."

Such caution was not wholly typical of Yao Wenyuan, who was a rather impetuous propagandist. He loved daring comparisons between ancient Confucian rulers and the Deng–Zhou group of leaders, and identified Mao symbolically as the first emperor of the Qin (Chin) dynasty (reigned 221 B.C.–209 B.C.). The first emperor carried out sweeping but much-needed reforms with no sentimental concern for human life, and, like Mao, hated intellectuals. He buried scores of Confucian scholars alive and burned their books, according to tradition. Mao was not much more lenient; indeed, the effect of his policies on intellectuals was greater than the first emperor's and accounted for persecution of innumerably more people.

Yao was also China's self-appointed censor of TV and radio. Through him the Gang suppressed much of the media coverage of Zhou's funeral and the commemorative activities that followed it—a policy that led to the Tiananmen Square riots on April 5, 1976. The party journal *Red Flag* did not report Zhou's obituary notice or the memorial speech (by Deng Xiaoping).[10] On the instructions of Yao Wenyuan, Xinhua killed a story on the national mourning for Zhou, which it had prepared for January 15. Many members of the public, it is alleged, telephoned the *People's Daily* to ask why it was not carrying more coverage of memorial activities for Zhou; in place of such coverage, Yao had instructed the paper to print a 5,000-word article on the leftist debate about education that had been brewing at Qinghua University for the past few months. The media even suppressed coverage of the crowds of mourners lining the streets along which Zhou's hearse passed on the way to the crematorium.

In 1976 Yao Wenyuan ordered compilation and publication of a book to be entitled *Khrushchev's Rise to Power*. This, it was subsequently claimed, was a veiled attack on Hua Guofeng, because it said that Khrushchev made his name in the field of agriculture, as Hua to some extent did in Hunan. It also mentioned the fact that Beria, Stalin's chief of secret police, tried to organize a coup d'etat after Stalin's death—supposedly a reference to the fact that Hua spent most of 1975 and the early part of 1976 in the role of minister of public security.[11]

The importance of the tiniest differences in formulation of political slogans was illustrated by the battle waged around Mao's so-called deathbed adjuration. The Gang claimed that some of his last words had been "Act according to the principles laid down." Hua Guofeng, however, who had seen Mao on April 30, said the Chairman had given him three written instructions:

"Take your time, don't be anxious."

"Act in line with past principles."

"With you in charge, I am at ease." (This last was to become the basis of Hua's legitimacy as party chairman and premier after Mao's death, and was the subject of a widely propagated oil painting.)

Hua read out the first two adjurations at a Politburo meeting, while Wang Hongwen and Jiang Qing took notes. Yao Wenyuan, according to the official account after the Gang's overthrow, even saw the original notes in Mao's handwriting, but nevertheless changed the second one in an internal party document to "Act according to the principles laid down."[12] Yao even altered the text of a commemorative editorial to give the impression that these were Mao's words.

Why, the Western reader may ask, was there such an important difference between the two texts—of which the one allegedly falsified was being quoted in the press as late as October 4, on the eve of the Gang's downfall? Only a Chinese Communist ideologist could satisfactorily interpret the full subtlety of the difference. Yao's version was taken to mean that Mao's successors were adjured by him to act according to his proletarian revolutionary line and policies, as explained in the editorial of the *Liberation Army Daily* on September 16. "Act in line with past principles" could perhaps be seen as a more flexible instruction, reflecting the mercurially shifting line that Mao pursued in practice.

The article "On the General Program," written on Deng Xiaoping's instructions, came under severe attack from the Gang of Four and their followers in 1976. The article referred to a number of important problems in railway administration, iron and steel production, national defense, agriculture, and specific problems of certain localities and work units, which had been raised in the Central Committee in 1975. It also referred to three directives issued by Mao in 1974, which concerned the theory of the dictatorship of the proletariat, stability and unity, and economic progress. The Gang printed tens of millions of copies of a preliminary draft of the article—which they were evidently circulating as material for teaching "by negative example"— and called it a "program to reverse [political] verdicts and restore capitalism," the favorite charges against Deng at the time. In February 1976 Yao Wenyuan personally made forty-seven annotations on the text of the article, and instructed that it be criticized by the writing group Liang Xiao and another such group, Cheng Yue. The leftists were angered by references in the article to the "bourgeoisie in the party" and to "sham Marxists," evidently considering these references to themselves. One part of the article read:

> Chairman Mao said [in 1974]: "Eight years have passed since the Great Proletarian Cultural Revolution. Now the best thing is stability. The whole party and the whole army must unite." We should study theory and grasp the line for the purpose of promoting stability and unity. Unite for one purpose, that is, the consolidation of the dictatorship of the proletariat. This must be fully realized in every factory, village, office, and school.

Yao Wenyuan added the comment "How about the revolution?" By this he meant that "promoting stability and unity" was a way of putting an end to the Cultural Revolution, which the leftists would have liked to see extended with all its aspects of disunity, strife, "class struggle," and disorder!

The Gang of Four's most obscure area of policy-making was in foreign affairs. Mao, Zhou, and Deng kept a firm grip on foreign relations and evidently considered it essential to present a united front to the outside world.

Like the Soviet Union, China avoids public criticism of any aspects of its past foreign policy, even though it was administered by people subsequently disgraced. Evidently this reflects a compulsion on the part of both nations to represent their foreign policy as totally consistent from the time of their respective revolutions till the present day—a sort of national face-saving attempt. And in China's case it is true that since the thaw with the West in 1971–72 there have been only two major shifts in her foreign policy: the splits with Vietnam and Albania. There have, of course, been changes of nuance, but the pro-Western stance continues unaffected by the professed Chinese concern for the problems of the Third World.

The Gang of Four all met visiting foreign dignitaries from time to time, but in general, in expressing their views, they confined themselves to the policy line laid down by the three top leaders. They opposed the boom in Chinese imports of foreign-made goods in the early 1970s, and they were scathing about foreign culture, although Jiang Qing and Wang Hongwen were both accused in 1977 of having imported luxury goods for themselves. It is difficult, however, to swallow allegations that they "opposed the unmasking" of the United States and the Soviet Union. In fact, their invective against the Soviet Union was a consistent feature of the Chinese media in 1966 until the late 1970s. And naturally before 1972 and President Nixon's visit to Peking, they poured out attacks on the United States. The reference below to party and state secrets most likely concerns Jiang Qing, who was criticized strongly for having given the series of interviews mentioned earlier to American scholar Roxane Witke, though Dr. Witke's book hardly seems to give away state secrets. Nonetheless, this passage from the Chinese press does accuse the Gang of meddling in foreign relations, and I reproduce it simply as a reference document.

The Gang of Four was opposed to Chairman Mao's great strategic policy of uniting the Third World, winning over the Second World [the developed countries apart from the two superpowers], and rebuffing the two hegemonists—American and Soviet.

They forbade the unmasking of the two hegemonists of the U.S. and the Soviet Union, and especially of the Soviet revisionists. They held up, suppressed, and forbade the publication of articles criticizing Soviet revisionism. They poured cold water on the struggle waged by the Taiwan patriotic compatriots to oppose Soviet revisionism and unmask the Chiang gang. They maintained illicit relations with foreign countries, paid no attention to party discipline and state laws, and bartered away important party and state secrets. . . . This gang of foreign lackeys looked upon foreigners and foreign goods as better than anything else. From the playing cards and fishing rods in their hands to the wigs on their heads and the dentures in their mouths, all were imported from abroad.[13]

Apart from the rather colorful final passage about the Gang of Four's tastes, this post-Mao analysis of their ideas on foreign policy seems diametrically opposed to everything previously known or assumed about the subject. If they really "forbade the unmasking of the two hegemonists," their writ did not run far, for China's foreign policy from 1971 on has been based on opposition to the Soviet Union. It was not the leftists but the "archrevisionist" Deng Xiaoping who, in the post-Mao era, called a halt to attacks on the Soviet Union's internal political, social, and economic order. It was the Deng government that quarreled with Vietnam and Albania and made unprecedentedly generous offers for a settlement with Taiwan. It was Deng's administration that invited foreign manufacturers of consumer goods—including such bastions of capitalism as Coca-Cola, Seiko, Sanyo, Mitsubishi, Rémy Martin and Hongkong's Dairy Farm (owned by the huge Hongkong Land) as well as the luxurious, Swiss-managed Peninsula Hotel—to come into China to participate in profit-making joint ventures. With the Gang still at the helm, none of these things would have been permitted, insofar as one can determine from their policy record.

One of the most truly ludicrous charges leveled against Jiang Qing—and a sign that the Gang of Four were not the only authors of political nonsense—was the allegation that because she praised the Great Wall of China, she supported the Soviet view that it was the country's true northern frontier. "Her sinister aim was to beat the drum for the vain attempt of the Soviet revisionist social imperialists to seize by force a large tract of Chinese territory as a gift in preparation for her to pledge allegiance and offer tributes to the new czar after her ascension to the throne as empress."[14] This extraordinary accusation—that Jiang Qing would abandon a large tract of Chinese territory to the Soviet Union—finds no confirmation in anything she is reported to have said.

In the attacks on Jiang Qing that featured prominently in the seven or eight months of media coverage following her arrest, it was frequently alleged that she had said it would be all right for China to have a new empress. She obviously admired the two previous women rulers, Empress Lü and Empress Wu, and anti-Jiang cartoons showed her imitating the nineteenth-century Empress Dowager Ci Xi (Tz'u Hsi). She affected long black gowns, which to the Chinese eye made her seem sinister. But she seemed unaware of the hatred her manner inspired in many of the other leaders, and was reported to have been completely astonished when she was arrested.

Although there is no question about Jiang Qing's major crimes against the Chinese people, many of the secondary allegations against her are of dubious validity. To the Western reader, it seems that the prosecutor preparing the case against her simply got carried away—no new phenomenon in Chinese justice, where the most dire and far-reaching consequences may be attributed to no more than a thought ascribed to the accused.

8

POLITICS VS. ECONOMICS

All socialist planned economies have to face the problem of priorities. Should heavy industry or light industry receive more investment? Should agriculture be subsidized, or should the industrial workers enjoy a higher living standard? And, the most troublesome dilemma of all, is it a political deviation to raise real incomes of the masses now, instead of investing in the future by spending more on economic development?

In the times of Marx, and later Lenin, industrialization—the breeding ground for communism—was essentially seen as concerned with the buildup of heavy industry, though textiles were also important. In the first half of the twentieth century, a country's military power was governed largely by its production of iron, steel, and fuels. Without Stalin's crash program to develop Soviet heavy industry in the 1930s, Germany would certainly have conquered Russia in World War II.

China fought its revolution mainly in the countryside; but when the Communists came to power, they already had at their disposal a significant heavy industrial base, built up by the encroaching imperial powers in coastal areas and by the Japanese in Manchuria, which Japan had seized in 1931. But even while rushing headlong into a program of further heavy industrial development with massive Soviet aid, Mao had doubts about the wisdom of overemphasis on heavy industry. In his 1956 speech on "the ten major relationships," he argued strongly in favor of developing the existing industrial base—consisting to a large extent of textile mills and light industries in coastal cities—through which the Western imperial powers had exploited cheap coolie labor and developed local markets for their products. Mao's argument in 1956 was that only by maximizing output from existing industries could more advanced ones be built up, laying a foundation for modernization of all industry and for the equipment of strong armed forces.

Shortly afterward, however, Mao became infected with the fever to "catch up" with the West, especially in steel production—even if it had to come from small and inefficient backyard furnaces. The predictable result was disaster, aggravated by the withdrawal of the Russian technicians in 1960. From then on, it became a matter of pride for China to develop herself autonomously, with only limited help from some West European and Japanese firms that braved American disapproval to sell her heavy industrial equipment and technology.

The Gang of Four's policy for industry was hypersocialistic and verging on anarchism. They believed it possible to make people work better and work more without giving them material incentives—other than gradual progress, mostly determined by seniority, up the eight grades of wages on which industrial remuneration was based. They opposed paid overtime, bonuses, prizes, and piecework, though such things persisted in some industrial enterprises and were periodically denounced by the leftists.

The Gang had a strangely ambivalent attitude toward increasing industrial production. If it could be done without substantial new investment, but simply through the zeal and political commitment of the workers, they praised it. But they denigrated technical achievement not based on political outlook. Mao Xinxian, a young woman textile worker at a Shanghai mill, set a record by weaving 400,000 meters of cloth without a single defect. She was persecuted, declared to be "an example of following the theory of productive forces" and accused of having "a low level of political consciousness of the struggle between the two lines" (Maoist and moderate).

The Gang of Four wanted to run even such a complex system as the steel industry on anarchistic, voluntaristic principles. Zhou Guenwu, secretary of the Party Committee at Peking Capital Iron and Steel Plant, said after the Gang's fall, "They forbade us to discuss production targets, to carry out inspection of products, to set consumption quotas, or to practice cost accounting." Jiang Qing allegedly tried to gain control of the Wuhan Iron and Steel Company, saying this would mean "grasping Wuhan and the [surrounding province of] Hubei."[1]

Mao had defined the policy for industry in a document of March

22, 1960, concerning the Anshan Iron and Steel Works—later to be known as the Anshan Charter. It laid down the five basic principles of running socialist industries: "Keep politics firmly in command; and strengthen party leadership; launch vigorous mass movements; institute the system of cadre participation in productive labor, and worker participation in management; reform irrational and outdated rules and regulations and maintain close cooperation among workers, cadres, and technicians; and go all out for technical innovation and technical revolution."[2]

On June 4, 1975, the Central Committee supplemented the Anshan Charter with a new seven-point program for the iron and steel industry, said to have been personally approved by Mao. The document demanded that investigations be made to discover "whether the ideological and political line is correct, whether the movement to study the theory of the dictatorship of the proletariat has really been launched, whether the masses have been fully mobilized, whether a strong core of leadership has been established, whether bourgeois factionalism has been overcome, whether the party's policies have been conscientiously implemented, and whether the sabotage of the class enemies has been effectively rebuffed."[3]

While these "Seven Whethers" could be seen as incorporating some leftist principles espoused by the Gang—dictatorship of the proletariat, mobilization of the masses—their main thrust was authoritarian and pro-party. The Gang was later quoted as having said the Central Committee document "had made several million metallurgical workers unable to lift their heads." But workers' reactions to the central instructions, cited in the *People's Daily*, clearly showed they were regarded as a necessary movement to increase production of arms and farm machinery and to overcome backwardness in the industry. The Gang, by contrast, is quoted as having said, "We would rather have the low speed of socialism than the high speed of capitalism." Zhang Chunqiao allegedly said, "There is no need to be afraid of a decline in speed. You can reduce the speed."[4]

The leftists despised any increase in industrial production unless it could be linked to their own political line: for instance, by showing that workers could run machines well beyond the machines' capacity and endurance, and solve technical difficulties by studying the thoughts of Mao—none of which dealt with problems of engineering!

In their extreme mood, the Gang and its supporters regarded efficient production in industry as a sign of political deviance—paying too much attention to output, not enough to ideology.

"At the instigation of the Gang of Four, some people brazenly charged into factories to smash up mess halls, occupy hostels, and cut off power, water, and food supplies, thus forcing the enterprises to suspend work and production. They would say, 'You don't know whether the products are being turned out in the name of the bourgeoisie or the proletariat. The more you produce, the greater will be your crimes.' " During a period of crash production, workers toiled round the clock, and the factory provided them with an evening meal—but the Gang's followers denounced this as a "material incentive."[5]

The Gang opposed strict time-and-motion methods of control in industry. Yao Wenyuan was quoted as having said in 1976, "Are we supposed to institute the kind of capitalist system that even counts the time spent by workers in the toilet?"

The leftists opposed "control, checking, and suppression"—the guiding principles of the Zhou–Deng moderates in their attempts to bring order into the near-chaotic industrial scene of the mid-1970s. The *People's Daily* defended this triple policy in the following terms after the downfall of the Gang:

> The personal-responsibility system at Daqing [oil field] stipulates that "all things are controlled by the people." Is that not "control"? The system of quality responsibility stipulates that "no work or products that fail to meet quality standards are accepted or allowed to leave the factory." Is this not "checking"? The system of safety in production stipulates that "it is necessary to wage resolute struggle against and deal blows at the class enemies who sabotage revolution and production." Is this not "suppression"? The question is: Who exercises control, checking, and suppression; how are things controlled, checked, and suppressed; and what matters are controlled, checked, and suppressed? It is erroneous to oppose control, checking, and suppression in one breath.[6]

The leftists' policy of disrupting industrial production for political reasons was summarized in the following phrases: "Don't carry out production for the erroneous line. Don't risk your lives for people following the capitalist road. Don't be afraid of strike, suspension of production, or disorder in society. Don't 'sew wedding gowns for others.' . . . To disrupt a factory or create confusion in an enterprise is to add another noose to the neck of the person following the capitalist road." Zhang Chunqiao was especially closely associated with these near-anarchist policies.[7]

The power struggle in 1976 severely affected production, but rapid recovery was reported after the overthrow of the Gang. The city of Hangzhou claimed that in March of 1977 its production rose by 65 percent over that of February. Recovery was particularly badly needed at the Hangzhou Silk Printing and Dyeing Mill, which was the scene of bitter factional conflict allegedly fomented by the Gang's main follower in that part of China, Weng Senhe. By mid-1977 they were overfulfilling quotas for production of big silk portraits of Mao and his successor, Hua Guofeng!

In Kunming, freight transport in April 1977 jumped 40 percent over that of March, for the railways had been particularly vulnerable targets for leftist agitation.[8]

The Gang was indifferent or hostile to attempts to improve living standards through increased production of consumer goods and textiles, calling them "bourgeois." Zhang Chunqiao was quoted as saying, "The Ministry of Light Industry exercises control only over hairpins."

The Chinese economy is founded on agriculture, which provides a livelihood for some 800 million of the country's estimated population of over one billion. Mao's revolution was rooted in the peasantry and their need for radical land reform. His postrevolutionary reforms—especially the people's communes—were central to his political thinking, disastrous though they were.

The Gang of Four knew little about agriculture, no more than would come up routinely at Politburo meetings. All of them were city-bred with urban outlooks. Though reform of the rural areas was Mao's great goal, they went along with it halfheartedly and were hostile to some aspects of it, as was disclosed after their overthrow.

The leftists did favor Mao's policy of trying to even out income differentials among the rural work force, though even Mao was obliged to retain such things as the work-point system (which paid stronger peasants better than weaker ones) and the peasants' private plots (which generated extra income for the hardworking). The Gang also supported Mao's emphasis on grain as the "key link" in the rural economy, opposing diversion of labor from grain-growing to the cultivation of secondary or cash crops and the breeding of livestock for meat and by-products. Their emphasis on revolutionary will for workers in industry was echoed by their statements on the peasants. It has been alleged that their policy was summarized in the adages "Production will go up automatically when revolution is carried out well" and "As long as revolution is carried out well, a fall in production is of little consequence." Although China suffered a chronic shortage of meat, they claimed: "For grain production to go up, animal husbandry must give way."

Yao Wenyuan is recorded as having questioned the wisdom of going all out for agricultural mechanization, saying it could not be achieved, even "in the main" by 1980—a goal announced shortly before Mao's death. With Mao ailing and barely lucid, Vice-Chairman Hua Guofeng (later premier and party chairman) took charge of agricultural policy and presided over two national conferences on agriculture in 1975 and 1976 respectively.

Although mechanization had been a goal from the 1950s on, Yao Wenyuan allegedly suppressed an editorial penned by Hua Guofeng in 1971 calling for more rapid progress in mechanization. The Gang was credited with having taken the line that mechanization could be carried out "only at the expense of the revolution."[9] Ironically enough, Deng Xiaoping and his supporters forced Hua's group to abandon the rapid-mechanization policy in 1978 on grounds of technical and economic difficulties.

Mao's ambitions for agriculture were symbolized by his choice of Dazhai—a poor production brigade on hilly ground in the northwest province of Shanxi—as the model. After the failure of the Great Leap and the downgrading of the people's communes as basic social units, Deng Xiaoping and Liu Shaoqi worked out new guidelines for agricultural work, which concentrated on providing material incentives for the peasants and reducing the extent of collective labor.

A production brigade is the intermediate unit of the three-tiered People's Commune. At the top is the commune headquarters, through which important decisions used to be made, a clinic and secondary school would be operated, and small industries would be managed. A typical commune might have authority over 15,000 to 25,000 peasants. The brigade accounted for about 600 to 1,200 peasants; and in communes regarded as "progressive," it undertook the accounting of people's labor and the amount they would be paid under a system of work points. Below the brigade is the production team, taking in one or several of the original villages of the area, with several teams to a brigade. On most communes accounting was done at the team level, with the villagers meeting every few evenings to discuss how many work points each of them should receive for the work done. The leftists considered the production team too small and inefficient, protecting peasant conservatism and fostering "capitalist" desires to make extra money by sideline production and private plots, where a pig could be raised or chickens bred, vegetables and tobacco grown, fruit gathered.

The commune system was all but abandoned in 1982. The topmost level lost its political authority and continues in a shadowy role that has yet to be completely determined. The brigades remain, but the accounting is done now by families or groups of families contracting with the production-team leadership to grow a fixed amount of grain or other produce for the next harvest, and keeping for their own use or for sale whatever else they have grown or bred.

Mao favored Dazhai because the people there all worked together as a brigade. The incomes of Dazhai peasants were nearly equalized, and they spent much time on collective projects such as irrigation schemes and the terracing of hills to make new farmland.

The basic objection to the Dazhai model—which hundreds of thousands of peasants from other parts of the country were sent to see—was that while arguably suitable for the harsh conditions of Shanxi, it was of little relevance to farming methods in rich coastal provinces like Jiangsu and Zhejiang.

Among those who did not care for Dazhai was Zhang Chunqiao, who reportedly said, "In Dazhai, hillsides are dug open to create farmland. But in Shanghai we don't have hillsides everywhere." Jiang Qing had her own model village in the Tianjin area, where she conducted social experiments in bringing literacy and culture to the peasants.

The First National Conference on Learning from Dazhai in Agriculture opened in Peking on September 15, 1975. Jiang Qing surprised the delegates by making a speech at the opening ceremony attacking provincial leaders for neglecting agriculture by not attending—though their absence had been decreed by the Central Committee, who had doubtless felt that the provincial leaders had their hands full coping with the mounting political strains in their respective provinces. Hua Guofeng, who presided, reported to Mao that Jiang Qing had demanded that a talk of hers on the novel *Water Margin* be circulated and a recording of 'it played. Mao is said to have dismissed her demands as "farts" and to have forbidden the printing or replaying of the talk.[10]

Hua Guofeng's final report on the conference aroused Jiang Qing's ire. According to Chen Yonggui, head of the Dazhai model production brigade and the politburo's "token peasant" at the time, she "viciously" told him and Hua, "That's a revisionist report." Nonetheless Mao ratified it, and it was issued as Central Committee Document

21/1975. Yao Wenyuan forbade publication of the report in *Red Flag*, even though it had been scheduled for printing. Zhang Chunqiao told officials in Shanghai to "stand firm" against the report, which recommended the widespread use of the Dazhai model for other agricultural units around the country. (Ironically, Dazhai and Mao's whole agricultural policy were overturned by the Deng group in 1979, and subsequently both Chen and Hua were disgraced in different degrees.)

Provincial leaders were confused as to how to react to the report, especially since followers of the Gang had spread rumors that Mao had in fact not approved it at all. Zhang Chunqiao openly forbade people to follow its recommendations. When Chen Yonggui addressed meetings on implementation of the report and on crop plans, Gang activists in Shanghai and Suzhou said that he "only knew how to work hard and sweat, and knew nothing about political line."[11]

The uncertainty surrounding agricultural policy affected production, especially in the six provinces of Yunnan, Guizhou, Sichuan, Fujian, Zhejiang, and Jiangxi. At the notorious trouble spot of Wenzhou in Zhejiang, "the situation in many places deteriorated to such an extent that the land was divided up and the commune members had to go it alone. Polarization of rich and poor reemerged, black markets became rampant, and the collective economy disintegrated."[12]

According to the mass-criticism group of the Ministry of Petrochemical Industry (now divided into the Ministries of Petroleum and Chemical Industry), the Gang of Four opposed the building of small, rural chemical fertilizer plants. This was surprising since Mao himself was understood to be in favor of small-scale industry in the rural areas. This is one of several areas of policy in which the Gang inexplicably appeared to differ from their demigod. They called the plants "air-raid shelters for the county party committees" and "fortified villages." They had them closed down in places, and in one county alone caused a loss of 500,000 yuan. Another factory, which had been commended by Hua Guofeng as an advanced unit, was denigrated by the Gang as "riding to fame on a few briquets." In Zhejiang, Wang Hongwen and Weng Senhe disrupted the biggest fertilizer plant in the province so that it failed to fulfill its production plan for three years in a row.

At the instigation of the Gang of Four, anarchism spread unchecked, and some of the chemical fertilizer plants were reduced to a state of not following rules or having no rules to follow. In some plants, the equipment was left unrepaired the whole year long and was not looked after by anybody, thus causing the percentage of equipment in good working order to drop constantly. In some plants, the consumption of raw materials and fuel greatly increased and productivity of labor declined, thus resulting in losses. In some prefectures, production in chemical fertilizer plants was suspended or partially suspended for a time. [A prefecture is a group of several counties administered jointly, usually to unite pockets of ethnic minorities. There are such minorities in Zhejiang.] In one prefecture, production at more than twenty small chemical fertilizer plants was at one time almost completely suspended.[13]

The Gang attacked Zhou Enlai for permitting the purchase of a foreign-built vessel, renamed M.V. *Geng Xin*. They favored the development of homegrown shipbuilding and the 30,000-nautical-mile ocean voyage made by a Chinese-built freighter, M.V. *Feng Qing*, in the summer of 1974. The Gang evinced great satisfaction at her successful voyage—but for this they were later denounced as having "picked peaches" (i.e., sought to glorify themselves through the achievements of others). They were also accused of having gratuitously blamed other people for saying the ship would not be safe on the high seas, and for recommending the import of some pieces of equipment. Zhang Chunqiao was quoted as having said, "The voyage undertaken by the M.V. *Feng Qing* is a victory, and the sinking of M.V. *Feng Qing* will also be a victory"—evidently expressing confidence in the Gang's ability to make political capital out of anything.[14]

Jiang Qing had no expertise in shipbuilding or navigation. Her intervention in the M.V. *Feng Qing* affair was politically motivated and intended as an attack on Deng, and she certainly chose a sensitive point. China's single most important infrastructural problem in the 1970s (and still today) has been the congestion at her major ports, estimated in the early 1980s to be costing her some U.S. $200 million per annum in slow turnaround of ships. *On the Docks*, a leftist stage work, was not the least bit concerned with slow turnaround, but with the ideological purity of the dock workers and with the trapping of saboteurs. A favorite leftist slogan for Chinese stevedores in the mid-1970s was "Don't become slaves to tonnage."

In 1973 Zhou Enlai called for major improvements in dock work to be put into effect during the next three years. But early in 1974, when the Shanghai Docks No. 5 District fulfilled its stevedoring quota ahead of schedule, the Gang sent people to supervise the composition of a big wall poster condemning "slavery to tonnage" and "following the theory of productive forces." They said the poster was "of national significance." Productivity at the No. 5 District slumped from 1974 on: Volume of goods handled dropped by 10 percent year by year, while costs rose.[15]

The Gang, as shown by press commentaries in 1974, was hostile to imports of foreign technology, claiming that "Chinese workers can make anything foreign workers can make" and declaring, "We should not crawl along behind other people's backsides!" They even demanded that a chemical fertilizer plant attached to the famous Daqing oil field, containing imported installations, be dismantled and removed.[16]

The Gang spread the word that foreign trade was dominated by a "right opportunist line" and that the Ministry of Foreign Trade was actually "the Ministry of National Betrayal." They claimed that things needed in China were being exported, and things that could be produced in China were being imported, and they denounced the "slavish comprador philosophy." For their own use, however, they imported high-class cosmetics, consumer goods, tonics, and even "reactionary and obscene" films from abroad. Their attitude, according to their detractors, was that "even the moon is more beautiful in Europe" and "foreigners' farts smell better."[17]

Wang Hongwen is quoted as having denounced the export of traditional handicrafts as "only seeking foreign exchange, but not building socialism." Zhang Chunqiao, on seeing an ivory carving on the theme "Chang-ê Flies to the Moon," commented: "May these big bosses and big designers become immortals at an early date. The farther away they are from the workers, peasants, and soldiers, the better." Jiang Qing banned the manufacture and export of folk art on the theme "Three Attacks on the White-Boned Demon" (a famous incident from the Monkey legend; later Jiang Qing herself was derogatorily referred to as the White-Boned Demon).

Jiang Qing also attacked the export of crude oil to capitalist countries (mainly Japan), though in the three years 1973–75 these exports never accounted for more than 0.66 percent of total world export volume of crude.[18]

In contrast, the Dengist view of foreign trade was succinctly expressed by an air-force man who wrote: "Everyone knows that it would be stupid of us to abandon the steam engine invented by Watt, and work out something of our own. It [self-reliance] does not mean, either, that we should refuse to use electric lights because they were not invented by us, and insist on using kerosene lamps."[19]

Chinese economic planning since the return to power of Deng Xiaoping has tried to remove the dichotomy of politics and economics, and instead marry them in a harmonious whole. Marxism, it is felt nowadays, does not demand endless sacrifices from the people: on the contrary, it is supposed to make their lives easier. But in times of national strain and stress, it is always tempting for the leaders of Communist countries to demand self-sacrifice from the people in the name of protecting socialism. Such a line is hard to sustain, however, when the country is at peace within and without.

9

CULTURE AND
THE PERFORMING ARTS

China's cultural life has been a focus of bitter political struggle ever since Mao laid it down (in his 1942 "Talks on the Yan'an Forum on Literature and Art") that culture must primarily serve the workers, peasants, and soldiers, and the cause of revolution and socialism.

Mao held fast to this principle for most of his life, which brought him into severe conflict with many artists, writers, scholars, musicians, actors, and other people involved in intellectual or creative work. Because of the cultural/intellectual orientation of three members of the Gang of Four (Jiang Qing, Zhang Chunqiao, and Yao Wenyuan), it was inevitable that they would become deeply involved in this struggle.

Mao was the originator of a famous saying on cultural and intellectual matters: "Let a hundred flowers bloom and a hundred schools of thoughts contend"—known for short as the "double hundred" policy. It is commonly believed that Mao thought up this slogan at the time of the intellectual ferment in 1956–57, but in fact it dated back to a directive he issued in 1951.[1] Although the Communist party had long conducted intermittent campaigns against right-leaning intellectuals and writers, and proponents of cultural freedom under socialism, the cultural climate in China was relatively mild until 1957. Peking opera, poetry, novels, playwriting, and music—both Western and Chinese—flourished, despite the loss of many intellectuals to Taiwan and the general disruption of cultural life by the Civil War, which ended in 1949.

The spate of criticisms of the party in the mid-1950s induced Mao to elucidate his cultural policy. On February 27, 1957, he laid it down that works of art and literature should be helpful to unity, to socialism, to the dictatorship of the proletariat, to "democratic centralism," leadership of the Communist party, and international solidarity with all peace-loving people.

From 1958 on, the agony of the Great Leap Forward, which brought China almost to its knees economically through ill-judged crash programs, pushed cultural matters into the background. But with the failure of the Leap, Mao returned to the attack with his so-called Two Directives. On December 3, 1963, he proclaimed that many fields of culture were "still dominated by dead men and that art inadequately serves the superstructure" (i.e., is not an effective tool of propaganda). On June 27, 1964, he said that most of the country's cultural associations "basically did not implement the party's policy over the past fifteen years. . . . In recent years they have even neared the brink of revisionism."[2]

It was always the contention of the leftists that the Hundred Flowers policy could be put successfully into effect only if a distinction was made between "fragrant flowers" and "stinking weeds." Only flowers (leftist works) should be published or performed; there was to be no liberalization for weeds. In practice this meant a weeding out of China's cultural garden, with disastrous effects. In the Cultural Revolution, artists, actors, writers, and intellectuals bore much of the brunt of the Red Guard onslaught, for they had no physical or organizational form of self-defense.

The net effect of the implementation of Mao's cultural policy, first through the Gang of Four and later through the left-dominated Ministry of Culture, was the temporary demise of most forms of Chinese culture, both traditional and modern. The Peking Opera was drastically revised in terms of subject matter, setting, and costumes, and for several years only eight works were cleared for stage performance in the whole of China. Western music came under a cloud, bookshops were denuded, and newspapers castrated. Traditional art and literature were suppressed in favor of "revolutionary" art and highly politicized leftist literature. But despite the cultural wilderness thus created, the leftists insisted that they were following the Hundred Flowers policy.

The most notable work suppressed early in the Cultural Revolution was the big ballet-oratorio *The East Is Red,* which in the mid-1960s served as one of the main cultural vehicles for propagation of Mao's personality cult. Produced both as a stage work and as a film, it is a highly effective and moving portrayal of the course of the Chinese

Revolution from the nineteenth century to 1949. Its famous theme song continued to be used as a jingle for everything from clocks to computers long after the show itself was banned. A whole generation of young Chinese grew up thinking of it as the most important tune in the world. The slogan of the title was used to name numerous restaurants, shops, and hotels.

The reasons for the suppression of this work are still unclear, but most likely Jiang Qing did not want it rivaling what she regarded as her own revolutionary stage shows, or playing up the importance of historical events in which she was too young to participate. The hero-worshiping theme also spawned such symbolic catchphrases as "facing the sun"—referring to sunflowers, which turn toward the light and are therefore the symbol (almost erotically expressed in dance) of China's marriage with Mao.

Nowadays the credit for the "reform" of the Peking stage (to the extent that it is any longer considered to have been useful or desirable, which is very limited) is given to Zhou Enlai, and is claimed to have been usurped by Jiang Qing. In 1958 Zhou visited North Korea and met with the Peking Opera Troupe of the Chinese "People's Volunteers," who had not yet been posted home after their intervention in the Korean War. He asked them what gift they would like to send back to China, and they reputedly responded by creating the opera *Raid on White Tiger Regiment*, whose theme was an incident in the war. On returning to Peking toward the end of the same year, the military troupe was merged with the Shandong Peking Opera Troupe, according to Lu Jingwen, a leading figure in the Shandong troupe. (Many of the "volunteers" were natives of Shandong.) Zhou examined the opera five times and "gave many important instructions" with regard to it, Lu stated. But later, he added, Jiang Qing and Zhang Chunqiao took over the new production, which "seriously sabotaged the integrity of the original opera, from the theme and the plot to the cast."[3]

(The author saw the work performed in Peking in 1973 and thought it a politically neutral thriller with much action and little ideology; but the Chinese can read ideology into anything.)

An intimate glimpse of the way in which Jiang Qing took control of the Peking Opera and other regional operatic styles was given by Zhao Yanxia, an actress with the Peking Opera Troupe. She wrote in the *People's Daily* in 1977 that Jiang Qing once said, "Model theatrical works are created by me"[4]—which was to some extent true, but which omitted to mention the technical and artistic expertise of the performers, who in the last analysis were responsible for making each work a success.

The opera *Shajiabang*, which dealt with the guerrilla war during the Japanese occupation, was adapted from a Shanghai-style opera called *Sparks Amid the Reeds*. The original version had been shown in dress rehearsal on December 5, 1963, in Jiang Qing's presence. She allegedly laughed at it, saying that "the staging of Peking Opera on contemporary themes is ludicrous"—which, if she really said it, was an extraordinary contrast to her subsequent views.

Around the same time, according to actress Zhao, Mao put out a statement criticizing those who were "enthusiastic about promoting feudal art and capitalist art, but not socialist art." As a result, the troupe members were sent off to visit military units to improve their knowledge of soldiering, and then painstakingly revised the work. After five months' rehearsal, Jiang Qing came backstage and berated the cast for putting the work on at all. However, on April 27, 1964, Zhou Enlai and Marshal Zhu De saw the performance and approved it. On July 23, Mao watched it and shook hands afterward with the cast, but suggested that its title be changed to *Shajiabang* (which is just a place name).

Jiang Qing, according to Zhao's account, then changed her stance and became enthusiastic about the opera. This is what the Chinese call "grabbing the banner" or "picking peaches"—i.e., taking credit for other people's achievements. Jiang Qing, Zhao concludes, "never designed a single plot, rewrote a line in the dialogue, or produced a singing passage."[5] The opera later entered the conventional repertoire of eight stage works put on in the Cultural Revolution.[6] The eight works were *The Red Lantern, Shajiabang, Taking Tiger Mountain by Strategy, Raid on the White Tiger Regiment, On the Docks, The Red Detachment of Women, The White-Haired Girl,* and a symphony based on the music of *Shajiabang*. (It is not clear why a symphony should be included in a list of stage works. A wag in Peking's foreign community once remarked that the ideal revolutionary stage work would be called *Taking the White-Haired Girl by Strategy Beneath the Sign of the Red Lantern.*)

The basic concept of reforming the Peking Opera seems to have come from Mao, whose policies in cultural matters were summed up in two slogans: "Weed through the old to bring forth the new" and "Make the past serve the present, and foreign things serve China." If actress Zhao's account is accurate, it would seem that Jiang Qing threw herself into this work in order to divert some of Mao's power and influence to herself, rather than out of a personal conviction that revision of the Peking Opera was necessary in itself.

The approach was to retain the singing style, the music, some acting methods and acrobatics of the old Peking Opera, while introducing new themes on modern subjects. But though the production of the eight works began in earnest in 1964 (with the National Festival of Peking Opera on Contemporary Themes), they were not, strictly speaking, the first such productions. *The Red Lantern*, for instance, was based on a Shanghai-style opera that itself was based on a film called *Revolutionary Successors*. *The Red Lantern* was shown at the National Festival and Mao watched it twice. Zhou Enlai, by contrast, saw it nine times and "gave many important views on how to revise it."[7]

Zhou seems to have taken a much more active watching role over the eight works than has hitherto been assumed. This was characteristic; and there seems little doubt that he kept a close eye on the stage works for which Jiang Qing claimed credit, because he realized she was using them to further her own political career.

In 1964 Jiang Qing began to take an interest in the production of *On the Docks*, an opera about class struggle and sabotage set on the busy wharves of Shanghai. She attacked two deviant political lines that she professed to have spotted in the work: the "theory of middle characters" and the "theory of no conflict."[8] In Maoist aesthetics, "middle characters" are those who are neither totally loyal to the revolutionary or socialist cause nor totally hostile to it—who vacillate, but in the end usually turn out all right. They are the artistic expression of the policy of United Front. Jiang Qing apparently insisted that such characters were unsuitable for the new Peking Opera: Every character must be either good (that is, good and revolutionary all the time) or bad (that is, counterrevolutionary and evil all the time). The only concession to reality in character portrayal in the approved stage works was the temporary hoodwinking of some members of the masses by the villain and his henchmen. But the masses (being by definition wise) are eventually led to victory by a heroic character, usually a party member or highly motivated young person.

Shanghai was also the origin of the dance-drama *Taking Tiger Mountain by Strategy*, based on an earlier work called *Tracks in the Snowy Forest*, which had come out in stage production and novel form in the early 1960s.[9] Mao and Zhou both made suggestions for the adaptation, but Jiang Qing's role in this is not specified.

"As to the four other stage works, Jiang Qing had no share in them until they were fully rehearsed and even successfully staged," a criticism group of the Ministry of Culture stated in 1977. "She only saw *Raid on White Tiger Regiment* during the 1964 Festival, and described it as an 'unexpected success.' " In the case of *The Red Detachment of Women,* "Jiang Qing saw only a rehearsal of this ballet [which had been praised by Mao and Zhou] on September 21, 1964. Before that she never bothered to talk about it."[10]

As for the symphony *Shajiabang,* "Jiang Qing visited the Central Philharmonic Society only once, in January 1965. Her aim was to see if the various instruments of the symphony orchestra were suitable for accompanying the Peking Opera. During the rehearsal, she never went near the hall where the musicians were practicing." Mao and Zhou eventually approved the production on July 30, 1968.[11]

Zhang Chunqiao, throughout this period, apparently played the role of image-maker for Jiang Qing. He rebuked the Shanghai School of Dancing for inviting her to see *The White-Haired Girl* only after it had been seen by Zhou Enlai. "Jiang Qing should have been invited to see it first," Zhang is quoted as saying. After Mao saw the ballet in April 1967, Jiang Qing received the cast and told them, "My ambition is to produce twenty plays and twenty films before I die." She also claimed credit for creation of the symphony *Shajiabang.*[12]

One of the most ludicrous episodes on the opera front was the appearance of a character in *The Red Lantern* who had supposedly been tortured. Jiang Qing asserted—reasonably enough—that since his knees were said to have been broken, he should not appear standing up. But when the troupe changed the scene accordingly, she berated the director for showing the injured man "sprawling on the ground."[13]

The catalog of petty complaints about interference by Jiang Qing is almost endless, despite the insistence of the post-1976 media that she really had very little to do with the eight works and their production. One actor had to be disheveled for her; another should wear his hat at an angle; another didn't know how to dismount from a horse properly; yet another should have a beard. But she rarely made constructive suggestions, insisting, "I can only make prescriptions, I am not a nurse."[14]

The Red Lantern survived from 1964 virtually in its original form with most of the original cast, which was small. *The White-Haired Girl,* on the other hand, was mutilated beyond recognition for nearly ten years, it is claimed, and other works were similarly treated.[15]

Jiang Qing allegedly boasted about underground work that she claimed to have carried out in Shanghai in the 1930s, hiding important documents under a stone in a cemetery (a characteristically melodramatic act), and wanted this scene portrayed in *The Red Lantern*.[16] She allegedly banned the song "New Fourth Army" because the words were written by Marshal Chen Yi (who narrowly escaped severe persecution by the Red Guards when he was foreign minister in 1967, and died of cancer in 1972), and she tried to have some scenes flattering to the North Korean Army cut from *The Raid on White Tiger Regiment*.

The extraordinary symbolic abstruseness of much writing and drama produced in the early 1970s is exemplified by the 1974 campaign to denounce the opera *Three Ascents of Peach Mountain*. Written in Shanxi provincial style, the opera symbolically praised the rightist agricultural policy of Liu Shaoqi (and Deng Xiaoping) as opposed to Mao's leftist line in agriculture. Liu's wife, Wang Guangmei, had once given him a report on conditions at a production brigade called Peach Garden, in Henan Province, and his espousal of greater economic freedom for the peasants in the early to middle 1960s was to some extent based on this report. Chosen as symbols for the opposing policies were a sick horse (intended to satirize Mao's line in agriculture) and a "big red horse" in healthy condition, representing Liu's line—or so the media hinted in 1974.

The opera's plot concerned the conscientiousness of a woman brigade secretary, who made good the losses incurred by another brigade in buying her people's sick horse. Symbolically, again, the horse was needed for work on an irrigation project called Great Leap Reservoir—the Great Leap having exemplified all the faults in Mao's farm policy.

The opera was banned, and Su Zhenhua, first secretary of the Provincial Party Committee, was purged (not the same Su Zhenhua who died in 1979 after serving as commander of the navy and a member of the Politburo).

One of the most contentious of the symbolic dramas was the film *Pioneers*, depicting the Daqing oil field workers' struggle with harsh conditions. It was banned as soon as Jiang Qing saw it, on the grounds that it prettified the policies of Liu Shaoqi and Bo Yibo (a veteran economic planner who was purged in 1966, was rehabilitated in 1979, and at time of writing is a leading state councillor and member of the Politburo). Jiang Qing criticized the film on ten separate counts, but it is now claimed that Mao said in 1975, "There is no big error in this film. Suggest that it be approved for distribution. Don't nitpick. To list as many as ten accusations against it is going too far. It hampers the adjustment of the party's current policy on literature and art."

A reader of the *Guangming Daily* was quoted by that newspaper as saying:

> When the film *Pioneers* was shown, the masses of workers, peasants, and soldiers applauded it. But the Gang of Four, who were bent on destroying the socialist cause and knew nothing about the hardships that the workers, peasants, and soldiers experienced in founding their enterprises, stayed in modern buildings in Peking. They had never experienced a sandstorm in the Gobi Desert, or seen a blizzard in the wilderness of northeast China. Much less did they know how petroleum was extracted. But they had to fabricate accusations against *Pioneers* in order to destroy it.[17]

The dance-drama *The Light Saber Society* (also translated as *The Small Dagger Society*) was banned by Jiang Qing on the grounds that it would compete with "her" model theatrical works—although Mao allegedly approved it in Shanghai in 1960 and Zhou Enlai specifically encouraged the acting troupe to develop the production further. In 1974, it is now alleged, Mao again made a favorable reference to the work, which satirized foreigners and their Chinese lickspittles in Shanghai in the late nineteenth century. The troupe, learning of this, asked permission to stage it again, but the Gang controlled Shanghai more tightly than any other part of China, and suppressed it. It was eventually shown in a new production in 1977, when the Gang was no longer around to censor it.[18]

Another target of the Gang's wrath was the film *Rosy Clouds over the Ocean*, which had somehow been made without Jiang Qing's interference or direction. It dealt with the heroic struggle of fisherwomen in their local militia to defend the fruits of socialism. Numerous accusations were concocted by leftist functionaries in the Ministry of Culture to prevent the film's release. Producers Xie Tieli and Jian Jiang boldly wrote to Mao and Zhou, stating their side of the dispute, but Jiang Qing forced them to give her copies of these letters. The two were due to be denounced at a criticism rally in the Ministry on October 12, 1976, but were saved by the overthrow of the Gang six days earlier.

According to the *Guangming Daily*, Jiang Qing did all she could to suppress the play *Ten Thousand Crags and Torrents*, which was first performed in 1938 and tells the story of the 1935 Long March.

She allegedly wanted all references to Zhou Enlai and Marshal Zhu De deleted, and said, "If they are not to be taken out, then put in Liu Shaoqi's name" (i.e., brand the play openly as revisionist).

A key event in the Gang's campaign to use the performing arts to attack Zhou Enlai and Deng Xiaoping was the filming of the movie *Counterattack*. Though suppressed in 1976 before it had a chance to be widely shown, the film was intended to provide heavy artillery rather than sniper fire in the left-right battle.

Counterattack was based on events at an imaginary school somewhere in the vicinity of the Yellow River, probably in Henan Province. It evidently dealt with the return of teachers and educators to their jobs after years of disgrace during the Cultural Revolution. They were derogatorily referred to as "the home-going contingent." The chief villain of the film, Han Ling, was originally portrayed as secretary of the school's Party Committee, then director of education for the whole province. Eventually the scenarists decided to portray him as first secretary of the Provincial Party Committee, ranking high enough to have his own chauffeur-driven Red Flag limousine. The higher the villain's position was made out to be, the more specifically the film would be seen as criticism of Deng, Zhou, and other high officials. The attack on Zhou was made explicit by the naming of one character after a secretary of Zhou's—though later it was thought prudent to change the name by using homophonic characters, a favorite trick in the system of carrying on political struggle through literature, criticism, and allegory.

The heroine, Jiang Tao, was made to resemble Jiang Qing (with the same surname). She boasted of having followed Mao on the Long March. The villain, Han Ling, when driving in his limousine to reassume his original duties, which had been curtailed by the Cultural Revolution, was confronted by Jiang Tao's "open-door education contingent." ("Open-door schooling" was the leftists' name for the system under which students spend a good part of the school year working in factories or communes, to make them better understand the problems and sentiments of the workers and peasants.) In the scenario, Han ordered his driver to reverse—a symbol of the return to power of disgraced officials and the "reversing" of Maoist policies. The Gang, it is said, refused to include a final scene in which Han Ling would be given the chance to change his ways and become a good leftist. This would negate the Left's assertion that a person acquires his or her political coloring from family background and environment; and that once a bourgeois, always a bourgeois.[19]

The complex political undertones of this celluloid allegory were allegedly compounded by the practices adopted by the people shooting it, stirring up leftist political currents in the vicinity of any filming location; harassing the local party setup, sending libelous letters, and dragging out background material damaging to the local power holders—even putting up big-character posters calling for their overthrow. They talked about Deng Xiaoping ("Xiaoping" means "little peace") as Deng Daping ("big peace"). The concept of "peace" in Maoism has overtones of capitulation to the enemy, amnesty for "revisionists," and opposition to the protracted nationwide process of struggle that Mao often held up as the true road to revolution and socialism.

Zhou Enlai, it is claimed, wanted to rescue some of the better films made before the Cultural Revolution, but Zhang Chunqiao and Yao Wenyuan opposed the idea. In 1972 Zhou is reported to have told leftist officials engaged in cultural work: "You should not be too rigid. Some [of the old] films are very good. Go and take a look."[20]

In modern China, a fresh evaluation of the cultural achievements of the period before the Cultural Revolution—the 1950s and early 1960s—is in progress. Some old movies are being remade, others studied for fresh release.

A striking example of the continuity of the Chinese system of political/literary allegory in the arts is the opera *Orphan of the Zhao Family.* Set in the feudal state of Jin in the spring and autumn period around 800 B.C., it tells the story of a villainous chief minister who quarrels with the noble family of Zhao and executes them *en masse.* Believing he has extirpated the line completely, he adopts as his heir a male child offered by a court physician. Unbeknown to him, the baby is the last survivor of the Zhao clan, whom the physician has saved by offering another infant for the slaughter. Fifteen years later, the commander of the Jin armies (who has been away in the wars for all that time) returns and learns of the massacre. At his suggestion, the physician teaches the boy about his past through the use of drawings, whereupon the adopted son understands his personal history and slays his foster father in revenge.

This opera was written in the Yuan (Mongol) dynasty, which ruled China from 1280 to 1368. Because the family name of the Song (Sung) emperors (who were overthrown by the Mongols) was Zhao, the opera was regarded by Chinese people as a patriotic allegory calling for the expulsion of the Mongols and the refounding of the native dynasty. Apparently the Mongol emperor Kublai Khan and his successors were never apprised of this symbolism, or they would surely have punished the playwright and performers.

At the start of the Cultural Revolution, the leftists banned the opera on the grounds that in one scene it showed a slave girl sacrificing herself for her mistress—not considered by the Maoists to be sound Marxism. But in all probability, they feared the work would be taken as an allegory of their witch-hunt against Liu Shaoqi and other prominent "revisionists," and a promise of their eventual return to power. The opera was produced again in 1981, to rapt audiences. But, to be quite logical, there is no reason why some of the audience might not have interpreted it as a call for the rehabilitation of the Maoists purged by Hua Guofeng and Deng Xiaoping, or of Hua when Deng demoted *him*. Such is the addiction to symbolism and allegory in Chinese literature and the arts.

The Gang allegedly suppressed not only the traditional Peking Opera but also many regional styles. The Chengdu Sichuan Opera Company had many of its new operas banned. In their place, the troupe had to perform "cheap copies of Peking Opera that were played to empty seats." The art of the Suzhou one-man ballad performers, popular in southern Jiangsu Province, was stifled by the Gang's insistence that they be accompanied by piano, cello, and accordion, which made it impractical for them to travel across country as they traditionally did. Only three out of twenty Suzhou ballad troupes survived at the time, but by 1977 more than 200 ballad singers were back in business touring southern Jiangsu. Vernacular operas in the style of Henan Province were banned by the Gang, but performed again after its downfall.[21]

All in all, the Gang of Four was little concerned with the fifty-odd ethnic minority groups, whose homelands they rarely or never visited. These minorities ranged in numbers from a few hundred to about 8 million (the Zhuang of Guangxi Region). The total population of non-Han (the Han are the ethnic Chinese) minorities is estimated at 40–50 million, with the majority living in areas adjacent to China's frontiers with North Korea, the Mongolian People's Republic, the Soviet Union, Afghanistan, Pakistan, India, Burma, Thailand, Laos, and Vietnam. This makes them politically sensitive, as does their adherence to their own languages and traditional customs despite Chinese pressure to adopt modern attitudes, embrace socialism, and live in harmony with the Han.

The Communist party's basic attitude toward the ethnic minorities, as adopted in the 1950s, was to permit them to follow their traditional ways so long as these did not challenge the authority of the Chinese state, and at the same time gradually encourage them to become integrated into it both culturally and economically.

During the Cultural Revolution, however, the minorities were often harassed by Red Guards or troops who were taught to regard minority customs as "feudal" and exploitative. It was demanded that they revere the Han Chairman Mao and turn their faces to Peking as the source of all inspiration and guidance. Minority public figures were persecuted or jailed.

From 1977 on, the party began to admit that its policies toward ethnic minorities had been less than wise. Significant concessions were made to minority sentiment. The Tibetans were allowed to revive the lama Buddhism to which they faithfully adhere, and grow their beloved barley instead of wheat, which Peking had favored. The Uighurs and Kazaks of Xinjiang were permitted to practice Islam without harassment or antireligious campaigns, and to revive the Arabic script as the universal medium for writing their Turkic languages. Nonetheless, racial disturbances continued in Xinjiang.

As part of this process, the party-controlled media began putting the blame for deteriorating Han-minority relations on the Gang of Four and its policies. Jiang Qing especially was criticized for violating the Constitution by trying to suppress the use of minority languages and music. She is alleged to have said once that those languages "don't sound familiar, they sound like foreigners' speech."

Zhang Chunqiao is claimed to have forbidden the use of minority written languages, with the exception of the Mongol, Tibetan, Uighur, Kazak, and Korean scripts. The Zhuang, Yi, Dai, Lisu, and Jingpo nationalities had their scripts banned.[22]

Jiang Qing regarded the minorities as historical invaders of China. "She restricted people of Han nationality from learning and performing programs of minority art, prevented cultural exchange between the minorities, and suppressed the literature and art of the minority nationalities." According to the *People's Daily*,[23] she disparaged "that little Xinjiang of yours" when meeting high officials from the region, which covers a sixth of China's land area!

The Gang's antiminority policies were to a large extent focused on their culture and music. The Jingpo (Kachin) minority of Yunnan, who number about 200,000, near the Burmese border, condemn the Gang for suppressing their language and script.

The party and the government published for us the writings of Chairman Mao, as well as various political and cultural works in the Jingpo language, and ran a Jingpo-language newspaper called *Tuanjie Bao* [Chinese for "Unity News"]. The Yunnan Provincial People's Broadcasting Station also broadcast Jingpo-language programs and transmitted in good time the instructions of Chairman Mao and the Party Central Committee to our remote frontier villages. In the schools of the Jingpo nationality, teaching was carried out in the Jingpo language. The Central Institute for Nationalities and the Yunnan Institute for Nationalities also set up a special course in Jingpo language to train group after group of Jingpo-speaking cadres. Our esteemed and beloved premier Zhou Enlai was greatly concerned with the question of using the Jingpo language. As early as 1957, Premier Zhou issued an important instruction on Jingpo-language work, which we always bore in mind. . . . However, the diabolical Gang of Four wielded the cudgel of Han chauvinism, and forbade us to use the spoken and written languages of our own nationalities. . . . There appeared a tendency to abolish the nationality language in individual places in our region, and as a result the propaganda work and cultural and education work of the party were seriously crippled, thus affecting national solidarity.[24]

Particularly telling is the attack on the Gang's cultural policies with regard to ethnic minorities. *The People's Daily* wrote in 1977 (summary of Xinhua, April 6):

Jiang Qing opened attacks on minority songs and dances in April 1973, asserting that there was "a disastrous number of them." Then her trusties in the Ministry of Culture went into action and ordered that "no more ballads" should be produced, referring to the rerendering of raw folk music of minority nationalities. They banned items depicting the rhythms of labor, rich in national flavor, on the grounds that they cannot reflect the spirit of the times." They even charged that the valuable music heritage created by the working people of minority nationalities had an "alien flavor." They particularly attacked the "twelve *mukams*"— traditional music of the Uighur people in Xinjiang. They forbade even the mention of Kazak songs, simply because there are also Kazaks in the Soviet Union. The Gang of Four tried to emasculate the national characteristics of minority dances. It is well known that the traditional dances of Uighur, Mongol, and Tibetan nationalities are distinctive for their head, shoulder, and waist movements. But the Gang insisted that when minority dances were presented, the dancer should not perform these movements.

Jiang Qing also issued another directive, banning most of the songs and tunes popular in the national minority areas. As the *People's Daily* later disclosed:

The results of investigation in four national minority areas, namely Xinjiang, Tibet, Inner Mongolia, and Yanbian (Korean Autonomous District in Jilin Province), showed that only four national minority songs could just be managed to be put on the air, while broadcasting of the other several hundred songs was forbidden because the "ancestors" of these old songs were suspected to be ditties and love songs.[25]

Zhou Enlai, by contrast, was said to have encouraged ethnic minorities to adhere to their own culture, while also learning that of Han China, and to play their own music. He supervised the production of the revolutionary opera *The Red Lantern* in Uighur, with Uighur music. Jiang Qing disparaged the work as "distorted," but did not actually try to suppress it, doubtless because of the protection Zhou extended.

In general, though, the minority homelands must have seemed remote indeed from the conspiracies and attempted mutinies centered on Shanghai and the Chinese heartland, and most of the Gang's artistic censorship focused on more prominent works and troupes.

The question arises: Through what channels did the Gang exercise its influence on China's cultural life? The chief one appears to have been the Ministry of Culture, which remained under leftist control until 1977. The Ministry's importance as a political organ is highlighted by the fact that in February 1976 it was entrusted with the conduct of a campaign to oppose Hua Guofeng's appointment as acting premier following the death of Zhou Enlai. Zhang Chunqiao and Jiang Qing summoned top officials of the Ministry on February 6 and gave them instructions. The Ministry officials discussed the matter among themselves and in May submitted a draft to Yao Wenyuan, who ordered some revisions. Headed "An Important Fighting Task," the article was to be signed Chu Lan. Articles like these are often "circulated internally" for the eyes of high cadres, without ever being printed for the general public. It is not uncommon for enemies to be attacked on the basis of such drafts of articles.

In any case, "An Important Fighting Task" was never published because the Gang was overthrown first. However, its general outline is known from a fierce critique published in December 1976. The article was aimed at discrediting elderly people who took part in the early revolutionary struggle (principally the May Fourth movement of 1919, before the Communist party had been formed). Evidently the article would have denounced them as "followers of the capitalist road," rather than using the less invidious term "bourgeois democrats," and this would expose them to political persecution such as had been used to overthrow Deng Xiaoping eight months previously. Though not directly attacked by the article, Hua Guofeng would by implication be accused of betraying the Maoist cause by throwing in his lot with the old revolutionaries, many of whom suffered at the hands of Mao.

The Gang's main interest in cultural matters was in drama, but the other arts did not escape either. Reputedly in an attempt to discredit Zhou Enlai (who had ordered the commissioning of paintings to decorate hotels and for export), the Gang's followers selected fully 300 works from the Peking Hotel, the International Club, and other places, and held an exhibition (not open to the general public, but only to high-level cadres and leftist activists) devoted to what they called these "sinister" paintings.

Among the paintings was one called *Welcoming the Spring Flower*, which showed a cock stretching its wings and crowing its welcome to the spring. This is a very common theme in the Chinese traditional style. Yao Wenyuan, however, said that the cock was scowling and sticking its tail up in the air as a sign of arrogance. "Is this a welcome to the spring?" he asked. "It is a sign of hostility toward the spring of socialism and to the prosperity that has emerged since the Cultural Revolution began. . . ." The Gang of Four specially attacked this work of an old painter from Jiangsu Province, and denounced the artist in the press. Their plan was to ferret out "the power behind the scenes," so as to direct their fire at Premier Zhou. Any painting that was not to the Gang's liking was declared a "sinister" one, and the painter then became a "villainous character," an "undercover agent," or a "bad egg," and his works were banned. Consequently, many artists no longer dared to paint.[26]

The Gang was also offended by a huge exhibition of Chinese traditional arts and crafts staged in October 1972 in Peking. They particularly objected to the ivory carving of the goddess Chang-ê flying to the moon (a favorite theme in popular Chinese art). After the fall of the Gang, the media pointed out that Mao himself had referred to the legend of Chang-ê in a poem he wrote—one of his best—extolling his late wife, Yang Kaihui. Doubtless this was part of the reason for Jiang Qing's hostility toward this and 13,000 other exhibits on show. (For a fuller description of the exhibition, see the *London Times* of October 25, 1972. The author visited it and was struck by the massive restoration of traditional themes.)

Another charge against the Gang of Four is that they suppressed some writings of Lu Xün (real name Zhou Shuren), the outstanding literary figure of prewar Shanghai, who died of tuberculosis in 1936. Though he was never a party member, the Communist party claims him as their own because he took their side on many issues while their fortunes were at a low ebb in the 1930s. But no single political party could encompass the sweep of Lu Xün's intellect or the power of his writing. In the early to middle 1970s, Lu Xün was the *only* prerevolutionary Chinese writer of the modern period whose works were sold in Chinese bookshops—apart from those of Mao and occasionally one or two works of the party's literary doyen, Guo Moruo.

Lu Xün posthumously became a key figure in the left-right struggle of the period 1973–76. In 1971 the Chinese Language Department of Nankai University in Tianjin compiled an annotated selection of Lu Xün's letters and essays, according to Li Helin, curator of the Peking Lu Xün Museum, which is associated with the Lu Xün Research Office under the State Council. When the collection was submitted to Yao Wenyuan for approval, Yao suggested publishing the letters separately, after the essays. Li says Yao's intention was to suppress the letters, which may well have contained material with which the Gang of Four were out of sympathy, or which was unfavorable to Yao's father, Yao Pengzi. After submitting an expanded collection of the essays, the Nankai scholars heard no more from Yao. In the meantime, a publishing house controlled by the Gang published two volumes of Lu Xün's essays; a volume of his selected letters; and a volume of selected short stories, poems, and essays. Zhang Chunqiao ordered that each volume be distributed in a million copies. Li says the intention was that the Gang should monopolize all publication of Lu Xün's works. Toward the end of 1975, he asserts, the People's Literature Publishing House published a "clean copy" of Lu Xün's letters, but the Gang forbade more than 200 copies to be printed. They also attempted to gain control of the Lu Xün Research Office, but by that time their days in power were numbered.[27]

In 1975 Lu Xün's son, Zhou Haiying, wrote to Mao to tell him of "serious problems" in the collection, compiling, and publication of his father's letters, and in annotation of his works and studies of him. He suggested that elderly people who knew Lu Xün well should be asked to take part in providing explanatory notes on some important people and events mentioned in the writer's works. Mao wrote a note expressing his agreement. Yao Wenyuan, who in 1972 had written a marginal note on a document to the effect that "from the viewpoint of today many deletions can be made" from Lu Xün's writings, would not have been pleased about this, and is in fact accused of having withheld an article on Lu Xün by Lu's widow, Xü Guangping.

In the political struggle over the role of art and literature in modern China, the wheel seemed to have come full circle in December 1981, when *Red Flag* published an article by Hu Qiaomu, head of the Academy of Social Sciences and one of Deng's top advisers on intellectual matters. He wrote:

A scientific analytical approach should be adopted toward Mao Zedong's Thought on literature and art. . . . Long-standing practice proves that these ideas expounded by Mao Zedong in his talks at the Yan'an [Yenan] Forum on Literature and Art are incorrect: subordinating literature and art to politics, an absolute separation of political criteria from artistic criteria, classifying human nature as formed in set societies in one single term as class nature, comparing the writers who opposed the Guomindang rule and came to Yan'an retaining petty-bourgeois habits of the Guomindang, and putting such writers on a par with the big landlords and big bourgeoisie. These have exercised unfavorable influences on the development of literature and art since the founding of the People's Republic.

Examples are Chairman Mao's repeated launching of mass criticism of art and literary workers, and his two instructions in 1963 and 1964 on literary and art work [the two instructions have now been officially considered incorrect by the Party Central Committee]. Erroneous ideas also led Chairman Mao to launch the "Cultural Revolution." It must be recognized that Mao lacked full understanding of or the proper confidence in contemporary writers, artists, and intellectuals in general and went so far as to regard them as part of the bourgeoisie.

By availing themselves of this mistake, the counterrevolutionary clique of Lin Biao and Jiang Qing carried out ruthless persecution of intellectuals. We must always bear this lesson in mind.

10

INTELLECTUALS, EDUCATION, AND SCIENCE

Apart from some top political leaders, the worst-hit victims of the Cultural Revolution were China's intellectuals. Symbolic of the old China, which revered learning, they represented a challenge and a source of resistance to Mao and the Gang of Four.

Mao knew and sometimes emphasized the importance of intellectuals in the period of revolution and socialist construction. A self-taught intellectual himself, he once said: "Those intellectuals who support Marxism and are relatively familiar with it are a minority. Those who oppose it are also a minority. The majority support Marxism but are not familiar with it, and support it in varying degrees."

This tolerant attitude was not characteristic of the way Mao handled the intelligentsia from the antirightist campaign of 1957 on. Under his aegis, the Gang of Four was reputed to have said that the best way to deal with intellectuals was "to press them down like a ball in water." In the immortal understatement of the *Guangming Daily*, this "seriously dampened their enthusiasm." The Gang also said of the children of peasants who went to university, "In the first year they are still country folk; in the second year they become urbanized; and in the third year they turn their backs on their parents."[1]

As was stated in the media in 1977, the Gang's policy toward intellectuals was one of "advocating that they should cast knowledge to the winds, and that the working people should not learn science or culture." The leftists are claimed to have said, "We prefer workers without culture to exploiters with culture and intellectual aristocrats." They called intellectuals "maggots that undermine the socialist base." Zhang Chunqiao was accused of having said, "It would be better for the intellectuals to forget everything they learned from primary school to college." Zhang Chunqiao is quoted as having said, "If the whole country becomes illiterate, that's a great victory." Ironically, all the Gang's members except Wang Hongwen were intellectuals in their own way.

The most concise summary of the Gang's policy toward intellectuals was a statement attributed to Zhang Chunqiao to the effect that those who aired views opposed to those of the leftists should be "accused of opposing [political] remolding, be branded as a social base of restorationist forces, and be sent to labor camp." (Many were.) Anyone who argued in favor of vocational education would be accused of "turning the clock back." Laboratory work and classroom teaching were denounced as "divorced from proletarian politics, from the worker-peasant masses, and from practice."

Intellectuals and people holding official positions were frequently sent to rural areas for extended periods of manual labor combined with political study. The so-called May Seventh schools for cadres and intellectuals (where they spent months on end growing their own food and studying Marxism-Maoism) were vaunted as "one of the newborn things of the Cultural Revolution."[2] Deng Xiaoping, on the other hand, dismissed the May Seventh schools as "concentration camps" and did away with them after his return to power in 1977. Subsequently, Party Schools were set up to improve the general educational level of cadres.

The leftists cast doubt on the patriotism and loyalty of Chinese intellectuals, an easy thing to do since many of them had studied the cultural life and scientific achievements of foreign countries, had traveled abroad, or had overseas connections. Zhang Tiesheng, a leftist student who became a national figure in 1974 for handing in a blank paper at an examination, said that in the event of a Soviet invasion of China, a large proportion of the intellectuals would "in all likelihood be out waving white flags as a sign of welcome."

Zhang Tiesheng was vastly eulogized in the leftist-controlled media in 1974–75. The Zhang Tiesheng affair exemplified the Maoist view that scientific knowledge and book learning were inferior to political fervor. At the time when Zhang Tiesheng turned in his blank paper, the debate about the value of formal book learning and examinations was raging behind the scenes: it broke out in wall-poster form in late 1975, with the denunciation of Zhou Rongxin, the minister of education. Decrying examinations was a way of preventing the rehabilitation of disgraced intellectuals, among whom university teachers and examiners formed a large proportion. But an exposé of his act and its motives was made in 1977 after the Gang's overthrow. It was claimed that he actually wanted to pass the university entrance examination but had turned in papers that earned low marks, answering only three questions on chemistry and physics. He was unable to answer the question "What is the minimum speed for covering a journey of fifteen kilometers in two hours?"—an astounding indicator of the low standards set for university entrance in the mid-Seventies.[3]

Zhang's real name, it was disclosed, was Liu Tieshang, and his father had been a partner and manager in a grain and oil shop in Liaoning before 1949, and was on terms of intimacy with a Guomindang officer. In the mid-Seventies this was a damning family background.[4] And in 1983, Zhang was tried for counterrevolutionary activities and sent to prison.

The Gang clung to the extreme-left view of education—that it should concentrate on teaching pupils "correct" political attitudes and zeal, and encourage them to take part in manual labor to "temper themselves" alongside the workers and peasants. In 1974 some schoolchildren became so aroused by the leftist political campaigns that they smashed windows and desks in their classrooms.[5] But to breed a new Red Guard movement lay beyond the powers of the Gang.

Policy toward intellectuals was reflected in the use of the term itself—*zhishi fenzi,* or "elements with knowledge." The term was not reserved for academics and creative artists but was rather taken to mean just about anyone with a high-school education. The intention was to dignify the bewildered, idealistic teen-agers who from 1967 on were packed off by the millions to primitive rural areas in order to get them out of the cities where they caused such havoc and where there was no work for them.

The party has since revised its policy on intellectuals, quietly dropping the idea that teen-agers who can just about write their own names are still to be considered as belonging in that category.

Nonetheless, popular prejudice against intellectuals as semiparasitic and unreliable members of society could not be rooted out so quickly after the intensity of the previous campaigns against them. By 1982, the party was still exhorting its branches to make sure intellectuals had been properly treated and restored to positions in conformity with their powers, knowledge, and experience. Many were still living in extremely reduced physical circumstances and denied the chance of work in their own fields of specialization. Some did not care to go back to teaching or writing, lest they be victimized again in some future leftist upheaval.

A legacy of the Cultural Revolution is the dire shortage of scientists and technicians. Many are still exiled in remote areas where their knowledge cannot be used. Others have become apathetic and their brains dulled by the decade of discrimination against them. Some no longer want jobs just anywhere in the country; they are bringing up families and do not relish separation from them. But there are more fundamental reasons for the continuing malaise of trained scientists.

Most Marxist schools of thought run up against the problem of natural science, for science and scientific methods may be taken to disprove the "scientific" base of Marxism, or—as the case may be—reinforce it. Marxism itself is a social science, which has no answer to the larger questions about the origins of life, the nature of matter and energy, the existence of intelligent beings in other universes, and other similar topics about which debate rages among scientists. Communist or Marxist regimes that try to enforce agreement between natural and social sciences often find themselves either favoring theories that are discredited in the rest of the world (Lysenko's biology and Stalin's philology) or rejecting theories that are widely accepted elsewhere. Freud is still rejected in many Communist countries because his theory that sexual and anal sensations during childhood govern personality development conflicts with the Marxist view that personality is a product of economic and social environment. Hence political and social connotations become inextricably entwined with acceptance or rejection of any developments in the natural sciences.

In 1973 Zhou Peiyuan (a leading Chinese physicist and public figure, who was attacked in the Cultural Revolution and rehabilitated in 1972 as vice-chairman of the Revolutionary Committee of Peking University), allegedly on the instructions of Mao and Zhou Enlai, wrote an article advocating the study of basic theories of natural science, which had been neglected from 1966 on. The Gang attacked this article; but in September 1975, Hua Guofeng, who was then minister of public security, "and other leading comrades of the Central Committee" defended Zhou Peiyuan. (Hua has a reputation for being knowledgeable in matters of technology.)

Yao Wenyuan took the view that Marxism was in danger of being supplanted by natural science, and said, "The foundation of basic theory is Marxist philosophy, and the most basic theory is Marxism. Divorced from Marxist theory, there is no theory of natural science." The Gang claimed that there was "someone behind" Zhou Peiyuan—

presumably meaning Deng Xiaoping, who had presided over the compilation of a report on scientific work in China in 1975. The theoretical group of the Chinese Academy of Sciences wrote after the Gang's overthrow:

Natural science comes from the struggle for production and scientific experiment. According to historical records, as early as several millennia ago there appeared the buds of natural science. In ancient Egypt, ancient Greece, and the Zhou and Qin dynasties in China, there were already scientific works in such diverse fields as agriculture, astronomy, mathematics, mechanics, and the calendar system. Beginning in the second half of the fifteenth century, ever greater progress was made in natural science. Could all these theories of natural science, which appeared before the emergence of Marxism, be written off at a single stroke by Yao Wenyuan?[6]

Though they understood the propaganda value of such scientific feats as building ICBMs and nuclear weapons and launching satellites, the Gang's basic approach to science was suspicious and negative. "The satellite flies up to the sky, and the red flag falls to the ground" was their favorite slogan regarding the dangers of too much emphasis on science and technology, which they considered made people lukewarm about class struggle and revolution.

The agents of the Gang of Four tried to pack the Academy of Sciences with people favorable to themselves. They are even accused of having sabotaged the work of the National Seismological Bureau, allegedly hampering its effectiveness on the eve of the Tangshan earthquake of July 1976, in which some half-million people were killed or badly injured.[7] In the period 1974–76, the subject of earthquake prediction had become politically significant. The media claimed that earthquakes had been forecast, and measures taken to minimize the damage they did, through nature observation on the part of the broad masses. When earthquakes were imminent, it was claimed, the water table in wells fluctuated and animals behaved eccentrically. But apparently no such warning signs were spotted on the day before the Tangshan earthquake, which caught the inhabitants of the city in their beds.

According to Professor Zhou Peiyuan, Premier Zhou Enlai supported the drafting of two reports on the question of strengthening basic scientific studies at Peking University and Qinghua University (which specializes in science and technology). One of these reports was published in March 1973, whereupon "a trusted follower of the Gang of Four came to the university to hurl all kinds of abuse, on one pretext or another, and give vent to his dissatisfaction with Premier Zhou's instructions on strengthening theoretical work." As a result, "the demands put forward in this report could not be realized in the main—the instructions given by Premier Zhou on many occasions, and the efforts made by the broad masses, again came to naught."

As 1973 was the year of Premier Zhou's last ascendancy, when many of the policies of the Cultural Revolution were being reversed or at least questioned, it is remarkable that in the vitally important field of scientific research even he was unable to make headway against the opposition of the Gang of Four and their antiscience, anti-intellectual followers.

The biggest clash between the Gang and its opponents over the question of science and education came in 1975, when Vice-Premier Deng Xiaoping ordered the drafting of a document called the "Outline Report on the Work of the Chinese Academy of Sciences." Evidently it dealt with the need to restore the traditional priority given to apolitical scientific research, both theoretical and practical, and to stop playing politics in the laboratory.

The Gang was suspicious of pure scientific research and theoretical work—partly because it was something they could not understand or control, and partly because of their Maoist belief in the power of the human will. They favored what they called "typical-product teaching" in science, which meant the study of run-of-the-mill problems of industry or agriculture. They recommended that science "should rest on engineering"—i.e., be visible and tangible in its results. (An interesting aside: The author ascertained, during a talk with two Chinese engineers in Shanghai in 1976, that they either had never heard of Einstein's theory of relativity or did not want to admit to knowledge of it.)

In late 1975, students at Beida and Qinghua University in Peking were instigated to attack the education minister, Zhou Rongxin, for allegedly trying to restore "bourgeois" forms of education such as emphasis on factual knowledge and strict examinations. Even foreign diplomats and correspondents were bussed out to the campuses to read and photograph the thousands of wall-posters covering many yards of specially erected signboards.

As became apparent from subsequent events, this campaign was just the starting point for a major assault on Deng Xiaoping, master-minded chiefly by Zhang Chunqiao and Yao Wenyuan. The posters sprang up at one Shanghai university and doubtless in other big cities too. The death of Zhou Enlai in January 1976, while it did interrupt the campaign, finally only deflected it from its earlier emphasis on education, and toward simply "the top party person in authority taking the capitalist road." Most people knew this referred to Deng. By February, students in Shanghai were admitting to their foreign colleagues that the posters were aimed at Deng—who was not, however, as yet specifically named in them. In April, the Tiananmen Square riot broke out in Peking and Deng was suspended from his official posts—as the alleged troublemaker.

The debate about education did not fade out just because Deng—who stood for practical learning with a sound theoretical background, and abhorred political posturing—was temporarily out of office. Education might be called the nub of the controversy and conflict out of which the Cultural Revolution was now hastening to its end with the death of Mao in September 1976. Still, the conflict continued. Zhou Peiyuan and his supporters had their chance to hit back at their former persecutors in an article published in the *People's Daily* on January 13, 1977. Going back to 1933, Zhou Peiyuan cited Mao as the authority for the integrity of scientific research, and also quoted Zhou Enlai as saying in 1956, "Without some research on theoretical sciences as the base, it is impossible to make fundamental progress and innovations in technology." Zhou Peiyuan claimed, "As far as I know, Premier Zhou gave verbal and written instructions on this topic on more than ten occasions."

American scientists of Chinese origin visiting Peking were greatly honored, and gave their encouragement to the renaissance of theoretical science in China; several of them were received by Mao in person. However, Zhou Peiyuan said: "The Gang of Four who stepped into Lin Biao's shoes interfered with and brought to naught Premier Zhou's instructions on strengthening the study of basic theories."

The same conflicts appeared in the field of medicine, where the Gang of Four made much of the all-Chinese successes in the use of acupuncture and other traditional therapies, whether hand in hand with or divorced from Western medicine. The Gang particularly emphasized the role of "barefoot doctors"—lightly trained, rural nursing personnel who provided grass-roots medical care and hygiene instruction in the rural areas, where qualified doctors were few and far between. Deng, by contrast, regarded the "barefoot doctors" as no more than a temporary expedient, and said they must "progress from bare feet to straw sandals, and thence to rubber-soled shoes."

Yao Wenyuan called China's hospitals "an asylum whereby followers of the capitalist road can evade the mass movement." In fact, he was quite right. Elderly cadres who could not face struggle-and-criticism sessions reported sick, and some of them stayed in the hospital for years on end. After the overthrow of the Gang, there was a mass exodus of these "invalids" from the hospitals.

Advanced technology became a major political issue for the Chinese Communists only after their victory in 1949 and their assumption of the dignity of government. For a decade they sucked in the technology of the Soviet Union and Eastern Europe, blending it with the knowledge of many distinguished Chinese scholars and scientists who had patriotically, or for reasons of sentiment or family ties, returned to help build the New China.

In 1960 the Soviet Union cut off aid because of the mounting political disagreements with Peking. China's pool of technology more or less survived, through autonomous research and modest trade in essential items available from Western Europe and Japan (to the displeasure of the Americans, who imposed severe restrictions on the nature and level of technology available to China whenever they could). But Western technology became more freely available from 1972 on, after the partial normalization of Sino-American relations, and around it developed a bitter internal debate.

Mao, Zhou Enlai, and other senior leaders understood the need for Western technology, though the pragmatists around Zhou were the more favorable to it. The Gang of Four and other left-extremists were at best lukewarm, at worst fiercely hostile to technology imports. This debate did not end with the overthrow of the Gang, but remained a central theme in the high-level policy debate that accompanied the massive development of China's foreign trade in the late 1970s and 1980s. Currently, a more cautious policy prevails.

The Dengists got rid of Hua Guofeng in 1982 partly by blaming him for having overordered from the West and Japan in the late 1970s. Now import policy concentrates on equipment that will help renovate existing industrial capacity in China, rather than on imports of whole turnkey operations as was done before.

11

THE PERSONALITY CULTS
OF HUA GUOFENG
AND ZHOU ENLAI

The cult of the leader's personality is fundamental to Maoist political strategy, though its model was the personality cult of Stalin. Mao told his old friend the American journalist Edgar Snow that he personally deplored the cult, but there was never any sign that he tried to stop it. His power to destroy almost any other leader or prominent person was rooted in the awe in which people held him as a human being and cult figure, to whom no other leader, except to some extent Zhou Enlai, could hold a candle.

The Gang of Four drew much of their power from their ability to present themselves as the true interpreters of Maoism. In this, of course, Jiang Qing's role was important, but it is now alleged that Mao had not been living with her for a good few years before his death, and that he had several times upbraided her for her political activity. If this is true, it is astonishing that she wielded as much power as she did.

When Mao died, it was important for the Gang to create a new cult. Jiang Qing would doubtless have liked to be its object, but other leaders must have balked at this. In the end the logical choice for a personality cult was Hua Guofeng, the little-known provincial administrator who had been rising steadily since he was brought to Peking by Mao to help investigate the 1971 Lin Biao incident. Hua joined the politburo in 1973, became minister of public security in 1975, and was appointed acting premier over the heads of Deng Xiaoping and Zhang Chunqiao when Zhou died early in 1976.

With his avuncular manner, his ready smile, and his tubby figure, Hua seemed not an unappealing leader, at any rate to people who had never suffered from his climb to power. His main problem was that he was an unknown—"Chairman Who?" as the wags of the diplomatic corps soon dubbed him.

As long as Mao was alive, the Hua cult could not get off the ground. But following the old Chairman's death in September 1976 and the appointment of Hua as his successor and as premier, the cult was rapidly built up in late 1976 and 1977.

Probably one reason for this was that Hua and his followers knew that Deng Xiaoping would be rehabilitated and restored to high office, despite his demotion and.the prolonged attack on his policies that had dominated the political columns from April through December 1976. Aware of Deng's great political strength and skill, the Hua faction—which included many members of the last Mao politburo— saw the cult as a good way of limiting Deng's power when he returned. But over the next four years, Deng regained all his old power and more besides. Hua was replaced as party chairman in 1981 by Hu Yaobang, and as premier in 1980 by Zhao Ziyang, both Deng's protégés. The Hua cult lasted only about a year while Deng was consolidating his position sufficiently to declare that there should be an end to all cults of living leaders.

Although Hua drew much of his strength from the support of the Gang of Four in 1976, the latter were not especially happy about the growing dimensions of his cult, which they doubtless feared would overshadow them.

Mao allegedly supported moves to use propaganda and publicity to familiarize the general public with Hua.[1] Yao Wenyuan, however, who was in control of most if not all of the media, used his influence to publicize the Gang of Four instead.

Hua was born in the northwestern province of Shanxi and arrived in Hunan with the advancing Communist armies in about 1949. He is thought to have caught Mao's eye when he supervised the organization of a permanent exhibition in Mao's parents' house at the village of Shaoshan, Xiangtan Prefecture. A substantial guesthouse was built to accommodate the masses of Chinese and foreigners who came to visit the holy spot. The villagers were pampered with irrigation aid, flood-prevention works, power generation, transport, and domestic water supply. Excavated soil was used to terrace fields on the hillsides, and camphor, maple, fruit trees, and tea shrubs were planted to prettify the environment and make the peasants look prosperous.[2]

By 1977 a total of 1 million *mu* (167,000 acres) had been brought under irrigation in the Shaoshan area, though by that time Hua was no longer in active control of Hunan Province, having taken over the leadership in Peking. Hua once intervened in the construction of a fifty-mile irrigation canal linking Shaoshan with Chizi in Xiangxiang County. When the local leaders despaired of the difficulty of the task, Hua told them: "This canal leads to Chairman Mao's home village. You must study well and carry forward the Communist style."[3] Hua was also credited with developing chemical fertilizer industries and an iron and steel industry in Hunan, as well as boosting coal and salt mining, building a railway to Shaoshan, and setting up a TV-set factory there.

In 1980, however, due to the gradual waning of Mao's (and Hua's) prestige under the Deng group's exposés of the weaknesses and faults of Maoism, the special prefecture created just for Shaoshan was abolished. There was a public scandal about the way in which the local government and party headquarters' assets were distributed to local officials—in the form of transistor radios and fountain pens, cash allowances, and cut-price furniture.[4]

Hua was closely identified with the movement to emulate the famous Dazhai production brigade in Shanxi, the more so perhaps because it was his native province. He dominated the National Learn-from-Dazhai Conferences held in 1975 and 1976, but later found his links with the famous labor unit a liability. At Deng's instigation, Dazhai was exposed as a fraud and strongly criticized for falsifying its statistics and accepting outside aid in what was supposed to be a wholly self-reliant operation. The model peasant leader, Chen Yong-gui, who had attained the status almost of a living saint, was disgraced and dropped from the Politburo.

The attempt to build up a cult of Hua Guofeng was reaching its apogee on New Year's Day of 1977, when the *People's Daily* and the *Guangming Daily* both printed the same six photographs. They showed Hua shaking hands with Mao, working while on a train journey (a classic pose of Mao's), comforting earthquake victims, attending anniversary celebrations in Lhasa (fifteen months before), talking to workers at a Tianjin power plant, and inquiring into production conditions at the oxygen plant of the Anshan Iron and Steel Company. Other papers showed pictures of him mingling with workers and peasants.

The paraphernalia of the Hua cult included the weaving of silk portraits of him in Hangzhou, and a set of pictures in the *People's Daily* showing him helping transplant rice on a commune in Hunan, inspecting a farm-machinery plant, drinking barley beer with Tibetan peasants near Lhasa, chatting with middle-school graduates after an earthquake in Liaoning Province, and inspecting the Shaoshan irrigation project in 1965.[5] This photographic blitz was part of a campaign to build up Hua Guofeng as a worthy successor to Mao.

Short-lived as it was, the cult of Hua Guofeng had to contend with a rival cult, doubtless propagated by Deng and his associates to assist in the discrediting of the Gang of Four. Although Hua quarreled with the Gang in 1976 because he had succeeded in leaping over their heads to the top position, he was known before then as a leftist, a confidant of Mao, and propagandist of the Mao cult. From the time of Zhou Enlai's death, the Deng group built up a cult of the late premier that served the dual purpose of covertly attacking the Gang of Four and keeping Hua Guofeng politically in his place. Everybody knew that Deng was Zhou Enlai's chosen successor, and it was Hua's appointment over his head that helped trigger the April 5 riots on Tiananmen Square.

Zhou stood for moderation, pragmatism, and humanity in Chinese socialism. He was also a superb survivor, though this meant that he often had to compromise on points of principle and doctrine with Mao and the leftist elements in the politburo. Whereas his survival of the Cultural Revolution could be seen as the result of his sellout of many colleagues and friends, it has rather tended to be seen in China as an important factor in moderating the movement's excesses and protecting people who would otherwise have been persecuted. Like any true revolutionary, Zhou could be ruthless in the extreme. But he succeeded all his life in projecting an image of grace, charm, and intellectual force that nowadays makes him the most respected and well-liked leader in the people's memories of the Revolution.

The Zhou cult (which still makes itself felt from time to time) emphasizes his modesty, his disregard for his own comfort and safety, his concern for the masses and for his colleagues in the party. It also emphasizes his discreet opposition to the Gang of Four's activities. He is credited with having drawn up plans for one of the most impressive achievements of Chinese science—the combination of Western and traditional Chinese medicine, through the convening of a national work conference on the subject in 1971.[6] The Academy of Medical Sciences said that it was Zhou who told Chinese medical workers that "it was imperative to pay attention to the traditional method of concoction so as to ensure that the effective ingredients would not be damaged."[7] He kept in his office a map showing the distribution of districts of China with a high incidence of esophageal cancer. (This was the inspiration for the national cancer map published in 1972.)

During the Cultural Revolution, though most doctors and researchers were under a political cloud, a small number of specialists were encouraged to continue research to buy glory for China in the international scientific community. More generalized research was neglected, and there was even a move to "bury specimens and destroy data,"[8] which Zhou opposed.

Zhou, like Mao, was praised for his plain life-style. When traveling around the country and staying in guesthouses, he "always took the simplest meal offered other passengers—a few slices of bread or a bowl of bean porridge—and would never let anything go to waste or drop a single grain of rice on the plate. . . . During the time of difficulties [in the Great Leap Forward] . . . he refused to eat fish or meat, nor would he drink tea. . . . He often ate steamed corn bread at home and very simple food when he was outside. He always used an old suitcase for twenty years on all his trips abroad. His staff wanted to change to a new one, but the premier refused. In his luggage was an old quilt that he had used for dozens of years. An air stewardess once noticed it and suggested that he use a new one provided by the airline, but Premier Zhou would not agree. All his shirts and underwear were worn thin and some were patched. He had a woollen coat since 1949, which had been turned inside out and remade, and which he wore until his final stay in the hospital."[9]

The frugal Zhou concentrated much of his political energy on protecting veteran heroes of the Revolution and trusted comrades from Mao's and Jiang Qing's shock troops, the fearsome Red Guards and behind-the-scenes manipulators like Zhang Chunqiao.

The most prominent person protected by Zhou was Foreign Minister Chen Yi, an outstanding wartime commander and one of only ten men appointed marshals of the PLA in 1955. The Gang had its sights set on his overthrow.[10]

The struggle came to a climax on August 11, 1967, when Chen Yi was brought to a public meeting to be criticized for his alleged crimes. Arrogant because they had Lin Biao, Chen Boda, and Jiang Qing as their behind-the-scenes bosses, the handful of persons who manipulated the meeting shouted "Down with Chen Yi" and displayed a streamer bearing the same slogan, in violation of the instructions given earlier by Premier Zhou on behalf of the Party Central Committee. When a group of thugs was about to make a physical assault on Chen Yi, Premier Zhou, who was present, ordered the guards to escort Chen Yi from the meeting hall, while he himself walked out in protest. This was the best he could do under the circumstances to help expose the enemy and educate the misled masses.

On another occasion, Lin Biao, Chen Boda, and Jiang Qing devised a scheme to force Premier Zhou to engage in exhausting talks with relays of the very people who had manipulated the August 11 meeting. The talks lasted eighteen hours, during which the premier neither ate nor slept. The thugs even threatened to intercept Chen Yi's car and storm the Great Hall of the People to seize Chen Yi. The premier indignantly replied, "If you dare try, I'll do whatever I can to stop you!"[11]

One of the most striking claims made for Zhou was that he was the moving force behind the construction of the numerous water-conservation projects that saved China from mass famine during the population booms of the 1960s and 1970s.[12] Rainfall in northern China especially is capricious and usually only just sufficient to ensure decent crops. It has normally been thought that Mao, in his capacity as the successor of the river-harnessing emperors of ancient times, made water conservation his greatest technical contribution to the feeding of the Chinese people. However, the theory-study group of the Ministry of Water Conservancy and Power stated: "In accordance with Chairman Mao's instructions, Premier Zhou personally presided over the authorization of policies and tasks for every stage of water-conservation work, the concrete arrangements for each upsurge in water-conservancy construction, the harnessing of each big river, and the building of many important projects. Regarding many important problems, he always went personally to the spot to acquaint himself with conditions, and went deep among the masses to conduct investigation and studies, listening to conflicting views from many quarters and studying things again and again before making decisions."[13]

Zhou is praised for having launched the move to drill pump wells against drought in northern China, and personally inspected the bridge collapse on the Yellow River at Zhengzhou in 1958. He issued instructions for the salvaging of the San Men Gorges Dam, begun with the aid of Soviet technicians and plagued with problems of silting.

Many water-conservation projects in China bear inscriptions by Mao, usually on the lines of "Do work on the Yellow River well," or

"Do work on the Hai River well." Zhou, it is claimed, refused to write an inscription for the big Miyun Reservoir near Peking, saying, "The credit for the construction of this reservoir should go to Chairman Mao's *revolutionary line*" (italics added). Not to Mao's knowledge of river control, or his personal contribution—just to his "line."

Disregarding Zhou's instructions, workers and staff at the Miyun Reservoir built an exhibition hall commemorating Zhou's involvement in its construction. "When he heard of this, the premier shook his head and said, 'I didn't expect that you would have done things like this'—and on his orders the exhibition was converted to a laboratory."

Zhou is also credited with having guided China's diplomacy and international relations along ideologically correct but, at the same time, mostly practical lines. He spoke French from his student days in Paris, a little English from a youthful stay in London, and had studied in Japan. He paid many visits overseas and was a man of the world in the most literal sense—unlike Mao, who had never been to any foreign countries except the Soviet Union and North Korea, spoke no foreign languages, and took an aloof, dogmatic line on foreign affairs. Hua Guofeng had no direct experience of the world outside China until he became chairman and premier after Mao's death and paid visits to Europe and Japan.

Zhou's military role was also significant, starting with his leadership of the abortive Nanchang uprising in 1927, whereas Hua was too young to have any military record of distinction.

Most of all, people were grateful to Zhou for his role in curbing the Red Guards and protecting some veteran revolutionaries (though it is true that he allowed many old comrades to suffer a bitter fate in the interests of remaining in power himself. He intervened only when he had good hopes for success.) In the early Cultural Revolution, Zhou used to go at 4:00 A.M. to the Peking Foreign Languages Institute every day to read the big-character posters there—doubtless to keep his finger on the pulse of the new movement. He visited Qinghua University—a hotbed of the movement—almost two dozen times between July 30 and August 22, 1966, and attended mass rallies. But he took the opportunity to warn the leftist activists against labeling all teachers and students who were not Red Guards "counterrevolutionaries." On his last visit he sat, it is claimed, for three hours in the rain, refusing the offer of an umbrella and wearing a Red Guard armband. He supervised arrangements for the millions of Red Guards who converged on Peking from different parts of the country to exchange "revolutionary experience"—ensuring they had food, shelter, clothes, and transport, and meeting with groups of them frequently late into the night. He served, in other words, as the lightning rod, and always cited Mao's pre–Cultural Revolution assertion that "differences should be settled by reasoning things out, not by coercion or force" (negated utterly by the practice of the movement itself, which depended above all on blind, undiscriminating coercion against all real or suspected enemies).

Zhou's lack of concern for his own comfort and safety was exemplified in a report about the earthquake that hit Xingtai Prefecture in Hebei Province in 1966: "Premier Zhou insisted on inspecting the places where the losses were most serious and the damage the greatest. On the evening of March 9, when Premier Zhou was listening to reports in the office of the Longyao County Party Committee, there was an aftershock of magnitude five. The house swayed and ceilings creaked, but Premier Zhou sat there completely composed."[14]

The Zhou cult is still used as an indirect way of criticizing others or scoring points. For instance, in June 1982 his widow, Deng Yingchao, published a front-page article in the party media recalling how she and Zhou had in the past even kept party secrets to themselves and not spoken to each other about them. This was probably a warning to high cadres—or possibly to a particular person—that loose talk about party affairs must cease.

All cults of personality are now outlawed in China. Deng Xiaoping is never called "invincible" in his thought or actions. But as of 1983, everybody knows he is boss.

PART THREE

PART THREE.

12

THE PLOT TO KILL MAO

During the Cultural Revolution, it was well-nigh impossible to conceive that any sane person could have tried to kill Chairman Mao Zedong. The other senior leaders were either subservient to him or suffered disgrace, exile, or imprisonment. Loyalty to Mao in person was proclaimed the greatest duty of all Chinese citizens.

Not only did Mao have the millions of Red Guards regarding him almost as a god and swearing eternal fidelity to him, the People's Liberation Army stood ready to obey his every command, and in return they were invested by him with a halo of glory and righteousness. In addition, Mao was heavily guarded wherever he went, and most of his movements were kept secret.

Even more astonishing was the fact that the alleged leader of the 1971 assassination plot was Mao's "closest comrade-in-arms," Defense Minister Marshal Lin Biao, hero of countless battles, the brain behind China's strategy of opposition to both the Soviet Union and the United States, and promoter of global revolution in partnership with the poor countries of the Third World.

The Ninth Congress of the Chinese Communist party in 1969 had named Mao as supreme leader, but into its statutes was written the law that Lin Biao would be his successor. Perhaps that clause gave Lin a motive to do away with Mao. But if the testimony at the trial is to be believed, the plot was formulated with extraordinary carelessness and ineptitude.

The essential feature of the plot was to have Chairman Mao's train bombed from the air at Shanghai, blasted with rockets and horizontal fire from antiaircraft guns, and, if that was not enough, roasted with flamethrowers, so that in the ensuing confusion Chairman Mao could be assassinated (see testimony on pp. 164–65.

In August of 1971, Mao had gone on a railway tour of southern China, during which he briefed local officials and army commanders on Lin Biao's alleged plans to revive the post of state chairman (which had lapsed with the disgrace and death of the last incumbent, Liu Shaoqi) in order to award it to Mao as a way of "kicking him upstairs."

News of Mao's activity got back to Lin Biao, who was staying at the seaside resort of Beidaihe, less than an hour's flying time from Peking. His son, Lin Liguo, who had been put in command of the entire air force, flew to Peking and conferred with Jiang Tengjiao, then chief political commissar of air-force units in the Nanjing Military Region. He showed Jiang Tengjiao a letter in Lin Biao's handwriting, which required Jiang to act in accordance with instructions to be relayed to him by Lin Liguo and the latter's aide, Zhou Yüchi. Lin Biao also wrote to the chief of the General Staff, Huang Yongsheng, hinting that a coup was afoot.

In addition to the fierce armed attack, an officer named Wang Weiguo was to hold himself ready to board the train and shoot Mao with a pistol if all else failed.

For reasons not disclosed during the public sessions of the trial, Mao decided to leave Shanghai early on his special train and return to Peking. Whether he had heard about the plot or merely wanted to get back to work is not known. But the armed attack never took place, nor did anyone board the train to shoot Mao.

The Lins had planned to fly south to Canton when the coup attempt failed. Their fallback plan was to set up a rival Central Committee in the southern city, together with the disaffected military commanders. But instead they panicked, and headed for the Soviet Union across Outer Mongolia, dying when the plane crashed. The officers who had helped plan the assassination bid—Zhou Yüchi, Li Weixin, and Yü Xinye—hijacked a helicopter and told the pilot at gunpoint to fly them south. The pilot tricked them by flying in circles and landing in the suburbs of Peking—for which he paid with his life; the plotters shot him. Zhou and Yü then shot themselves, while Li fired in the air and was captured, eventually giving testimony at the trial.

The interrogation of Jiang Tengjiao shows how vague the planning of the coup was. It is not explained why the various military officers wanted Mao dead. The testimony shows them working almost independently on various schemes, with only quite sketchy liaison. But all factions seem to have been disorganized. Li Zuopeng, chief political commissar of the navy, deliberately let the Lins make their escape bid, contrary to the instructions of Zhou Enlai.

Jiang Tengjiao, former Air Force Central Headquarters commander, gives testimony.

JUDGE: Jiang Tengjiao, Article Forty-one of the indictment accuses you of the following: that after reading Lin Biao's personal instructions on September 8, 1971, you did specifically, until September 11, plan and conspire with Lin Liguo and Zhou Yüchi to assassinate Chairman Mao Zedong, and did accept Lin Liguo's commission to act as commander of the front line in the Shanghai district.

JIANG: Uh!

JUDGE: Where did you see Lin Liguo on September 8?

JIANG: At Peking West airfield.

JUDGE: Who else was there?

JIANG: Zhou Yüchi and Li Weixin [another officer].

JUDGE: Did Lin Liguo give you Lin Biao's personal instructions to read?

JIANG: Yes, I read them.

JUDGE: What kind of pen were they written with?

JIANG: Red ballpoint.

JUDGE: What were the contents?

JIANG: I was to proceed in accordance with the orders transmitted by Comrades Lin Liguo and Zhou Yüchi.

JUDGE: Bring in the criminal in custody Hu Ping [formerly deputy chief of the Air Force Headquarters staff]. . . . Hu Ping, did you see Lin Liguo at Peking West airfield on September 8, 1971?

HU: Yes.

JUDGE: Give an accurate account of the events of that evening.

HU: Jiang Tengjiao phoned me—

JUDGE: Louder!

HU: All right. He phoned and told me to make available a B-28 aircraft. Around nine in the evening, Lin Liguo arrived on this aircraft. Before he left the aircraft, Zhou Yüchi came hurrying up and went into the cabin. I don't know what they talked about. After a while they both came out and told me, "Just lately Chairman Mao has been taken seriously ill while traveling outside Peking. He can't cough up his phlegm, and it's very hard for him to speak." They meant me to understand that Chairman Mao was critically ill. Lin Liguo said, "In a situation like this, the struggle for power at the top is extremely intense. Our party has never in its history ceased to struggle to seize power or seize it back." He added: "For security reasons, Lin Biao will not leave Beidaihe."

Then he took from his pocket Lin Biao's "black" [evil] instructions and gave them to me to read. They were written in red ballpoint. The handwriting was Lin Biao's. The bit I can remember now is the beginning, the first half, which was the order to act according to the instructions of Lin Liguo and Zhou Yüchi. I don't remember the rest, but it was signed by Lin Biao, with the date, which I can't remember either. After I'd read it, Lin Liguo said, "These are Lin Biao's orders. This is a very important matter." He wanted me to think up a way of ensuring Lin Biao's safety. I said, "Lin Biao and Chairman Mao are confirmed [in their political positions] in the Party Statutes." Then Zhou Yüchi said, "For Lin Biao's safety, you'd better get two aircraft ready for me to fly to Hongqiao airfield [at Shanghai]. The pilots should be people intensely loyal to Lin Biao and technically first-rate. And inform Beidaihe airfield." I said, "All the pilots who fly Lin Biao have been checked out and there's no problem about any of them." Lin Liguo said, "Check them out nonetheless." Before this, they had all told me that at the Lushan Conference,[1] Wu Faxian plotted with Chen Boda to oppose Lin Biao, and they told me to watch out for Wu Faxian and not get caught out by him. I pointed out, "If Wu Faxian finds out about movements of aircraft, I won't be able to account for them." Zhou Yüchi said, "Don't worry about that. When the time comes, Ye Qün [Lin Biao's wife] will be able to sort it out."

JUDGE: Where had Lin Liguo come from that day?

HU: From Beidaihe, Shanhaiguan airfield.

JUDGE: Show Lin Biao's personal instructions of September 8 to Jiang Tengjiao.

JIANG: This . . . looks like it.

JUDGE: How did you react to these instructions?

JIANG: I said three things: "For justice, for the Revolution, act resolutely!"

JUDGE: Do what resolutely?

JIANG: I haven't said yet what—

JUDGE: What command did Lin Liguo bestow on you?

JIANG: He wanted me to go to Shanghai as commander of the front line.

JUDGE: To command what?

JIANG: The implementation of the plot to kill Chairman Mao.

JUDGE: Read out the confession made on August 1, 1980, by the criminal in custody Li Weixin.[2]

COURT READER: "On September 8, 1971, a bit after eleven o'clock at night, the counterrevolutionary element Zhou Yüchi phoned me and told me to go immediately to the Air Force Academy, pick up Jiang Tengjiao, and come to Peking West airfield. A short while after we got there, around midnight, the counterrevolutionary element Lin Liguo came to talk with Jiang Tengjiao. When I brought some hot water in for them, I heard Lin Liguo say, 'The situation just now is very tense. The direct target is the chief (meaning the ambitious schemer Lin Biao), so we must carry out project 571 [the assassination of Mao]. The chief has entrusted me with carrying it out.' Then Lin Liguo took out a piece of paper and gave it to

Jiang Tengjiao to read. Later, when we went to the Air Force Academy, Lin gave this piece of paper to Liu Shiying [former deputy chief of the Air Force Headquarters Office], as well as Liu Peifeng, Chen Hongzheng, and me to read. For the first time I realized that this was a counterrevolutionary personal instruction from Lin Biao. Lin Liguo said to Jiang Tengjiao, 'We want you to be the general commander of the Southeast. . . . Do a good job!' Jiang Tengjiao said, 'I will certainly act resolutely in accordance with instructions from the chief and from you!' "

JUDGE: [to Jiang Tengjiao] What course of action did you plan?

JIANG: On the evening of the eighth, after Lin Liguo showed me Lin Biao's counterrevolutionary instructions and I had committed myself to their side, we sat down and he said they had thought up three courses of action. One was to attack the special train Mao was traveling in with flamethrowers and bazookas. The second was to use 100mm antiaircraft guns to fire point-blank at the train. The third was for Wang Weiguo[3] to go to see Chairman Mao, take a pistol along, and shoot him on the train.

JUDGE: Did you go on and discuss any other ideas?

JIANG: We couldn't reach agreement that evening and didn't come to a conclusion. On the ninth, we went on discussing it, and the question of bombing a bridge was raised—that was Zhou Yüchi's idea. In the afternoon we discussed other suggestions.

JUDGE: Did you discuss blowing up fuel tanks?

JIANG: That was brought up on the previous evening, after the other three ideas. We ate—it was getting overlate. Everybody left the room to eat; only Zhou Yüchi and I stayed behind. . . . Zhou Yüchi asked me whether the fuel tanks could be bombed, and I said I wasn't sure, but anyway they could be set alight. The ensuing confusion would be splendid, because in the conflagration we could seize the opportunity to act, and assassinate Chairman Mao. We planned that when Chairman Mao's train came into the station, we would say there had been an accident involving the fuel tanks, and troops were guarding him. But that plan wasn't approved that evening either.

JUDGE: Did you give this plan to Zhou Yüchi, and did he give it to Lin Liguo?

JIANG: As soon as they saw it, they agreed to this course of action. But later on I said the plan was no good, because after the fuel tanks were bombed, the guards on the Chairman's train would come to take over.

JUDGE: Did you really plan to bomb the fuel tanks? Had you drawn up a plan to this effect, and they then agreed to it? [without waiting for reply] . . . Did you go into the question of code words and passwords to be used between Shanghai and Peking?

JIANG: . . . We decided on a couple of methods.

JUDGE: What were they?

JIANG: If Chairman Mao entered Shanghai, we would say, "Wang Weiguo is sick." If he left Shanghai, we would say, "Wang Weiguo has recovered."

JUDGE: Lin Liguo and Guan Guanglie [the political commissar of a military unit in Henan Province]—did they discuss the question of bazookas?

JIANG: Lin told Guan straight out, "Send your Forty-first Flamethrower Company to Shanghai and give me command of it. . . ."

JUDGE: Read out the criminal in custody Guan Guanglie's confession of November 22, 1971.

COURT READER: "On September 11, 1971, Lin Liguo, Zhou Yüchi, Jiang Tengjiao, and Wang Fei[4] met in a small conference room at Peking West airfield and had discussions. On the same day, at about one-thirty P.M., Yü Xinye was ordered by Lin Liguo to drive me to Peking West airfield to take part in their counterrevolutionary activity. Jiang Tengjiao was taking an active role, and was the most reactionary. When I went into the room, Jiang cheerfully complimented me by saying, 'You're someone with real power!' His idea was to get me willingly to move my troops and weapons to take part in a counterrevolutionary coup. Lin Liguo asked me about the quantity and performance of my rockets and flamethrowers, and Jiang interrupted, saying, 'This is just the right stuff to attack a train with!' When I told them I couldn't move my weapons and troops, Jiang said very aggressively, 'I'll get such and such a regiment to attack the train, and gain merit!' "

JUDGE: [to Jiang] Did you hear that clearly?

JIANG: Yes.

JUDGE: When did you look into the question of attacking the train? And did you suggest blowing up any bridges?

JIANG: We looked into it on the forenoon of the ninth.

But it wasn't only Lin Biao's group of conspirators who lacked organization and cohesion. Li Zuopeng provides another glaring example of the way in which lack of communication and organizational confusion engendered chaos.

LI ZUOPENG

Li Zuopeng's main crime was to have facilitated the escape of Lin Biao from Shanhaiguan naval airfield. As first political commissar of the navy, Li had the power to defy Zhou Enlai's order that Lin not be permitted to take off in his personal Trident airliner, and the testimony is mainly concerned with the guiles he used to facilitate Lin's escape.

Li, a native of Jiangxi Province, became prominent in the late 1940s as a key commander in the northeast China civil war theater. After the Communist victory in 1949, he was sent to Guangdong Province, first as a member of the military government on Hainan Island, where he acquired experience of naval affairs and coastal defense. He was named vice-admiral in 1955, vice-commander of the navy in 1964, a member of the National Defense Council in 1965, and first political commissar in 1967.

Had Lin Biao and his family not been killed in the crash of the Trident in Mongolia, Chinese history might have taken a very different course. If the plot to assassinate Mao had succeeded, and Lin become Chairman of the party—as he was by then designated in the very Party Statutes—it is possible that the Sino-American rapprochement might never have taken place. It may be speculated that Zhou Enlai's contacts with Henry Kissinger were the last straw for the fiercely anti-Western Lin Biao. In this sense, Li Zuopeng has his small but vital part in history.

Lin Biao's Escape: Interrogation of Li Zuopeng, Former Politburo Member, Deputy Chief of the General Staff, and First Political Commissar of the Chinese Navy

JUDGE: Article Forty-three of the indictment before the Special Court states that on September 13, 1971, at 0020 hours, when Lin Biao's special aircraft [Trident] number 256 was preparing to take off but had not yet started up its engines, when the airfield commander at Shanhaiguan naval airfield telephoned to ask his instructions, Li Zuopeng took no measures to prevent it from taking off, giving the excuse that it could be "reported directly to Premier Zhou Enlai" in order to gain time and enable Lin Biao to board the plane and flee the country. Li Zuopeng, when Tang Hao, commander of the Shanhaiguan airfield, phoned you before Lin Biao's special plane took off, and asked you what to do if it took off without prior clearance, what did you reply?

LI: I've tried to recall this many times, but it simply didn't happen.

JUDGE: You mean he really didn't report to you, and you didn't reply to him?

LI: I can't remember.

JUDGE: Can you affirm that it didn't happen?

LI: I can't remember.

JUDGE: Did it really happen?

LI: I can't affirm that either. I can't remember what happened.

JUDGE: Call the witness Tang Hao.

TANG: Comrades Shi Yaolong, Zhao Yanghui, Tong Richeng [other officers], and I went to the control tower. Comrade Li Wanxiang [officer in charge of the control tower] had just been taking a call from Li Zuopeng. He reported to us what it was about, and we saw his notes. Then we went to the downstairs room in the control tower and used a secure telephone to call Li Zuopeng. I reported my name and duties to him and asked if the past few calls to the airfield had been from him. He said they were. He repeated the content of his conversations with Li Wanxiang. I asked him what to do if the aircraft took off without prior clearance. He said we should "immediately report to the premier."

JUDGE: Had you ever before called the premier direct from the airfield to ask for instructions?

TANG: No. At our level we had no way of contacting the premier. We didn't know how to get through to him.

JUDGE: Call the witness Zhao Yanghui [an officer at the airfield]. [to Zhao] Please tell the court about your telephone call to Li Zuopeng early on the morning of September 13.

ZHAO: I was on the parking apron and saw the aircraft starting its engines. I ran to the control tower and rang Li Zuopeng from downstairs. I reported to him that the engines had been started and the plane was rolling down the taxiway. He asked me where the plane was now—

JUDGE: Slow down a bit.

ZHAO: All right, all right. Li Zuopeng asked where the plane was. I went to have a look and told him it was on the runway. Then it took off, and I said, "Commander Li, what are your instructions?" He replied, "Well, that's it."

DEFENSE COUNSEL: How long did this conversation last?

ZHAO: One or two minutes. You can see out from the downstairs room.

JUDGE: We shall now investigate the charge in Article Forty-three of the indictment to the effect that after Lin Biao escaped, Li Zuopeng falsified the record of the telephone conversation. Accused Li Zuopeng: On September 13, did you see what your secretary Liu Zhixiang noted down about the report by the officer in charge, Li Wanxiang, on the control-tower shift on the night of September 12–13?

LI: Yes.

JUDGE: Did you personally alter it?

LI: Yes.

JUDGE: You clearly reply that you personally altered it?

LI: I may have altered a word on the top, but I can't remember what it was.

JUDGE: Read out the testimony given by Liu Zhixiang [formerly Li Zuopeng's secretary] on April 25, 1972.

COURT READER: "I answered the telephone, took notes on the conversation, and gave Li Zuopeng an oral report. Li emphasized that it was sufficient for one of the four leaders [Premier Zhou Enlai, Chief of the General Staff Huang Yongsheng, Air Force Commander Wu Faxian, or Li Zuopeng himself] to give clearance for the aircraft to take off. It was the first time he'd said that. When he spoke to Li Wanxiang, he'd said that all four of the leaders had to give joint clearance. He asked me to check up with Shanhaiguan airfield, to get Li Wanxiang to verify [the new version of the order]. . . . Li Zuopeng viciously altered the record of the conversation in his own handwriting, altered the instruction to read that "if any single leader, whoever it was, gave clearance, it should be reported to Li Zuopeng." Then he got Liu Zhixiang to copy it out over his signature and send it as a report to the premier.

JUDGE: Read out the testimony given by Li Wanxiang on April 7, 1972.

COURT READER: "In the afternoon of the thirteenth, Li Zuopeng's secretary phoned me and asked me to verify the contents of Li's telephone call. He told me to think very carefully whether the instruction about all four leaders giving joint clearance didn't actually say that one of them on his own could give clearance. I told him that I had understood from Li's previous two telephone calls that it had to be a joint clearance, and that's how I'd heard it and recorded it. If someone was wanting to alter the record now, there was clearly a conspiracy."

The Trident took off at 0032 on September 13, 1971, heading northwest. A little after 0100, Premier Zhou Enlai ordered the grounding of all planes throughout China. Toward dawn, the Trident ran low on fuel over the People's Republic of Mongolia, a Soviet satellite, and caught fire on crashing when the pilot tried to make an emergency landing. Lin Biao, Ye Qün, Lin Liguo, the pilot, and probably some aides were killed.

Or so says the official record. Other rumors have circulated to the effect that Mao, on learning of the Lins' flight, tried to talk to Lin Biao over the plane's radio, but Lin would not speak to him. Mao, according to this report, had jet fighters scrambled that chased the Trident over the Mongolian border and shot it down.

Besides being held responsible for Lin Biao's escape, Li Zuopeng was also accused of helping to overthrow Luo Ruiqing, former chief of staff and internal-security chief.

JUDGE: The accused, Li Zuopeng, is charged with slandering and persecuting Luo Ruiqing, [formerly] secretary of the Chinese Communist Party Central Committee, vice-premier of the State Council, and chief of staff of the Chinese People's Liberation Army. Li Zuopeng, did you, together with Wang Hongkun and Zhang Shaozhuan [see below] write a letter slandering Luo Ruiqing to Lin Biao?

LI: Yes.

JUDGE: What was the main content?

LI: I'm not sure, I can't remember too well.

COURT READER: "Vice-Chairman Lin Biao, we have something to report to you. We feel that Comrade Luo Ruiqing has for some years now been making serious errors with regard to the problem of leadership of the navy, and is harboring big ambitions."

JUDGE: What did Lin Biao tell you about his estimation of the Luo Ruiqing question?

LI: He said it was meritorious to oppose Luo Ruiqing.

JUDGE: Article Sixteen of the indictment accuses you of slandering and persecuting Ye Jianying, member of the Politburo, secretary of the Party Central Committee, and vice-chairman of the Military Affairs Commission. [It states that] you did conspire with Wang Hongkun, second political commissar of the navy, and with Zhang Shaozhuan, chairman of the navy political department, to write a letter to the Central Committee slandering Comrade He Long, to coincide with allegations that Liu Shaoqi, Deng Xiaoping, and Tao Zhu were scheming to subvert the party and army. Accused Li Zuopeng, did you on April 3, 1968, together with Wang Hongkun and Zhang Shaozhuan, write a letter slandering Vice-Chairman Ye Jianying?

LI: This is correct, but the letter was written by them, and then I signed it.

JUDGE: Give him the letter to read.

LI: Yes! It's my [signature].

HUANG YONGSHENG

The former chief of the General Staff of the PLA was found guilty of unjustly proposing that the late Marshal Peng Dehuai, one of Mao's early victims, be stripped of all posts, sentenced to life imprisonment, and expelled from the party. He was also convicted of having tried to frame Marshal Ye Jianying on a charge of trying to stage a counterrevolutionary coup. He and Wu Faxian, it was said, jointly framed Luo Ruiqing as a counterrevolutionary in 1968 after the general had been dismissed from his post as chief of the General Staff. Huang also concocted reports of a counterrevolutionary underground party organization in Canton. He was found guilty of participating in Lin Biao's coup bid.

JUDGE: The court will investigate questions related to the accusations in Articles Forty-one and Forty-four of the indictment against Huang Yongsheng. Huang Yongsheng, in 1971, before the incident of September 13 [the flight of Lin Biao], including the period from September 5 to 12, 'what kind of relations did Ye Qün [Lin Biao's wife] have with you?

HUANG: Lin Biao didn't get in touch with me often. I used to be in contact with Ye Qün by telephone.

JUDGE: On September 10, who sent you the letter that Ye Qün gave you marked "personal delivery"?

HUANG: Wang Fei [described as "responsible for operations in Peking in the projected coup d'état"].

JUDGE: Read out Wang Fei's signed confession of December 8, 1971.

COURT READER: "Zhou Yüchi went to a small adjoining room and he gave me a big mailbag full of things. On the front was written 'Hand delivery only to Chief of Staff Huang,' and on the back there was a 'top secret' sticker. I didn't pay attention to the sender's name—I don't remember what it was. Zhou told me to deliver it to Huang Yongsheng and said he was in the Peking West Guesthouse. . . . When I delivered it, I was to tell Chief of Staff Huang that it was from Jingcao and Liguo. I asked who Jingcao was. Zhou said it was a pseudonym used by Ye Qün in contacts with Chief of Staff Huang, and would be recognized at once. He said Chairman Ye and Lin Liguo were very solicitous about Chief of Staff Huang and told me to tell him to take care of his health. I tried to get out of it, but Zhou insisted, and I had no alternative but to take it home.

"On the evening of the ninth . . . a bit after eleven, I got to Huang's place at headquarters and give him the stuff. He was just reading a document. I said, 'These things are from Jingcao and Lin Liguo. . . .' I said I'd been told to say they [Ye Qün and Lin Liguo] were very concerned about his health and he should take care of himself. . . . Huang said, 'Thank you very much.' Then I said, 'The Chairman [Mao] gave an important order while he was out touring and Lin Liguo wants to tell you about it. The order was given while the Chairman was talking to Liu Xingyuan [deputy political commissar of the Canton Military Region] and Ding Sheng [another senior officer of the Canton Region], and it wasn't to be passed down, given out, or spoken about on the telephone.' Huang said, 'Oh, not even on the telephone?' "

JUDGE: Before Lin Biao fled, did he write you a letter in his own handwriting?

HUANG: Yes, yes, he did.

JUDGE: What was the content?

HUANG: This is roughly how I remember it. At the beginning it was written in red ink: "Dear Comrade Yongsheng, I've been thinking a lot about you." That was the first part. "I'm concerned that you should look after your health. If there's any problem, send for Wang Fei." That's more or less what it said. Without having it in my hand, I can't recall it in detail, but that was the broad sense.

JUDGE: Read out and show the letter Lin Biao wrote to Huang Yongsheng in his own handwriting.

COURT READER: "Dear Comrade Yongsheng, I've been thinking about you a lot. Always be optimistic and look after your health. If anything comes up, you can discuss it with Wang Fei. Yours ever, Lin Biao."

This letter was found in the helicopter that was [transporting the conspirators who were] fleeing.

JUDGE: Huang Yongsheng, I ask you further: When Lin Biao decided to have Chairman Mao assassinated, and Ye Qün and Lin Liguo sent you the package to be delivered only to you, while Lin Biao wrote you this personal letter, what were your relations with Lin Biao?

HUANG: Well, that's hard to say. Lin Biao and I—I didn't have any special relations with him. I had organizational contacts with him, relations between superior and subordinate, working relations, nothing special.

JUDGE: Huang Yongsheng, I ask you again: Going by that personal letter Lin Biao sent you, what was your position in the Lin Biao–Jiang Qing clique?

HUANG: I admit I was a member of the Lin Biao counterrevolutionary clique.

JUDGE: The indictment accuses you of having had detailed contacts with Ye Qün—on September 10, 1971, five telephone calls in one day. Is this true?

HUANG: As I recall, it wasn't five times but six.

JUDGE: Six phone calls?

HUANG: My impression is that there were six.

JUDGE: Read out the testimony of the Military Affairs Commission central switchboard operator Ma Taoying and six others.

COURT READER: "Before the criminal Lin betrayed his country and fled to the enemy side, Ye Qün, Huang Yongsheng, Wu Faxian, Li Zuopeng, and Qiu Huizuo made many telephone calls, conducting counterrevolutionary liaison. Our records show that from September 6 till 12 alone, the number of calls routed through the central switchboard of the Commission was fifty-six, not including automatic calls. Out of these, Ye Qün used a secure phone to call Huang Yongsheng sixteen times, spoke five times with Wu Faxian, ten times with Qiu Huizuo—thirty-one calls in all, total time nine hundred and forty-nine minutes. Apart from conversations between Ye Qün and Huang Yongsheng, Huang spoke to Li Zuopeng seven times. On September 10, Huang phoned Ye Qün three times, while Ye Qün phoned Huang twice. Of these five conversations, one lasted ninety minutes and another one hundred and thirty-five minutes."

JUDGE: [to Huang] Is it true that one of your calls to Ye Qün lasted one hundred and thirty-five minutes?

HUANG: Yes, yes, yes.

JUDGE: What did you talk about?

HUANG: We were consulting in detail, word by word, about the speech Lin Biao made at Beidaihe on August 16, 1971.

JUDGE: According to our investigations, what you have just said does not correspond at all to reality. For we have established that when you were supposed to be going through the speech word by word with Ye Qün, in reality Premier Zhou Enlai had already looked over Lin Biao's August 16 instructions, and the final draft was [completed] on September 5. Therefore, when you say that you were discussing the draft word by word with

Ye Qün on September 10, that is impossible. I now propose that the court listen to the reading of relevant parts of the photostat of Premier Zhou's comments in his own handwriting on the final draft of Lin's August 16 instructions. On September 5, the premier, having passed the draft, had the Central Committee Office pass it, and sent a copy to every member of the Politburo, so there was no way in which Huang Yongsheng could have been going over it word by word [at the time he said]. I propose an extract should be read to the court and a copy given to Huang Yongsheng.

COURT READER: Premier Zhou Enlai's comments on the draft of Lin Biao's speech of August 16: "Urgent document. . . . Have it printed and distributed to the comrades on the politburo; get me four copies. Zhou Enlai, September 5, 1971."

JUDGE: [to Huang] When did Premier Zhou make these comments?

HUANG: You—you—let me see—I can't read it too clearly—1971, this—this—what—what—September 5? . . .

JUDGE: After the premier made these comments, the Central Committee Office immediately had it printed and distributed.

HUANG: This word, I—this—this—

JUDGE: On August 16, Premier Zhou Enlai, Huang Yongsheng, Zhang Chunqiao, and Ji Dengkui[5] went to Beidaihe to report on their work to Lin Biao. Huang Yongsheng was to report on preparations for war—training and other such matters. Lin Biao gave some instructions. On August 30 the Military Affairs Commission work group sent Lin Biao a copy of the draft record of his talk on August 16. On September 1 the MAC Office straightened out the draft according to your suggestions, Huang Yongsheng. It was sent to Comrades Wu Faxian, Ye Qün, Li Zuopeng, Qiu Huizuo, Li Desheng, Ji Dengkui, and Zhang Caiqian [commander of Nanjing Military Region] . . . with a request for their opinion. On September 3 Ye Qün telephoned to suggest revisions in the draft. On the fifth, Premier Zhou amended another five passages . . . consisting of a total of eight words, which is what you've just seen. In the end the draft was finalized and Premier Zhou approved it and [had it] issued to the politburo members . . . marked "absolutely secret." On September 5 it was issued to them. At seven P.M. that day, Premier Zhou wrote a letter to Chairman Mao asking him to look it over and comment. At seven-thirty Chairman Mao approved it in his own handwriting. . . . This matter has been many times investigated; there's a dossier on it that may be consulted. You say that on September 10 you were going over the speech word by word with Ye Qün. Is that the case? Is it? Absolutely not! From the police interrogation right down to the judicial investigation, the question of those one hundred thirty-five minutes—you have been asked about those one hundred thirty-five minutes, asked several times, but you keep saying the same thing. . . . After a long time, you change your story and say that a thing that had already been done five days before occupied you for a hundred and thirty-five minutes on the phone? The evidence before the court cogently elucidates the content of those hundred and thirty-five minutes on the telephone. [Your version] is untrue. Your explanation does not stand up. We're warning you again: You must answer the court's questions truthfully. Article 44 of the indictment accuses you of destroying evidence after Lin Biao's flight. Is that true?

HUANG: I burned two documents.

JUDGE: You burned two documents.

HUANG: Two documents, which had nothing to do with Lin Biao.

Later a cleaner testified that Huang had spent days burning documents in his living quarters, and that the air reeked of smoke and the lavatory pedestal was scorched black.

QIU HUIZUO

Qiu Huizuo (the surname is pronounced roughly like English "chew") was mainly accused of setting up a "kangaroo court" and center for detention and interrogation in the General Logistics Department of the armed forces. Between 1967 and 1971, the court was told, 462 people were tortured until they confessed to whatever they were accused of or were "framed and persecuted." He also attacked the General Political Department (chief commissars' office) of the People's Liberation Army and attempted to steal their archives.

In his final plea, Qiu Huizuo said: "I unreservedly plead guilty. . . . My crimes are historical facts which are unalterable but, as a man, I can turn over a new leaf. I am determined to continue reforming myself."

WU FAXIAN

Wu Faxian, former air-force commander, distinguished himself in court mainly by his eagerness to cooperate with those planning to convict him. Taking into account the nine years he had already spent in custody, he could expect to serve the remainder of his seventeen-year jail term till 1989 unless remission was granted. Wu was found guilty of framing Marshal He Long and General Luo Ruiqing, and of making false charges against leading air-force officers, detaining and persecuting 174 of them—among whom Gu Qian, chief of staff of the Air Force Command of the Nanjing Military Region, and Liu Shanben, deputy superintendent of the Air Force Academy, were "persecuted to death." He was also convicted for having let Lin Biao put his son, Lin Liguo, in charge of the air force.

Wu Faxian's Defense

TV COMMENTATOR: The Second Special Court this afternoon heard defense pleas. Wu Faxian was the first to appear. Wu Faxian's lawyers, Ma Kechang and Zhou Hengyuan, appeared for him.

JUDGE: Defense pleas will now commence. The prosecutor will speak first.

PROSECUTOR: Chief Judge and procurators. With regard to the function and legal responsibility of Wu Faxian in throwing in his lot with Lin Biao and joining the Lin-Jiang counterrevolutionary clique, I wish to make the following points. . . .

TV COMMENTATOR: The prosecutor speaks about the accused Wu Faxian's crimes in following Lin Biao, taking part in Lin Biao's counterrevolutionary conspiratorial activity, his secret instructions to Lin Liguo to form the "united fleet," and his long-term association with Lin Biao.

PROSECUTOR: . . . fully illuminates the counterrevolutionary criminal activity in accused Wu Faxian's zealous support of Lin Biao and his long-term attempts to subvert the party, the state, and the armed forces, to bring disaster on the country and its people, to overthrow the sovereignty of the People's Republic of China and the socialist order. In Lin Biao's counterrevolutionary clique, he functioned as a leader. According to the Criminal Code of the People's Republic of China's appropriate provisions, he was a principal culprit who committed the crime of organizing a counterrevolutionary leadership clique and the crime of conspiring to overthrow the government. In order to protect the socialist order and guard the authority of the dictatorship of the proletariat, I ask the court to punish him according to the law. That is all I have to say.

JUDGE: Accused Wu Faxian, you may speak in your defense now if you wish.

WU: The prosecutor's account of my crimes is all based on fact, as is the evidence. I have confessed to them already. I have no submission to make. My crimes have been described with absolute accuracy!

JUDGE: Let us hear the defense.

TV COMMENTATOR: Wu Faxian's defense counsel speaks about Wu Faxian's position and function in the Lin Biao clique and the question of his attitude in admitting his guilt. He points out that although Wu was a principal culprit in the Lin Biao clique, his crimes must be distinguished from those of the main culprits, Lin Biao and Ye Qün. At the same time, the accused has found it possible to repent his crimes and submit to the law. His attitude was fairly good and it is hoped that in determining the sentence this will be taken into consideration. When defense counsel had finished, the prosecutor made a supplementary speech about Wu Faxian's attitude in admitting his guilt. He said he had no difference of opinion [with defense counsel].

JUDGE: Accused Wu Faxian, you have the right to make a final statement. In other words, you have the right of a final plea. Have you any statement to make?

wu: President of the Court, I do not wish to plead for myself. I really do admit my guilt.

JUDGE: Now you may leave the court and await the court's verdict after it has completed its deliberations. Take the culprit away.

In this inconclusive manner the case against the military defendants was presented. But the People's Liberation Army suffered a heavy blow to its prestige, which aided the Deng Xiaoping ruling group's subsequent moves to cut down the political role of the military in Chinese society. The high commanders arraigned for treason had shown themselves incompetent and unable to coordinate a plot which, with the resources at their disposal, should they have been better applied, would certainly have brought about Mao's violent end and probably led to the establishment of a military dictatorship in China. The PLA's competence was on trial, as much as its loyalty.

PART FOUR

13

THREE VICTIMS

Everybody in China experienced the Cultural Revolution differently. Some gained by it, climbing onto the leftist bandwagon and entering the ranks of the party or government apparatus. Youthful Red Guards traveled the length and breadth of the country "making revolution." But for most people it was a frightening and horrible experience.

Most of the trial transcripts deal with the victimization of top leaders, middle-ranking bureaucrats, and ordinary people up to the point when they were jailed, "put in the cowpen," or exiled to remote and impoverished rural areas. There is on the whole not much detail about the treatment of public figures after they disappeared from view in 1966 and 1967.

The Chinese media have, however, printed descriptions of what happened to a number of disgraced leaders and their families. Three of these accounts are presented below in summary form—the cases of Liu Shaoqi, He Long, and Luo Ruiqing. Here we can sit at table with the Liu family and listen to their doubts and fears about the great movement swirling around outside (and sometimes inside) the walls of the top leadership's residential compound, the complex of parkland, lake, and villas called Zhongnanhai. We can watch Lin Biao and Qi Benyü conspiring to overthrow Luo Ruiqing, chief of the General Staff of the People's Liberation Army, and see the septuagenarian war hero Marshal He Long neglected in the hospital until he dies from lack of treatment.

After the disastrous failure of the Great Leap Forward—a headlong economic surge that Mao ordered in 1958, which brought the country to the verge of starvation by 1961—Mao withdrew from the front of the political stage. Zhou Enlai, Deng Xiaoping, and Liu Shaoqi drew up new agricultural guidelines that shifted some of the burden of collective labor off the peasants' shoulders and permitted them to work for a modest personal profit as well as for the state. But Zhou, Deng, and Liu reckoned without Mao. He evidently did not forgive the emasculation of his pet social experiment, the people's communes. He probably blamed others for the failure of his backyard-iron-furnace scheme which relied on the peasants to provide iron and steel later found useless because of poor quality. He regarded the relative mildness of the social and intellectual climate in the early 1960s as backsliding. In 1965 obscure literary debates in the press began to foreshadow the terrifying mass movement Mao was aiming for—the Cultural Revolution.

He chose as his most prominent victim Liu Shaoqi, Head of State of the People's Republic of China and an eminent revolutionary who had written a book sold all over China, *How to Be a Good Communist* (now once more being sold in the bookshops).

LIU SHAOQI

Liu Shaoqi, the blackest warlock in the Maoist demonology, was a remarkable man. Born in 1898 in Mao's native province of Hunan, he quite probably knew Mao at the teachers' college in the provincial capital of Changsha. In 1919–1920 he studied Russian in Shanghai and was sponsored to go to Moscow for training as a revolutionary. Returning in 1922, he worked as an agitator among coal miners and Shanghai workers, and in 1925 became vice-chairman of the Chinese Federation of Trade Unions. After ten years as a Marxist agitator, he joined Mao at his guerrilla base in Jiangxi and became a member of the party politburo. He stayed behind when Mao and his forces left on the Long March, and worked in North China before joining Mao at Yan'an in 1937. Liu had an excellent record as a political commissar with the Red Army. He continued with his work in trade unions until the Communist victory in 1949, when he became deputy leader of the government and armed forces, standing in for Mao in 1950 when the latter went to Moscow to seek aid. In the 1950s Liu visited Moscow several times and was important in the buildup of the Sino-Soviet alliance and Soviet aid to China. In the 1960s he traveled quite widely in Asian countries—Burma, Cambodia, North Vietnam, North Korea, Pakistan, and Afghanistan—usually with his beautiful American-born wife, Wang Guangmei.

Liu evidently held views different from those of Mao on many issues. He and Deng Xiaoping had to sort out the mess left over from Mao's disastrous Great Leap Forward in the early 1960s. Liu believed in cultivating allies among the quasi-feudal, bourgeois, or junta-type regimes of east and south Asia, while Mao had his doubts about them. Liu probably tried to heal the Sino-Soviet split, which Mao reveled in.

On December 5, 1980, the Peking *Workers' Daily* printed a lengthy account of Liu's treatment, written by his children. It is summarized below.

On June 4, 1966, Mao sent a small number of "experimental work groups" to take charge of the Cultural Revolution movement at Peking University. Liu, according to his children's account, reacted cautiously, saying he had no experience of such things and would take a wait-and-see attitude. He telephoned many times to Mao, who was in the eastern resort city of Hangzhou, but received no clarification from him. Meanwhile the movement in secondary schools, universities, and colleges was spreading, and there had already been killings and suicides. Liu and Party Secretary-General Deng Xiaoping flew to Hangzhou to consult Mao, who gave Liu authority to handle the situation as he saw fit. On returning to Peking, Liu immediately convened an enlarged meeting of the Politburo Standing Committee. To inform himself of the state of the movement and the performance of the "work groups," Liu visited the No. 1 Middle School attached to the Peking Teacher Training College. The Head of State interpreted the movement as a continuation of the socialist education movement that preceded it, failing to see that it was a political campaign organized by Mao's entourage and aimed directly at him and other senior leaders. He believed it was merely a way of cutting down on bureaucratic work styles and isolation of cadres from the masses. He proclaimed that the movement was to be divided into three stages— "struggle, criticism, and rectification"—and would be concluded by the end of 1966. He invited students to submit criticisms of their teachers but banned physical violence, saying indiscriminate conflict was not the goal of revolution.

After a while, however, Liu realized that a trap was being laid for him by Jiang Qing, Kang Sheng, Lin Biao, and Chen Boda, and told his children, "This is the beginning of a big split right across the country, and it cannot be ignored. It may be that there are some high-ranking cadres behind it."

On July 16 Mao flung himself back into the public limelight by taking a long swim in the Yangzi River. He returned to Peking three days later. On July 24 he criticized Deng and Liu at a meeting. Meanwhile, Liu told a rally of some 10,000 activists at the Great Hall of the People, "You're not very clear in your minds, you don't really know how to conduct the Great Proletarian Cultural Revolution. When you have asked me how to go about changing things, I have always answered that I don't know myself."

On August 5 Mao wrote his famous wall poster entitled "Bombard the Headquarters" (meaning the party leadership of Deng, Liu, and others). At the Twelfth Plenary Session of the Eighth Central Committee, Liu was demoted from the number two position to number eight. Noticing the concern on the faces of his children, Liu told them, "Don't worry. Your father knows how to recognize his errors."

The children were themselves swept up in the Red Guard movement and went around with other youngsters confiscating property from "bourgeois" families. Their father forbade them to do so, showing them the state constitution, and said, "I have nothing against your smashing the 'four olds,' but you mustn't search houses and confiscate property."

In October, at a meeting of the Central Committee, Liu made a self-criticism that was praised by Mao, but the latter's favorable comments were deleted when the text of the self-criticism was circulated to party cadres around the country. An upsurge of criticism of Liu began in the capital and provinces. Liu, however, still had faith in Mao, and told his wife, "They have such a one-sided approach that the Chairman will have to criticize them sooner or later." But he warned the children: "We will have to put up with being criticized for a few months longer."

Meanwhile, inside the Zhongnanhai leadership complex in central Peking, a big-character poster was put up attacking Marshal Zhu De, the foremost wartime commander, as a "black commander" and "big warlord." Liu was sickened by this and went to see Premier Zhou Enlai about it, offering his resignation as Head of State. Zhou told him, "It's no good, you can't do it. This is a matter for the National People's Congress" (which had last met in 1964).

"Jiang Qing scurried off to Qinghua University," Liu's children wrote, "where she made a threatening speech, saying that the nature of the Liu Shaoqi affair had been agreed upon long ago as one of antiparty and antisocialist behavior, and that getting round to dealing with him was only a matter of time. At present they were afraid that the ordinary people could not shift stance so suddenly, thus they had to proceed step by step."

Liu began to lose his appetite and had pains in his heart. The children were beaten up and ostracized at school. Liu's second son, Liu Yunruo, was thrown in jail. His eldest son and eldest daughter were exiled to a remote border region and could not write home. But Liu still kept faith in the people. He said, "When I was in charge of the Central Committee's work, I had to take on very important responsibilities, and this meant taking responsibility for any errors. Now the masses are angry because they believe I didn't make a proper job of the work they entrusted to me. If the masses go too far in taking things out on you, you should try to understand the masses and not fight against this, and you mustn't harbor grudges. In the future you will come to realize that the Chinese people are really the most wonderful people."

On January 6, 1967, Red Guards lured Wang Guangmei out of Zhongnanhai by telling her that her young daughter, Pingping, had been run over on her way home from school and had a broken leg. When Wang (whom Zhou Enlai had warned not to leave Zhongnanhai) rushed to the hospital with her husband, she found no sign of Pingping, but instead encountered two of her other children.

Wang Guangmei rounded on the Red Guards who were watching them, and they said they had acted on orders from Jiang Qing. Liu took one of the children home to find Pingping waiting at the door, weeping miserably. With the aid of Premier Zhou Enlai, Wang Guangmei was released by the Red Guards and returned to Zhongnanhai.

Later in the month, Red Guards burst into the Lius' house and stuck wall posters and slogans all over the courtyard. Liu was subjected to struggle-and-criticism sessions. At one of these, a Red Guard challenged him to recite a certain quotation from Mao's works from memory. Liu—who was chairman of the editorial board responsible for publishing Mao's selected works (up till 1949), replied, "If you ask me to recite single sentences, I can't do it. You can ask me what the contents of this or that article by Chairman Mao are, about the historical background of the time when it was written, what problems it dealt with, what effect it had at the time, or what new original ideas it contained from the theoretical point of view, for these things alone are the quintessence of Mao Zedong Thought."

Late at night on January 13, Mao sent a car to fetch him for a talk in the Great Hall of the People. In a concerned manner, he asked about Pingping's leg. Liu told him it had all been a trick. He made a confession of his "errors" and said he had resigned his official posts and wanted to go away to become a farmer. Mao listened in silence, smoking a cigarette, then advised him to "read a few books." He recommended works by Hegel and Diderot. When Liu took his leave, Mao merely said, "Study well, and look after your health." Returning home, Liu told his children that Mao had been "very kind" to him.

Two days later Red Guards again invaded the Lius' home, sticking up posters and forcing Liu and his wife to stand on a table and be denounced out in the freezing courtyard. Liu told them he had never opposed Mao's thought, though he admitted to having had "differences of opinion" with the Chairman from time to time.

After midnight Zhou Enlai telephoned and told Wang Guangmei she would have to "stand a test." She was moved by what she saw as the premier's concern for her and Liu. The next morning Red Guards from the telephone exchange in Zhongnanhai rushed in saying they had come to take away the Lius' telephone. Liu leaped up and said, "This telephone is the property of the Political Bureau, and without the personal approval of Chairman Mao and Premier Zhou, you are not permitted, nor do you have the authority, to remove it." The Red Guards left in a huff. But next day they returned and ripped out the telephone cord. The Lius were now isolated from the rest of the leadership.

The children took to stealing out of Zhongnanhai in the early morning to buy unofficial newspapers and flyers from Red Guards and copy down the texts of wall posters to report on them to their parents. On March 28 Liu was so infuriated at the public accusations against him that he wrote to Mao to complain. Typically, the Red Guards accused him of having once expressed approval of the controversial movie *Inside the Qing Court,* which the leftists had denounced as revisionist, and said he had once called himself a "red comprador."[1] Seething with rage, Liu saw himself branded as "China's Khrushchev" and "the number one person in authority taking the capitalist road." At struggle-and-criticism sessions that Liu was still forced to attend regularly, Red Guards would slap him in the face and on the mouth with the *Little Red Book* of quotations from Mao every time he tried to argue his case. They told him, "You're not allowed to spread poisonous ideas."

Liu's supply of sleeping pills was reduced by the guards and he suffered from insomnia. He was becoming physically weak.

On April 8 Wang Guangmei was informed that she had to go to Qinghua University to make a self-criticism. While she was having dinner with the children, Liu appeared from his room, clinging to the wall and ashen-faced, with sweat running down his face. A doctor was summoned and he gave Liu a few pills, then went off in a hurry. The children wrote:

As we gazed at father's pale, thin face, there rose before our eyes a scene from the previous year, when father, having contracted a serious illness, had been chatting with us after recovering. At that time he called us children and his personal staff to his side, and said, sighing with emotion, "It looks as though I won't live much longer, and so I must make the best use of the time I have left to be able to do a few things. If only Marx[2] will give me another ten years, we will be able to really build China into a rich and strong country." Father went on to describe to us what he envisaged: how we would rectify the bureaucratic style of work within the party; how we would reform education, implementing two educational systems—one full-time and one part work, part study; how we would raise production capacity to develop the national economy; how we would narrow the three great gaps,[3] and so forth. Father said that, for example, we would use the big oil fields that had been discovered in Shandong and Hebei to build up an industrial base, and that this would enable desolate and out-of-the-way villages to be developed into new-style industrial cities. Here, there would be electricity, oil, and road and rail networks, and this would give an impetus to the modernization of neighboring rural areas. We would need to pay attention to the recruitment of female industrial workers so that not only female commune members would be left to work in the fields. Not only did father have splendid visions, he had also worked out solid and down-to-earth measures for putting his ideas into practice.

On April 10 a rally of 300,000 people was held at Qinghua University to denounce Wang Guangmei. She was struck and kicked and made to wear a cheongsam, with a necklace of Ping-Pong balls.

As summer approached, Zhongnanhai was besieged by a forest of Red Guard tents in the street outside. The Lius' older children traveled around the country, as Red Guards could do without paying for tickets, on "liaison" work. They witnessed some of the violence in big provincial cities and reported what they had seen to Liu. By this time he was so exhausted that Wang Guangmei had to write his self-criticisms for him.

Zhou Enlai did what he could to quell the demonstrators, attempting to speak to them at the gates of Zhongnanhai. But Jiang Qing, so the Lius' children say, personally led the mob around to a different gate whenever Zhou appeared at one.[4] Zhou told the Red Guards, "I am staying in Zhongnanhai and I'm not coming out. Zhongnanhai is where the Party Central Committee is, and if you think you are going to storm it, you will have to do it over my dead body." Nonetheless the mob succeeded in kidnapping a number of provincial party first secretaries who happened to be in Peking, and Central Committee department heads. They were at the gates. Posters appeared attacking Marshal Zhu De and Chen Yun, a right-leaning economic planner. The Lius' cook, Hao Miao, who had been with them for eighteen years, was arrested on charges of being a secret agent.[5]

Liu's six-year-old daughter, Xiaoxiao, was ready to go to school, but it was thought dangerous. Wang Guangmei asked Liu, "If we are arrested, can we ask them to let me bring Xiaoxiao to the prison?" Liu said no. So Wang Guangmei took Xiaoxiao to an aunt's place and entrusted the child to her.[6]

Going for a meal at the staff canteen on July 18, the Lius found a big-character poster announcing that there would be a struggle session against Liu Shaoqi that night, on the instructions of Jiang Qing and Qi Benyü. After the meal, tens of thousands of people gathered outside the gates and the Lius were denounced. Liu tried to wipe the sweat off his face, but the handkerchief was snatched from him. Meanwhile, their home was searched. After the rally, Liu was confined to his office and Wang Guangmei to the rear part of the house. Their children were allowed neither to see them nor to leave the house.

On August 5, 1967, the leftists ordered struggle-and-criticism sessions in the courtyards of the houses of the Lius and of Deng Xiaoping and Tao Zhu and their wives. Kang Sheng's wife, Cao Yi'ou, attended in person to witness their humiliation. Recordings and film of the sessions were made for nationwide distribution. The guards ordered the children to attend and see their parents being denounced. Liu and Wang Guangmei were struck and kicked and made to stand or sit in unbearably uncomfortable positions. A Red Guard grabbed Liu Shaoqi by the hair to make him raise his head for a photograph. Xiaoxiao ran away in terror and was hauled back by a Red Guard. The session lasted over two hours. Liu's face was bruised and swollen. Wang Guangmei struggled free and embraced her husband. It was the last they ever saw of each other; they held each other's hands in a gesture of farewell. The Red Guards tore them apart and hung a cartoon round Liu's neck, showing a noose and the pens and fists of the young agitators.

On August 7 Liu wrote to Mao to complain. There was no answer. Liu's leg had been injured and he could barely walk. Wang Guangmei had a head injury but was made to carry bricks and do other work.

On the morning of September 13, the children were summoned to their school to be criticized for giving their parents information about the situation. They were not allowed to see their parents. On the same day, Xiaoxiao and her aunt were expelled from Zhongnanhai and Wang Guangmei was arrested and imprisoned. Blows rained down on Xiaoxiao when she showed up at school, and she had to be rescued by a soldier. The children of other prominent leaders were receiving similar treatment. Liu's son Yuanyuan and the son of Peng Zhen, with no source of income, tried to sell their blood at a hospital, but were refused because they had no identification. They escaped through windows onto the roof of their five-story house when Red Guards came to haul them out.

Pingping, who had been imprisoned, was later taken to Shandong Province. Yuanyuan was sent to Shanxi, to work on communes. The peasants treated them well, giving them food, and helped Yuanyuan to escape. Hiking at night with only a few soya beans to eat, after three days he caught a train to Peking. Pingping, learning from her brothers' and sisters' letters that they would be permitted to visit their mother, dashed to the rail station, but was prevented from boarding the train.

The children wrote to Mao in 1972, and he instructed the special case group to let them see their mother. The group also informed them that their father was dead. (He died of pneumonia in Kaifeng, Henan Province, on November 12, 1969.) The children were allowed to visit their mother, who was in solitary confinement in a maximum-security prison near Peking for political transgressors. "When it was time to part," the children wrote, "the guards dragged mother back and we wept and cried, 'Mother, mother!' She turned her head, her face covered with tears, and nodded to us from the other side of the prison window."

Wang Guangmei was rehabilitated in 1979—three years after the arrest of the Gang of Four—and attended a session of the trial. She was appointed a member of the largely honorific Chinese People's Political Consultative Conference. A fluent English speaker, she was made director of the foreign-affairs department of the Academy of Social Sciences. (She had lost none of her flair or style. Appearing at a reception in Peking, she wore hip-hugging black pants with a decorative gilt pen stuck in the pockets on either side.)

The children traveled to the place in Kaifeng where Liu had been detained, but it was unoccupied. In 1976 they were told of an urn containing the ashes of an unknown person at the Babaoshan cemetery in Peking, resting place of notable people. They inspected the urn, but found no identifying marks. They were angered to see that Kang Sheng's urn occupied a place of honor. Though Kang died in 1975, he was not publicly denounced until late in 1980. Liu's children stripped the urn of the party flag draped over it. It had saliva marks and burns from cigarettes, they claimed—"the way in which the angry people expressed their indignation!"

They decided to accept the ashes of the unknown as those of Liu. "Even if the ashes were not father's, they must have been the ashes of an innocent person persecuted to death by Lin Biao, Jiang Qing, Kang Sheng, Chen Boda, and company." Yuanyuan poured some of the ashes into the Jinshui River outside the former Imperial Palace in the center of Peking on September 30, the eve of National Day.

As time went on, they learned more details of the treatment of their father and mother. While under house arrest, Liu once shuffled out of his room to see if he could learn anything of his wife and children, but all the children had left and Wang Guangmei was in prison. A guard pushed Liu over and removed his belt to prevent further such reconnaissance. The guard was doubled, and warned not to show any leniency to Liu. He became very weak, could hardly walk or feed himself, and had stomach ailments from the steamed bread and hard rice he was given to eat. He shook all over. Doctors denounced him as "China's Khrushchev" even while treating him. They stopped his supply of vitamins and a drug he was taking for diabetes. He became bedridden and could barely limp to the lavatory. His leg muscles atrophied. The children later wrote:

> Under the glaring lights in the room, father, did you know that your wife was being locked up in a dark, sealed cell? She was not able to straighten her spine, her hair was falling out, and she was coughing up blood. She had been sentenced to die by Lin Biao and company. Your eldest son, Liu Yunbin, had died a tragic death more than one year before. Your eldest daughter, Liu Aiqin, was locked up in a "cowpen"[7] and was being brutally beaten. Your second son, Liu Yunruo, was suffering from vertebral tuberculosis and had been tortured to the brink of death. Nineteen-year-old Pingping was being kept in solitary confinement. Seventeen-year-old Yuanyuan, who had just been released from prison, was trudging with difficulty in the monstrous wind

and sandstorms of the Yanbei area (Shanxi Province). Tingting, who was even younger, was bearing tremendous political pressures in solitude and struggling hard. Your beloved Xiaoxiao was being discriminated against everywhere she went. She had to endure pain and humiliation.

Eventually Liu could eat nothing and had to be fed through a tube in the nose. In this condition he passed his seventieth birthday. And on that day he was informed that he had been expelled from the party. Anger at this drove his physical condition further down. Zhou Enlai tried to help by sending two experienced nurses to look after him.

In October 1969 Lin Biao ordered that Liu be moved. The half-naked patient was removed under cover of darkness and flown to a maximum-security prison in Kaifeng, former capital of the Northern Song dynasty. He was dumped on a stretcher on the basement floor, and his pneumonia recurred. The Peking guards who had accompanied him were ordered back to the capital, taking with them Liu's medicines. A short while later, Liu's former chief bodyguard, Li, received word that he had died, and dashed down to Kaifeng to take charge of the body.

"Father was lying on the basement floor and his body was covered with a white bedsheet. The white hair, which was over a foot long, was disheveled. His mouth and nose were deformed and there were signs of hemorrhaging on his chin."

The prison guards had refused to send him to the hospital for treatment on the grounds that they did not know he had pneumonia. They ordered that he be cremated immediately because he had a "deadly contagious disease." The corpse was driven off in a jeep with its legs dangling out the back. The special case group, after warning all concerned to maintain absolute secrecy, ordered a banquet to celebrate their "accomplished mission."

HE LONG

Lin Biao suspected Marshal He Long of wanting to gain control of the air force. He told Li Zuopeng, "You must watch He Long. He is actually Luo Ruiqing's behind-the-scenes boss. He has adopted all vicious means to rally a group of people to oppose me." Li Zuopeng and Wu Faxian both wrote letters to Lin Biao *at the latter's dictation,* calling Marshal He by such names as bandit, warlord, defeatist, military usurper, mass murderer, "time bomb," one with illicit relations with foreign countries and Soviet revisionism, plotter of a coup d'état, etc.

Marshal He scoffed: "They do not have any real evidence. Their evidence is fabricated. . . . They want to remove all the old comrades so as to isolate Chairman Mao and put their men around him."

Lin Biao's wife, Ye Qün, incited Song Zhiguo, commander of a guards division, to write to Lin Biao, who ordered the letters printed and circulated. Among the accusations was the charge that although He Long kept photographs of himself, his wife, and Luo Ruiqing under the glass top of his desk at home, he kept none of Mao. He was accused of close links with the already disgraced Luo Ruiqing, Peng Zhen, and Yang Shangkun. He kept a pistol under his pillow at night and carried it on him during the day. He counseled intensive training and such disciplines as pistol shooting for Chinese soldiers, not political work. Kang Sheng accused him, in the summer of 1966, of trying to stage a mutiny in the Peking Military Region and building pillboxes in the suburbs. Kang also threw suspicion on He Long's acquisition of guns from the Physical Culture and Sports Commission, and suggested he was planning to assassinate Mao. He Long was accused of negotiating with a Guomindang emissary as long ago as 1933, whereas in fact he had the Chiang Kai-shek agent executed. He Long—obviously a hot-tempered man—heard of this allegation and shouted, "Damn it! They should be shot! This is a frame-up, a mere frame-up!" In a more sombre mood, he said to his wife, Xue Ming, "What will our party do? What will our country do?" Out walking one day, he struck a portrait of Lin Biao with his stick, saying, "You scoundrel, now you start fabricating charges against others." He called Kang Sheng "a wily old fox."

Marshal He refused to admit to the charges against him by writing self-criticisms. He was apparently under some form of house arrest, because it is said he was given only one small bottle of water a day, even in the summer. He needed more water because he had diabetes and was seventy-one years old. He had to wash and clean his teeth with the same small bottle. Given mainly boiled cabbage and radishes to eat, Marshal He suffered from malnutrition, but a doctor who was called did nothing more than confiscate his medicine. On March 27, 1968, he was sent to the hospital. However, Qiu Huizuo ordered that "medical treatment should be subordinate to the handling of the trial," so the doctor wrote that he was "pretending to be ill" and suggested he be treated by an army doctor.

He Long commented, "They just want to kill me slowly. It's murder without bloodshed."

He had a bad case of uric-acid poisoning. He vomited all the time and his breathing speeded up, and despite his diabetes he was given large amounts of glucose solution intravenously (fatal to a diabetic). Over his objections, he was again taken to the hospital that had said he was shamming illness. In the afternoon of June 9, 1968, they summoned his wife and told her, "The patient is dead."

It seems Ye Qün had a vendetta against He's wife, Xüe Ming, who at Yan'an in 1943 had denounced her as a Guomindang secret agent. In November 1969, according to the report in the *People's Daily*, Ye Qün phoned Wu Faxian and said, "Xüe Ming knows too much about me. Remove her to a place farther away from Peking and put her in air-force custody." Wu did as instructed, and Ye Qün ordered Xüe Ming incarcerated at an air-force officers' training college at Guiyang, in China's remote Southwest. They told the escorting squad that Xüe Ming should be made to do manual labor, be strictly supervised, and be forbidden to write letters.

Xüe Ming survived and was rehabilitated in the 1970s. Interviewed by a *People's Daily* reporter in 1980, she said: "I have no personal grudge against the Jiang Qing and Lin Biao cliques. They wanted to destroy our state and nation. What they destroyed included much more than just He Long!"

LUO RUIQING

The *People's Daily* account of the downfall of Luo Ruiqing is reprinted here verbatim, since it is not lengthy and conveys the atmosphere of conflict and revenge inherent in all the official accounts of the trial and the events leading up to it.

Iron Spring and Loyal Soul: Factual Account of How Comrade Luo Ruiqing Was Framed and Persecuted by the Lin Biao and Jiang Qing Counterrevolutionary Cliques

"When you understand me, you will know that I do not fear the clouds that cover the sky. The sun will shine as always on the travelers." Comrade Luo Ruiqing wrote this poem at the time he was being humiliated and tortured. He did not write this poem by chance.

The facts revealed at the trial in the Second Tribunal detail how Lin Biao, Ye Qün, Wu Faxian, Huang Yongsheng, Li Zuopeng, Kang Sheng, and Xie Fuzhi collaborated with one another in framing and persecuting Luo Ruiqing, and enable those who did not know the truth to feel the impact of the "clouds that cover the sky." They also make those who always held Comrade

Luo Ruiqing in respect understand more deeply his loyalty to the people.

The dark clouds of frame-up and persecution began to gather around Comrade Luo Ruiqing in 1965. He was then secretary of the Secretariat of the Party Central Committee, vice-premier of the State Council, and chief of the General Staff of the People's Liberation Army [PLA].

Obviously, he was one of the many major obstacles that Lin Biao had to overcome in order to usurp military power. Lin Biao began testing Luo Ruiqing by soft and hard tactics. Luo Ruiqing had to make his choice: He could go and seek refuge with Lin Biao, but by doing so he would be boarding a pirate ship, even if he could hold on to his personal fame and position for the time being; or he could firmly hold on to the position assigned him by the party and defend principles that must be upheld without fail, but by doing so he would become a thorn in Lin Biao's flesh. He had to choose one or the other.

The loyal general took a brave step. He disagreed with Lin Biao's expression of "giving prominence to politics." What would happen to the army if it did not grasp military work? He also disagreed with Lin Biao's statements on "the highest and most lively" and "the pinnacle." Could there be "the second highest and the second most lively"? How can an idea develop if it has reached its "pinnacle"?—and so forth.[8]

The contradiction sharpened. Lin Biao, together with Ye Qün, was determined to remove Luo Ruiqing so as to clear the road for the complete usurpation of military power.

Hatchet men were needed to frame other people. A high-ranking one was needed to frame and topple Luo Ruiqing. Lin Biao and Ye Qün singled out Wu Faxian, who was the air-force commander.

At that time, Lin Biao did not hold as high a position as he later did, when he was deputy supreme commander. Afraid that Wu Faxian would waver at a critical juncture, Ye Qün used both soft and hard tactics. First, she used hard tactics.

She phoned Wu Faxian: "You must fully expose Luo Ruiqing's activities in the air force. You should reveal what Liu Yalou [see below] said about Luo Ruiqing before he died." She was giving him clear-cut hints and she suggested a specific approach. She added: "Lin Biao asks whether you will join him or Luo Ruiqing."

He knew what she meant. He thought that Lin Biao, who was

on the rise, did not have full confidence in him. Thus he expressed his loyalty immediately: "Join Lin Biao, of course. Am I not going astray if I join Luo Ruiqing? Please tell Lin Biao that I certainly will join him. You should watch what I do in the future."

She also used soft tactics.

Ye Qün told Wu Faxian, "Lin Biao has promoted you from grade six to grade five."

At that moment, Wu Faxian was most willing to board Lin Biao's pirate ship. He did not hesitate to tread on Luo Ruiqing's body and climb to the pinnacle of personal power.

When two people have a conversation and later one of them dies, the content of the dialogue cannot be verified. Ye Qün made use of the fact that the dead cannot bear witness to fabricate a vicious piece of evidence for the purpose of persecuting Luo Ruiqing.

In late 1965 and early 1966, Ye Qün summoned Wu Faxian on two occasions and dictated, for him to take down, the so-called four opinions Luo Ruiqing wanted Liu Yalou [former commander of the air force] to relay to her [Ye Qün]. The "four opinions" were:

1. Lin Biao will have to appear on the political stage sooner or later, whether he likes it or not—if not now, then in the future.
2. You must take good care of Marshal Lin's health.
3. From now on, Lin Biao would not have to concern himself too much with the affairs of the army. It is better to let Chief of General Staff Luo handle the military.
4. Luo should handle everything. Lin Biao must let him do so.

Anyone with a clear mind will know at one glance that if Luo Ruiqing indeed said those things, he really wanted to seize military power, because Lin Biao was the minister of defense at that time.

Ye Qün told Wu Faxian to use these "four opinions" to explode an "atomic bomb."

Wu Faxian did what he was told. From late 1965 to March 1966, he gave two talks and wrote a letter alleging that Luo Ruiqing had indeed given the "four opinions," thus "fully showing Luo Ruiqing's ambition to have a hand in party affairs and seize military power. . . .

Ye Qün fabricated false evidence, as well as false evidence to the false evidence.

She also came up with witnesses. She told Li Zuopeng to groundlessly accuse Luo Ruiqing of "having disgraceful secrets, engaging in conspiratorial activities, and having ambitions of occupying the leadership of the navy," among other things.

Such serious false accusations, rumors, and slanders were poured on the general like buckets of dirty water. The feeling of being a victim of injustice and the pain of being unable to defend himself and falling prey to a plot made him unable to control himself.

After the "Cultural Revolution" began, Premier Zhou Enlai instructed Wu Faxian to send Comrade Luo Ruiqing to the airforce general hospital and give him proper protection.

Wu Faxian immediately reported this to Ye Qün, who said in answer, "This won't do! You have always opposed Luo Ruiqing. Now you want to shield him. How are you going to account for this?" So Wu Faxian started to look for excuses to fool Premier Zhou and stall for time. One minute he said that there was no suitable room in the air-force general hospital; the next minute he said that the hospital was not safe because it was close to the road. In this way Comrade Luo Ruiqing fell victim to endless rounds of criticism-and-struggle, personal humiliation, and bodily harm.

Kang Sheng and Xie Fuzhi also fanned the flames and openly denounced Luo Ruiqing as "a hidden traitor" who "maintained illicit relations with a foreign country" and was a "fake party member."

The more violent the storms, the more Comrade Luo Ruiqing was convinced that he must wage an unrelenting struggle against enemies lurking inside the party. He thought: "I must stay alive in order to make the party and the people understand my heart and to see the sun coming out after the dark clouds have been dispersed." The more his enemies wanted him to die, the more meaningful Comrade Luo Ruiqing found his life.

In order to achieve this goal, Comrade Luo Ruiqing requested an operation on his leg in June 1968. On August 3 the Luo Ruiqing special case group reported this request to Ye Qün, Jiang Qing, Chen Boda, Huang Yongsheng, and Wu Faxian.

On the morning of August 4, Ye Qün phoned Wu Faxian and

said, "About Luo Ruiqing's operation—Lin Biao did not approve and wanted it postponed. Lin Biao said that because Luo Ruiqing had not given us any information, we must try hard to carry out interrogation and struggle to obtain the information we want . . . if the operation were unsuccessful, we would not be able to write anything."

The postponement of the operation was a torture as well as a threat.

The wound in the general's left leg festered and did not heal. "Why don't you confess that you attempted to usurp army leadership and oppose the party, that you organized an antiparty clique and colluded with spies? Once you confess, we will treat your leg and make you comfortable."

The general remained silent.

They dragged the general in and out all day, resorting to all possible tactics, from several persons taking turns at interrogation to mental torture. The general grew weaker and weaker. Despite his high fever, he had to drag his legs and walk to the toilet, leaning with one hand on the wall, in the middle of the night. The guard was impatient with his slow pace and pushed him. The general fell on the cement floor and broke his leg.

They had to perform the operation. On the operating table, they removed the thighbone, which could have been fixed; the general lost his chance to have an artificial left leg attached. How those devils feared that he would stand up straight!

The case that was the talk of the town implicated Comrade Luo Ruiqing's wife, Hao Zhiping; her parents; and her seven children.

Hao Zhiping went to Yan'an when she was sixteen. She had never experienced such a grave injustice before. She was imprisoned for six years from the second half of 1966.

"In early 1968—on the eve of the Chinese New Year—Luo Yü, Luo Ruiqing's son, was arrested. He remained in prison for five years. Luo Ruiqing's other children also suffered all sorts of torture, insults, and hardships.

At the end of 1973, when Comrade Luo Ruiqing regained personal freedom, he told his children: "How painful it is for a Communist party member to be unjustly attacked and framed and prevented from working for the party! During these years I have almost forgotten how to laugh."

History is merciful. If the general knew that the principal

culprits of the Lin Biao–Jiang Qing counterrevolutionary cliques were being punished according to the law, he would surely smile with satisfaction and consolation!

The thing people regret is that the general survived for only a short time after this misfortune.

Ah, General Luo Ruiqing! What a faithful hero! The extraordinary test has shown that you were a tough fighter in opposing Lin Biao, Jiang Qing, and company—a mob of big thieves who attempted to usurp the party and state.

14

THE SENTENCES

A packed courtroom housing both the civilian and military tribunals of the Special Court tensely awaited the sentencing of the ten defendants on January 25, 1981.

Court President Jiang Hua's voice rose to nearly a shout as he pronounced, "Jiang Qing is sentenced to death!"

Mao's widow yelled, "You—" and was promptly silenced by two policemen who handcuffed her and bundled her from the court.

Jiang Hua continued: ". . . with a two-year reprieve and permanent deprivation of political rights." (Political rights in China theoretically include the right to vote and to receive a fair trial.)

Zhang Chunqiao listened to his identical sentence impassively.

Yao Wenyuan's eyes boggled as he was condemned to twenty years' imprisonment and deprivation of political rights for five years. Wang Hongwen showed no emotion when he was sentenced to life imprisonment and permanent deprivation of political rights.

Chen Boda drew eighteen years and five years' deprivation of rights.

Among the military defendants, Huang Yongsheng received a sentence of seventeen years and deprivation of rights for five years; Wu Faxian seventeen years and five years' deprivation; Li Zuopeng seventeen years in prison and five years' deprivation; Qiu Huizuo sixteen years and five years' deprivation; Jiang Tengjiao eighteen years and five years' deprivation.

Chen and the military defendants would have their sentences docked by the nine years they had spent in jail. Yao Wenyuan would presumably benefit from the four years he had been in detention. Jiang Qing, Zhang Chunqiao, and possibly Wang Hongwen would not benefit.

When last heard of at the time of writing in 1983, Yao Wenyuan was putting on weight from lack of exercise as prison librarian at the maximum-security Qin Cheng prison near the Ming Tombs outside Peking, where many of the Gang of Four's victims had spent years in solitary confinement. Zhang Chunqiao was seriously ill with throat cancer and was receiving treatment. Wang Hongwen was at a labor camp in Shanxi Province, northwest China. But these reports could be erroneous.

Jiang Qing was said to be in prison at Guilin, a famous tourist resort and beauty spot in southwest China. She was making dolls for about five cents apiece and was allowed to save the money. Later she was reported transferred back to prison in Peking.

On January 25, 1983, Jiang Qing and Zhang Chunqiao were reprieved and sentenced to life imprisonment, though there was no evidence that either had recanted.

15

CONCLUSION—
JUSTICE ON TRIAL

The trial of the Gang of Four was an important, some would say central, event in the political development of modern China. It cleared the air of much of the gloom and misery left over from the Cultural Revolution, vindicated large numbers of unjustly persecuted people, cleared the reputations of a few of those who died, and laid the blame squarely on the shoulders of the erstwhile leftist faction in the party. It left little doubt in most people's minds about the degree of support Mao's wife must—as she repeatedly claimed—have received from him. It did, however, bring out enough evidence of Mao's misgivings about her, and her ability to hoodwink him, to save a little face for him and for the entire nation.

The trial also pointed up the dangers of letting military commanders have too much political power. It exposed the style and methods of the conspirators. It served as a kind of apology to the people of China, and an explanation to the rest of the world, for the country's extraordinary behavior from 1966 until 1976.

However, as a showpiece of the new legal system put into effect less than a year before—on January 1, 1980—the trial was a disaster. The party-controlled media mounted an intense campaign to prove that the trial was held within the framework of the new Criminal Code and Code of Criminal Procedure. If so, why was it necessary to have a special court at all? At the least, this course of action signified that the leaders had doubts about the efficacy of the new codes, which were based mainly on Soviet and West European legal systems.

Top commentators, explaining the applicability of the new criminal codes to the trial, were ambivalent with regard to the comparison between Chinese standards of justice and those of other countries. On the one hand, they would assert that such and such a practice was common in the legal systems of other countries—thereby reflecting the widespread belief in China that "foreign things are better than Chinese products." At the same time, Fei Xiaotong (one of China's top social scientists, who served as a lay assessor on the panel of judges) claimed that foreign standards need not apply to Chinese law.

Great play was made with the announcement that the court would try the defendants only for their crimes under the law—not for any political "mistakes" or "errors of line" they may have made. This was quite unrealistic since many of the crimes of the Gang of Four were conducted in a legal vacuum, and were at the same time greatly lauded in the national political media, held up as shining instances of the continuing revolution in action.

It could not be shown that any member of the Gang of Four actually killed anyone with his or her own hands; their crime was to have issued instructions that resulted in so much death and persecution. Their responsibility was above all political, and some of their actions were inspired solely by political considerations. When a judge berated Jiang Qing for having had Liu Shaoqi's house searched—on the grounds that the 1954 State Constitution did not permit the Head of State to be treated in this way—he was merely quibbling at what everybody in the courtroom knew: By late 1966 the Constitution was completely inoperative, and Mao had either approved or ordered the overthrow and maltreatment of Liu and his wife, Wang Guangmei, of which the house search was merely a part.

The other great weakness of the trial was its inability to measure up to the new standards of objectivity proclaimed in the Code of Criminal Procedure. The new laws specifically rule out the extortion of confessions to convict the person in the dock—the most fundamental of all Chinese traditional ideas of justice, and one for which most Communist regimes show a strong liking. The military defendants were in prison or jail for nine years before being put on trial, as was Chen Boda. In general, they had learned from their interrogators what they should say in court in order to win lighter sentences.

Jiang Qing, however, had evidently made no confession, nor had Zhang Chunqiao. Even after four years in detention, both were defiant. Yao Wenyuan was still in the process of mentally sorting out his political recantation and finding excuses for the way he acted while in power. Wang Hongwen was the only one of the four who cooperated fully with the court, though he still drew a longer term than expected.

Perhaps he was considered lucky to have escaped the death penalty for planning an armed coup d'état.

China was not, in fact, devoid of a legal system before 1980. A long list of crimes and misdemeanors came into being from 1949 on, and although they were not published in a codified form, they were effective in the main. Until the Cultural Revolution, courts sat, passed judgment, commuted or upheld death sentences, and sorted out litigation with foreign companies engaged in trade with Chinese government organs. In the high Cultural Revolution (1966–71), the courts ceased to function and lawyers were in disrepute. From the early 1970s on, however, courts again became active, though fewer disputes or prosecutions actually came before them than before. Civil disputes were handled for preference at the level of the Street Committee, the party branch, or other administrative organs. Many of the less severe criminal offenders were dealt with "administratively" by the police without recourse to court proceedings, and were sent to reformatories.

As at the Nürnberg trial of German war criminals after World War II, there was great difficulty in assigning blame to defendants who claimed that they were merely following orders and had no freedom of choice, or that they "did not know" what horrors and crimes their obedience, and the obedience of those below them, brought about.

The Gang of Four's actions resulted in death and misery for hundreds of thousands—more likely millions—of people. They had numerous collaborators and willing instruments. One would have expected the trial to have been the prelude to many other trials, especially in certain provinces where the human damage was greatest—trials of policemen, leftist cadres, prison governors, newspaper editors, Red Guard leaders, or vandalizers of art treasures and monuments. But few such trials have been reported, despite earlier assurances that they would take place. Some people responsible for persecution of others have gone to jail—a few of them made appearances at the trial—while others have been released and returned to normal life. Intermittent press reports even tell of them openly working to regain their former authority, feasting old associates and interfering with party and government affairs.

The difficulty of enumerating the victims of the Cultural Revolution is shown by the pedantically specific figure of 720,511 people "unwarrantedly persecuted," compared with the obviously rounded figure of 34,800 "innocent" people whose deaths were caused in one way or another by the Gang's activities. In the so-called East Hebei frame-up alone, 84,000 people were said to have been "ruthlessly persecuted" and 2,955 lost their lives, according to the official count.

Several places are singled out as having suffered particularly disastrous infighting and loss of life: 346,000 victims in Inner Mongolia, 7,100 in Guangdong, 80,000 in the armed forces, and 211,100 "personages in various circles." In the east China city of Ji'nan, the figure for victims is given as 383, while in Shanghai it is 741 (surely an understatement). Because of the mixture of rounded and unrounded figures, the total of 729,511 was arrived at quite arbitrarily. In some places figures are given only for those "persecuted to death," without any figure for the lesser fate of those "framed and persecuted." The same applies to the armed forces, who counted 1,169 people "persecuted to death," but none "framed or persecuted." This is clearly anomalous. The same applies to returned overseas Chinese, about whom it is recorded only that 281 were "persecuted to death" but no figure is given for those "framed and persecuted." This is absurd, for it is common knowledge that the overseas Chinese suffered worse than most people because of the envy aroused by their superior living conditions. The survivors left in droves in the 1970s.

The worst aspect of the trial was the meager or rather nonexistent defense, which dwelt mainly on the defendants' admissions of guilt and—above all—their behavior in court. If the defendant cooperated with the court—as did Jiang Tengjiao—that would be grounds for a plea of mitigation. If he or she challenged the evidence or testimony or the very legality of the court, as Jiang Qing did, that would be treated as contempt and could contribute to the sentence. Not a single defense witness was called. The defendants in some cases seemed to be aware of the details of the charges against them only when they read the indictment, which was served on them three weeks before the trial opened. None of the prosecution witnesses was cross-examined by defense counsel. At most the judge would warn a witness to speak truthfully. Since much of the proceedings was in the form of recordings and epidiascope projection of documents, there was no means of cross-examination even if the defense had intended to conduct it.

The trial of the Gang of Four was, in brief, a classic showpiece of what totalitarian regimes regard as justice for their political enemies. Its chief merit was that it was loosely scripted, and much of the testimony gave the strong impression of being rooted in fact—albeit tendentiously presented—and not merely in the imaginations of the interrogators and prosecutors. That, perhaps, is something to be welcomed.

BIOGRAPHICAL NOTES

DENG XIAOPING

Born 1904, Sichuan Province. As a young man, Deng studied and worked in France and the Soviet Union, returning to China in 1926. He became a guerrilla commander and in the early 1930s joined up with Mao in Jiangxi and took part in the Long March. Deng held important military commands in the anti-Japanese war and the Civil War. After the Communist victory, he was appointed to head the party's Southwest Bureau, which included his native province, and later took on numerous responsibilities in Peking, including the post of secretary-general of the party (abolished in 1967 and restored in 1982).

Deng was very active in the ideological dispute with the Soviet Union—though Khrushchev admired his ability—and in the ensuing unsuccessful negotiations, and he did what he could to moderate Mao's excesses in economic policy, especially agriculture. He is famous for the saying "It doesn't matter whether the cat is white or black as long as it catches mice." This became the ideological banner of his pragmatist leadership faction.

In 1967 Deng was denounced as a "revisionist" and disappeared, resurfacing in 1973 and quickly taking over the reins of leadership from Zhou Enlai, who was fighting cancer. The Gang of Four schemed to have him overthrown again and in 1976 they succeeded in blaming him partially for the April 5 riots on Tiananmen Square. After the overthrow of the Gang, Deng returned to power stronger than ever, and guided China onto the path of economic and social reform, dis-

mantling Mao's political system in the process. He purged the politburo of leftists, and in 1981 enabled Hu Yaobang to take over the
party chairmanship from Hua Guofeng, Mao's chosen successor. At
the time of writing, Deng was still the effective leader of party and
government.

KANG SHENG

Kang Sheng, sometimes known as "the evil genius of the Cultural
Revolution," was born into a poor peasant family in Shandong Province in 1899. He joined the Communist party while studying at Shanghai University and became a labor agitator in the city. In 1933 Kang
went to Moscow for further study and training, until he returned to
China and joined Mao Zedong's forces at Yan'an in 1937. His Moscow
training made him the most suitable person to organize Party security,
and he is believed to have run the Party School at Yan'an. After the
Communist victory in 1949, he helped administer his home province
and other parts of East China. He spent the late 1950s in Peking and
became heavily involved in the Sino-Soviet dispute. From 1966 he
helped organize the Cultural Revolution in collaboration with Jiang
Qing, whom he had befriended at Yan'an. Kang Sheng is thought to
have been responsible for many of the most vicious intrigues of the
period, but he was in failing health and died in 1975. His wife, Cai
Yi'ou, was accused of looting state-owned libraries and museums to
add to her private collections. Though given full Party honors at his
funeral, Kang was denounced in 1980 and would have joined the
Gang of Four in going on trial had he still been alive.

LI FUCHUN

Born in 1899 or 1900 in Hunan Province to a family of minor literati,
Li underwent training in France and Russia, took part in the Long
March, and held high office in northeast China. He specialized in
economic planning on the Soviet model and was considered a political
moderate. He married Cai Chang, one of the most famous of China's
women revolutionaries.

LIN BIAO

Born in 1907 in Hubei Province, son of a small landowner and busi-
nessman, Lin was later to become one of the Communists' outstanding
military commanders. He joined the Red Army in 1927, took part in
the Long March, and commanded the Fourth Field Army in the Civil
War. After a prolonged illness, he was named marshal of the People's

Republic in 1954 and defense minister in 1959 when Peng Dehuai was removed from the latter post. In the 1960s he became famous for his theories on the "encirclement" and defeat of the superpowers by the global Third World. Lin was a central figure in the Cultural Revolution group and vigorously promoted the personality cult of Mao Zedong. He was named Mao's "close comrade-in-arms" and successor. Lin and his wife and son were killed on September 13, 1971, while attempting to flee to the Soviet Union in a Trident jet after allegedly trying to assassinate the Chairman. His wife, Ye Qün, was also a prominent figure in the Cultural Revolution.

MAO ZEDONG

Most famous of all Chinese revolutionaries, in the last two decades of his life Mao developed a megalomania and apparent paranoia that led him onto a policy course nowadays recognized as having been near-disastrous. Entombed in a crystal sarcophagus in his mausoleum on Tiananmen Square in Peking, Mao is still regarded with veneration for his revolutionary career from the 1920s till 1957. His personality cult set new records in the annals of dictators.

Born in 1893 in Shaoshan village, Hunan Province, Mao came of peasant stock. He read widely in his youth, developing patriotic ideas that later formed the basis of his revolutionary thinking. He served as a soldier, studied on his own, and became an assistant librarian at Peking University. In 1919 he returned to Hunan and joined with others in studying Marxism. He was a founding member of the Communist party at Shanghai in 1921. Pursued by the authorities, he set up his first guerrilla base at Jinggangshan, Jiangxi Province, in 1927. He remained in that general area, resisting Guomindang attempts to encircle and crush him, until late 1934, when he led his depleted forces out on the Long March to the northwest. They arrived at their destination late in 1935, by which time he was the recognized leader of the Communist party. He married Jiang Qing in 1940. During the anti-Japanese war, Mao's forces sporadically cooperated with his old enemy, Chiang Kai-shek; but with the defeat of Japan, all-out civil war broke out, leading to Communist victory and the proclamation of the People's Republic on October 1, 1949.

With the exception of his treatment of landlords, which was harsh—many being executed—Mao pursued generally mild internal policies until 1956, emphasizing economic construction and aid from the Soviet Union. But in 1956–57 he masterminded the crushing of dissident intellectuals in the Hundred Flowers movement and the Antirightist

Campaign. In 1958 he launched the people's communes and the Great Leap Forward. Growing ideological disputes with the Soviet Union resulted in the withdrawal of Soviet technicians in 1960, and by 1961 China was on the brink of economic collapse, with starvation widespread.

Mao's long-term associates Liu Shaoqi and Deng Xiaoping did what they could to repair the damage over the next five years while Mao to a considerable extent withdrew from public life. In 1966 he unleashed the Red Guard fury on his old comrades and on the nation as a whole, virtually dismantling the organs of party and state, wrecking the educational system, and writing off China's foreign relations. The armed forces had to be called on to quell the Red Guards in 1977–78, and Defense Minister Lin Biao became Mao's "closest comrade-in-arms" and named successor. Lin allegedly plotted to assassinate Mao in 1971, and died while attempting to flee to the Soviet Union. In 1972 Mao received President Richard Nixon in a historic reconciliation with the United States, which now became China's main ally in the global political confrontation with the Soviet Union.

In the early to middle 1970s, Mao's leftist entourage, headed by Jiang Qing, increasingly took control of national policy against the opposition of Deng and Zhou. In 1976 Mao allowed Deng to be disgraced a second time, and named Hua Guofeng his successor. Mao died on September 9, 1976, and less than a month later the Gang of Four was overthrown.

PENG DEHUAI

Born in 1898 in Hunan Province, of a rich peasant family, Peng was one of the Revolution's most prominent military commanders, and an early victim of Mao's paranoia. As right-hand man to Zhu De, Peng fought successful engagements in the Jiangxi period, the Long March, the anti-Japanese war, and the Civil War. He commanded China's "volunteer" army in Korea. Peng fell afoul of Mao in 1959 for criticizing the latter's policies, and was dismissed from the post of defense minister, which he had held since being promoted to marshal of the People's Republic in 1954. He continued to carry out minor functions despite having been dubbed "head of an antiparty clique." In 1966–67 Red Guards paraded him through the streets of Peking. Peng was accused in 1970 of having "consistently opposed the party and Chairman Mao, maintained illicit foreign relations, and committed countless crimes." Huang Yongsheng, one of the defendants at the trial, who was chief of staff at the time, proposed that

Peng be expelled from the party and sentenced to life imprisonment. Peng died in 1974 and his reputation was officially rehabilitated in 1978.

TAN ZHENLIN

Born in Hunan Province in 1902 or 1903, Tan was an outstanding military commander and subsequently an expert on agriculture; the Gang of Four tried repeatedly to discredit him. Tan joined Mao's forces in Jiangxi in the late 1920s and was left behind to carry on guerrilla operations in the old base areas while Mao led the rest of his forces on the Long March to the northwest. After 1949 he held top administrative posts in east China. He showed more leftist leanings than Deng or Liu, for instance in his keen support of the Great Leap Forward in 1958–61. Tan was attacked by the Red Guards and was branded a counterrevolutionary in 1968. He was rehabilitated in 1973 as a member of the Central Committee and chairman of the Fourth and Fifth National People's Congresses (1975 and 1978 respectively). Tan died in 1983.

TAO ZHU

Born 1905 or 1906 in Hunan Province, Tao joined the Communist forces in Canton in the 1920s and may have taken part in the Long March. After 1949 he rose steadily through the party hierarchy in the central-south region. In 1966 he was summoned to Peking to assist his fellow Hunanese Mao Zedong in organizing the Cultural Revolution, but within a few months was branded a counterrevolutionary and disappeared. Tao died in 1969, and his good name was restored in 1978.

YE JIANYING

Born 1898 or 1899 in Guangdong Province, of a Hakka merchant family, Ye joined the Communist party in 1927 and took part in the Long March. He was prominent in the period of Communist-Guomindang cooperation during the Japanese invasion of China, and later in the administration of the central-south region. He was regarded as almost a cult figure of the People's Liberation Army in the postwar period and was named marshal in 1954. Since 1978 he has served as chairman of the Standing Committee of the Fifth National People's Congress—China's closest equivalent to a head of state.

ZHOU ENLAI

Born in 1898 in Jiangsu Province, of a gentry family, Zhou was China's greatest modern statesman. He survived Mao's paranoia by never aspiring to the number one position, and was frequently able to temper some of Mao's political excesses.

After education in China and Japan, Zhou studied in France and visited other European countries. He helped run the Canton Military School with Chiang Kai-shek in the mid-1920s, later joining forces with Mao and leading an unsuccessful uprising in the city of Nanchang. Zhou took part in the Long March and became a prominent figure at the wartime headquarters of Yan'an and in contacts with the Chongqing-based Guomindang.

From 1949 on, Zhou bore heavy responsibilities in the spheres of economic planning, administration, and relations with the Soviet Union and Third World countries. He made a powerful impression at the 1954 Geneva Conference on Indochina. Zhou played a central role in the ideological break with Moscow, but in 1969 had an emergency meeting with Soviet premier Aleksei Kosygin that effectively put a stop to the mounting warfare on the Sino-Soviet frontier.

Zhou signed the 1972 Shanghai Communiqué with Richard Nixon, ending more than two decades of fierce Sino-American hostility. Together with Deng Xiaoping, he presided over the country's recovery from the disruption of the Cultural Revolution and the restoration of its foreign relations, as well as sponsoring a big jump in China's foreign trade in the early 1970s. The Gang of Four tried repeatedly to undermine his standing with Mao, but failed. Zhou died of cancer in 1976.

NOTES

ABBREVIATIONS USED IN CHAPTER NOTES

GMRB — Guangming Ribao (*Enlightenment Daily*)
JFJB — Jiefangjün Bao (*Liberation Army Daily*)
RMRB — Renmin Ribao (*People's Daily*)
Xinhua — Xinhua She (*New China News Agency*)

CHAPTER 1

1. The term "cadre" is used loosely in China to indicate anyone who does nonmanual work, but it has overtones of "party cadre"—a party member who exercises authority in his allotted sphere of activity. In the military, it means an officer. The word is imprecise and charged with ambiguity, especially when cadres in general are being reproached for self-indulgent life-style or arrogance toward the general public. Under Mao, all cadres were sent to "May Seventh schools," where they grew some of their own food and studied the works of Mao and Marx.
2. The Eighth Plenary Session (plenum) of the Eighth Central Committee of the Chinese Communist party was held in August 1959.
3. A writers' association.
4. Disgraced for his play *Hai Rui Dismissed from Office*, which was thought to be an attack on Mao.
5. Among the leading persecutors of Liu and his wife was Qi (pronounced "Chee") Benyü, a Marxist historian and polemicist, and associate editor of the party's theoretical journal *Red Flag*. He was a member of the Central Cultural Revolution Group and a right-hand man of Jiang Qing until he was denounced in 1968 as one of the masterminds of the left-extremist May 16 movement (which was too far left even for Mao's taste).
6. The TV commentator described the editorial this way: "The editorial deals with the need to make continuing efforts to carry out the Great Proletarian Cultural Revolution to the end. When Chen Boda approved it, he changed the subject matter to 'sweeping away all ghosts and monsters.' He introduced this slogan in the editorial, saying that leading cadres at all levels, the broad masses of intellectuals, and the broad

masses themselves were representatives of the bourgeois class—bourgeois specialists, bourgeois scholars, authoritarians, sectarians, ghosts, and monsters—and should all be swept away, utterly routed, and totally discredited."

7. A university professor.

8. Blitz interrogation consists of giving the person under interrogation no respite, but continuing with relays of interrogators, shouting and threatening, shining lights in the face, pushing and slapping. The person under interrogation is told he or she will suffer a cruel fate unless he or she confesses.

9. By contrast with genuine Red Guards, who performed most of their agitation openly.

10. In October 1966, the various branches and offices of the Chinese Communist party were in a defensive stance, neither approving nor resisting the house searches being carried out (allegedly on Mao's instructions) by Red Guards. They were recording events neutrally, fearful that they would themselves come to the same pass. It is not known which individual composed document 99.

11. To "put someone in the cowpen" meant to isolate him or her, imposing humiliating tasks such as cleaning latrines.

12. Subsequently premier, after Zhou Enlai's death in 1976, Hua was gradually ousted from his official posts over the next six years, being demoted in 1982 to mere membership in the Central Committee. He was regarded as a leftist and opportunist.

13. In September 1982, the party chairmanship was abolished and Hu became secretary-general, nominally the top post, but still outranked in practice by Deng Xiaoping.

14. Roxanne Witke, *Comrade Chiang Ch'ing*. Boston: Little, Brown, 1977.

15. *GMRB,* 12 March 1977.

16. Guo Fenglian.

CHAPTER 2

1. Marshal Peng, an outstanding military leader and a popular hero, commanded the Chinese "People's Volunteers" in the Korean War. During a 1959 meeting at Lushan, in Jiangxi Province, he criticized Mao's handling of economic problems, which had brought the country near starvation. He was demoted and sank into obscurity, dying on November 29, 1974. (His reputation was posthumously rehabilitated in 1978.)

2. One of Mao's entourage.

3. M.V. *Feng Qing* was a China-built ocean freighter that was given much publicity as a symbol of Chinese self-reliance when it sailed on a long maiden voyage.

4. The "Counterattack" was a campaign of media materials and mass meetings designed to show that Deng Xiaoping and his associates were right-

ists who were sabotaging Mao's leftist policies and were whitewashing senior officials who had been disgraced in the Cultural Revolution.

5. It is not made clear where Wang had been, or on exactly what day he returned to Peking.

6. Presumably fanning local political conflicts through agitation in the media.

7. They were derogatorily referred to as "the home-going contingent"— after the landlords who ran away when the Red Army was approaching, and came back under the protection of the Guomindang forces when the Communists left.

8. Respectively first secretaries of party committees in the provinces of Fujian, Jiangxi, and Jiangsu.

9. One of Shanghai's main newspapers.

10. "Going against the tide" was a slogan popularized by Wang Hongwen at the Fourth National People's Congress in 1975. The phrase means sticking to one's principles as a Communist even if by doing so one puts oneself temporarily in the minority.

11. Marking the fifty-fifth anniversary of the founding of the Chinese Communist party.

12. It is unclear from the transcript which of the three people he mentioned sent him the letter.

13. "Big-character posters" or *dazibao* were the main propaganda weapon of the leftists in the Cultural Revolution. They were used to smear one's opponents, support new movements, and generally stir up the political situation. The *dazibao* process was a development of the traditional Chinese practice of putting up posters to air grievances or issue official warnings against wrongdoers. They were declared illegal after the burst of poster-writing in 1978–80, which was used by Deng Xiaoping to attack his leftist opponents and pull the public over to his side.

CHAPTER 3

1. Angling (with an expensive imported rod) remained Wang's favorite hobby.

2. Xinhua, 6 June 1977.

3. *RMRB*, 3 June 1977.

4. Ibid.

5. Ibid.

6. Ibid.

7. *RMRB*, 18 May 1977.

8. *Peking Review*, 25/1977.

9. *RMRB*, 18 May 1977.

10. The trade unions had resisted the Red Guard movement because it eroded their power and they were denounced and subsequently disbanded. They reappeared again from 1973 on. It seems that trade-union

activists had gathered at the Diesel Engine Plant to seek safety in numbers.

CHAPTER 4

1. Tang Wensheng, also known as Nancy Tang, is a partially American-educated woman, probably in her late thirties at the time of writing, who used to interpret in English for Mao and Zhou Enlai. She disappeared from the scene soon after the fall of the Gang of Four, as did her close associate Wang Hairong, a niece of Mao's.
2. The "February Adverse Current" in 1967 was a short period during that month when attempts were made by bureaucrats, senior army officers, and others to rehabilitate their colleagues who had been overthrown in many different parts of the country. The Adverse Current was soon defeated and the attacks on senior leaders were intensified.
3. Former secretary of the Shanghai Municipal Party Committee and vice-chairman of the Municipal Party Committee and Revolutionary Committee, leftist, tried and imprisoned in 1982.
4. The enumeration of nine nefarious activities does not fit the punctuation. Reason unknown.
5. Second secretary of the Municipal Party Committee, tried and imprisoned in 1982.
6. Huang Tao, an aide of Zhang's.
7. A main feature of Deng Xiaoping's attempts to straighten out the Chinese economy in the mid-1970s was the restoration of rules and regulations abolished in the Cultural Revolution, causing great waste and many industrial accidents.
8. An extreme-left Red Guard faction that sought to overthrow Premier Zhou Enlai. It was disbanded and some of its members imprisoned after the 1971 Lin Biao episode.
9. A Red Guard faction at Qinghua University; it named itself after Mao's base area in Jiangxi before the Long March.
10. Kuai regarded himself as the "Old Grandfather" or head of the Qinghua Red Guards. However, there were rival factions who fought each other with blunt and sharp objects, catapults made from bicycle inner tubes, and even firearms. Later Kuai's faction was suppressed by the army and he was jailed as an ultraleftist conspirator. It is not clear whether he was at liberty by the time he gave testimony at the trial. See William Hinton, *Hundred Day War*, Monthly Review Press, 1972. Kuai was tried and imprisoned in 1983.
11. A Chinese saying meaning "to give no quarter," "to show no mercy."

CHAPTER 5

1. "The prosecution charged that, on Chen Boda's instructions, Xie Fuzhi, then the minister of public security, fabricated the case of a bogus

'Chinese Communist party (Marxist-Leninist),' alleging veteran revolutionaries Zhu De to be its 'secretary,' Chen Yi the 'deputy defense secretary and concurrently minister of defense,' and (economic planner) Li Fuchun the 'premier.' Its members were supposed to have included Dong Biwu (the late acting chairman of the People's Republic), Ye Jianying, and other leaders. They were alleged to have had 'illicit relations with foreign countries' and were attempting to 'stage a coup.'

"Asked if he had any grounds for these allegations, Chen Boda replied that he suggested 'tracking down the behind-the-scenes boss' without any foundation and was responsible for concocting the frame-up." *A Great Trial in Chinese History*. Peking: New World Press, 1981.
2. Evidently Lu's wife.
3. *A Great Trial in Chinese History*, p. 75.
4. Ibid.

CHAPTER 6

1. The last Head of State was Liu Shaoqi. After his disgrace, the post was abolished and the chairman of the Standing Committee of the National People's Congress became the Head of State for protocol functions, whereas high-level talks or negotiations were conducted by Mao, Zhou Enlai, and other leaders. The post was held by Dong Biwu, Zhu De, and Ye Jianying in succession. In 1981 Sun Yat-sen's widow, Soong Ching-ling, was declared honorary Head of State on her deathbed. The restoration of the post was made specific at the time of the Twelfth Party Congress in September 1982, but the incumbent to succeed Marshal Ye was not named at time of writing.
2. "United front" is a set of Communist political tactics somewhat similar to "right opportunism." It emphasizes the party's need to unite with patriotic or philanthropic elements in the interests of overthrowing a dictator or resisting aggression by another country. Examples of a united-front approach would be Stalin's political tactics in World War II and Deng Xiaoping's rehabilitation of writers, artists, scientists, etc., who were disgraced in the leftist Cultural Revolution. China's present foreign policy of friendship with the Western developed countries and Japan, and with the Third World, to oppose Soviet expansionism is another example of united-front tactics.
3. *RMRB*, 26 May 1977.
4. Ibid.
5. *RMRB*, 24 Jan. 1977.
6. *GMRB*, 20 Jan. 1977.
7. *RMRB*, 29 Feb. 1977.
8. Xinhua, 28 Dec. 1976.
9. Ibid.
10. Ibid.

11. Ibid.
12. *GMRB*, 10 Mar. 1977.
13. *RMRB*, 30 Jan. 1977.
14. Ibid.
15. Ibid.

CHAPTER 7

1. *RMRB*, 22 Feb. 1977.
2. *GMRB*, 3 Jan. 1977.
3. Cited by Xinhua, 20 May 1977. The most blatant cases of this were in the Campaign to Criticize Lin Biao and Confucius, in which both historical and literary debate served to mask severe power struggle, but which foreigners were enjoined to follow literally, without looking for the political double entendre. This was the case even in such a flagrant attack on Zhou Enlai as the historical denunciation of the twelfth-century B.C. duke of Zhou. (The allusion was the more blatant since during World War II, when there were contacts between the Communists and the Guomindang in Chongqing, Zhou was sometimes nicknamed Zhou Gong—"Duke of Zhou," or "Venerable Zhou.")
4. *RMRB*, 11 Jan. 1982.
5. *RMRB*, 11 Jan. 1977.
6. *RMRB*, 13 July 1977.
7. *JFJB*, 12 June 1977.
8. *RMRB*, 5 Jan. 1977.
9. *RMRB*, 30 Dec. 1976.
10. Xinhua, 7 Jan. 1977.
11. *RMRB*, 9 Feb. 1977.
12. *GMRB*, 24 Dec. 1976.
13. *GMRB*, 7 Feb. 1977, reprinted from *JFJB*.
14. *GMRB*, 3 Mar. 1977.

CHAPTER 8

1. *RMRB*, 23 Mar. 1977.
2. *RMRB*, 23/24 Mar. 1970.
3. *RMRB*, 12 Feb. 1977.
4. Ibid.
5. *GMRB*, 29 Dec. 1976.
6. *RMRB*, 17 Feb. 1977.
7. *RMRB*, 26 May 1977.
8. Xinhua, 3 June 1977.
9. *RMRB*, 30 May 1977.
10. Xinhua, 24 Dec. 1976.
11. Ibid.
12. Ibid.

13. *RMRB*, 26 Mar. 1982.
14. *RMRB*, 17 Jan. 1977.
15. *RMRB*, 5 July 1982.
16. Xinhua, 28 Dec. 1976.
17. *RMRB*, 2 Jan. 1977.
18. *GMRB*, 18 Mar. 1977.
19. *RMRB*, 19 May 1977.

CHAPTER 9

1. *GMRB*, 13 Dec. 1976.
2. *RMRB*, 28 May 1967.
3. *GMRB*, 16 Dec. 1976.
4. *RMRB*, 2 Jan. 1977.
5. Ibid.
6. Actually, from the early 1970s on, there were more than eight because the regional troupes began to stage their own shows again. The monopoly of the eight works was effective mainly in the high Cultural Revolution of the late 1960s. *GMRB*, 8 Feb. 1977.
7. Ibid.
8. Ibid.
9. Ibid.
10. Ibid.
11. Ibid.
12. Ibid.
13. Ibid.
14. Ibid.
15. Ibid.
16. Ibid.
17. *GMRB*, 4 Dec. 1976.
18. Xinhua, 1 Jan. 1977.
19. *GMRB*, 25 Dec. 1976.
20. Ibid.
21. Xinhua, 26 May 1977.
22. *GMRB*, 25 Mar. 1977.
23. *People's Daily* (quoted by Xinhua, 14 Mar. 1977).
24. *GMRB*, 25 Mar. 1977, article attributed to Gang Pang of Jingpo nationality.
25. *RMRB*, 2 Feb. 1977.
26. Xinhua, 24 Mar. 1977.
27. *GMRB*, 23 Nov. 1976.

CHAPTER 10

1. *GMRB*, 24 June 1977.

2. Other "newborn things" included barefoot doctors and revolutionary stage works.
3. *GMRB*, 30 Nov. 1976.
4. Ibid.
5. Xinhua, 3 Dec. 1976.
6. *RMRB*, 16 Mar. 1977.
7. *RMRB*, 30 Jan. 1977.

CHAPTER 11

1. *RMRB*, 3 Mar. 1977.
2. Xinhua, 2 Feb. 1977.
3. *GMRB*, 2 Jan. 1977.
4. *RMRB*, 25 Feb. 1982.
5. *RMRB*, 20 Dec. 1982.
6. *RMRB*, 9 Jan. 1977.
7. Ibid.
8. Ibid.
9. Xinhua, 12 Jan 1977.
10. Xinhua, 11 Jan. 1977.
11. Ibid.
12. *GMRB*, 15 Jan. 1977.
13. Ibid.
14. Xinhua, 7 Jan. 1977.

CHAPTER 12

1. The Second Plenum of the Ninth Central Committee, August 1970.
2. One of the officers who helped Lin Liguo prepare the assassination bid.
3. Political commissar of PLA Unit 7341.
4. Described as "responsible for operations in Peking in the projected coup d'état."
5. Politburo member, leftist. Ji was in charge of Henan Province and was active in agricultural affairs and ideology. Deng Xiaoping ousted him from the politburo in 1978.

CHAPTER 13

1. A comprador (from the Portuguese meaning "buyer") is a native merchant or agent who arranges business on behalf of foreigners. In the context of nineteenth- and early twentieth-century China, it has acquired a derogatory note, indicating a mercenary lickspittle who profits from the exploitation of his fellow Chinese by foreigners. It is not clear why it should have been applied to Liu Shaoqi, except as a general term of abuse.
2. Mao and other Chinese leaders have jokingly referred to Marx as though he were God in heaven. "Going to see Marx" means to die.

3. Between town and countryside, industry and agriculture, and physical and mental labor.
4. The author is very skeptical of this claim.
5. Hao appeared at the trial as a prosecution witness.
6. *Ayi* or auntie is commonly used by children to address an adult woman whether she is a relative or not.
7. To "put someone in the cowpen," meant to isolate him or her and impose humiliating tasks such as cleaning latrines.
8. According to his posthumous detractors, Lin Biao was obsessed with ideas of individual genius, which he ascribed to his son, Lin Liguo.

INDEX